Gaelic Games, Nationalism and the Irish Diaspora in the United States

Gaelic Games, Nationalism and the Irish Diaspora in the United States

PAUL DARBY

UNIVERSITY COLLEGE DUBLIN PRESS
Preas Choláiste Ollscoile Bhaile Átha Cliath

First published 2009
by University College Dublin Press
Newman House
86 St Stephen's Green
Dublin 2
Ireland
www.ucdpress.ie

ISBN 978-1-906359-23-2

Cataloguing in Publication data
available from the British Library

The right of Paul Darby to be identified as
the author of this work has been asserted by him

Typeset in Ireland in Adobe Garamond,
Janson and Trade Gothic by
Elaine Burberry and Ryan Shiels
Text design by Lyn Davies
Index by Jasne Rogers
Printed in England on acid-free paper by
Athenaeum Press Ltd, Gateshead

Contents

List of Illustrations

Preface

The seed for this book was sown shortly after I followed a well-trodden emigrant path across the Irish Sea to take up a lecturing position at Liverpool Hope University in September 1997. Prior to my own emigration I was in the midst of a career in Gaelic football, both for my club, Naomh Éanna, based in Glengormley on the outskirts of Belfast and my county, Antrim. Although the move to Liverpool brought me closer to Anfield and my other great sporting love, I was saddened by the prospect that, for the foreseeable future at least, I would not be regularly involved in a game that had been a central part of my life up to that point. A phone call within a week of my arrival from Adrian Loney of the John Mitchels Gaelic Football Club (GFC) in Birmingham and a kind invitation to turn out for that club, led to a sooner than anticipated resumption of involvement in Gaelic games. On arrival at Pairc na h'Éireann, the home of Gaelic games in Warwickshire, for my first outing with John Mitchels I was taken aback not only at the quality of the facilities but also by the warmth of the welcome I received and the sense that, psychologically at least, I had returned 'home'.

At around the same time, a casual conversation with a student from County Kerry about the relatively high proportion of Irish students at Liverpool Hope led to the formation of a Gaelic football club at the college. Since then the club has provided Irish students, male and female, not only with opportunities to play competitive Gaelic football but, equally importantly, with a sense of the familiar in otherwise unfamiliar surroundings. On a personal level, my involvement with John Mitchels and the student team at Liverpool Hope did much to help me settle in England and alleviate the pangs that I felt for home, family, friends and Gaelic sport. For this I remain grateful. My experiences with those whom I played with and against also sensitised me to the significance of Gaelic games in the lives of the long and short-term Irish emigrants in the United Kingdom and as such they contributed, in no small measure, to this book.

In the summer of 2000, a generous research grant from Liverpool Hope and an opportunity to spend a summer playing for Notre Dame GFC in Boston, allowed me to combine my personal involvement in Gaelic games with a growing academic curiosity about the history and significance of the Gaelic Athletic

Association (GAA) amongst Irish immigrant communities. I am very grateful for the financial assistance that facilitated this first phase of my fieldwork for this book and for the encouragement of colleagues at Liverpool Hope at the time, particularly Gavin Mellor, Nick Gilson, Steve Atkins and Graham Baldwin. I am particularly indebted though to a number of individuals associated with Notre Dame GFC who looked after the practical arrangements of my stay in Boston and acted as 'gatekeepers' during my research there, most notably Maurice Walsh, Hugh Meehan and Liam Byrne. I am also grateful to all those who passed through Delaware Place and Napleton Street in Brighton, MA, during the course of my stay for making my ethnographic research so enriching and enjoyable.

Beyond ethnography, I adopted traditional historical methods to uncover the development of Gaelic games in Boston and availed of a range of repositories and archives. A number of individuals were particularly helpful in pointing me in the right direction in this regard. At the John J. Burns Library at Boston College, Dr Robert O'Neill and John Attebury provided advice and access to the library's special Irish collections and archives. Tim Lynch of the Irish Institute at Boston College and the staff at the College's Thomas P. O'Neill Jr. Library were also very accommodating in helping with my numerous requests for assistance, as were staff at Boston Public Library (Brighton and Copley branches). I also had the opportunity to spend time with individuals involved in the administration of Gaelic games in Boston and without their views this book would have lacked necessary depth and insight. John Hehir, former president of the North East Division Gaelic Athletic Association (NEGAA), and Connie Kelly, former public relations officer (PRO) of the NEGAA deserve special mention for sharing with me at length their views and memories of the development of Gaelic sports in Boston and for their hospitality and kind words of encouragement. Thanks also go to Kieran Conway, Mark Stokes and Olivia Cahill of *The Irish Emigrant*, a weekly newspaper for Boston's Irish community, who gave so freely of their time and considerable knowledge of Gaelic sport in the city.

By the summer of 2002 I had moved back to Northern Ireland to take up a lecturing position at the University of Ulster at Jordanstown. Although this move allowed me to resume my playing career in Gaelic sport at home it did not diminish my academic interest in analysing the significance of Gaelic games for sections of the Irish diaspora in the United States. Financial support, gratefully received, from the University of Ulster allowed me to undertake two research trips in 2003 and 2004 to assess the history and role of the GAA in New York. Whilst there, I was ably assisted by a number of individuals. William Colbert, director of the American Irish Historical Society and Dr Marion Casey and Scott

Spencer at Glucksman Ireland House, New York University (NYU), provided access to various archives and help with my numerous queries. Staff at New York Public Library and the Tamiment Institute Library at NYU were also invaluable in helping me to track down important documents and newspaper articles. My research in New York was also enriched by a number of men who, over the years, have devoted much time, energy and dedication to ensuring the preservation and development of Gaelic games in the city and beyond. These include: Liam Bermingham; Seamus Dooley; Monty Maloney; Terry Connaughton and Noel O'Connell, all of whom have held, and continue to hold, high-ranking positions within the New York GAA. Kieran O'Sullivan of the Limerick hurling club and Fergus Hanna, executive publisher of the Irish emigrant newspaper, *Home and Away*, also helped me understand the role of Gaelic games within the New York metropolitan area. It would be remiss of me not to mention Phil McCleery at this point who provided great company whilst conducting research in New York.

The two final phases of the research for this book were supported by funding from the British Academy which allowed me to spend time in Chicago and San Francisco in July and August 2005 and August 2006 respectively. In Chicago I owe thanks to the librarians at the Chicago Historical Society, the Harold Washington branch of the Chicago Public Library and the Newberry Library, particularly Katie McMahon. Joe Begley, former chairman of the Chicago Central Division of the North American County Board of the GAA (NACB) and honorary president of the NACB, and Eamonn Kelly, PRO of the NACB, were especially helpful in introducing me to key players in the development and history of Gaelic games in Chicago. The insights of Harry Costello and Lisa Krueger, rúnái and treasurer of the Chicago central division respectively were also gratefully received. A special word of thanks must go to Tommy Dolan, former chairman of the NACB, who not only officiated in a number of games during the long, hot August day that I visited Chicago Gaelic Park, but also spent a couple of hours with me talking about his experiences of playing, watching and organising Gaelic games in Chicago and throughout the US. He also ensured that my visit to the superb facilities and playing fields at Gaelic Park included a run out in a challenge game for the American Patriots, a team comprised exclusively of American-born Chicagoans. I thank my 'team-mates' for their good humour and patience and for reassuring me that should emigration from Ireland to the US stop tomorrow, competitive Gaelic games would continue to be played on American soil.

San Francisco was the furthest I had travelled during the research stages of this project but it was a city where I was made to feel very much at home by the

GAA fraternity. Liam Reidy, PRO of both the San Francisco GAA (SFGAA) and the Naomh Padraig club, acted as my 'gatekeeper', easing my access to various Gaels in the city as well as tracking down some important documents and information on the GAA in the city. His predecessor with the SFGAA, Eamon Gormley, was equally helpful and introduced me to some of the leading figures in San Francisco Gaelic games circles, past and present. These included: Malachy Higgins, chairman of the SFGAA; Joe Duffy, Chairman of the Ulster GFC and treasurer of the NACB; Mike Moriarity, former chairman of the SFGAA and John O'Flynn, chair of the Irish Football Youth League of San Francisco. I thank each of them for broadening my understanding of the GAA in the US and for contributing so enthusiastically to this project. I am also indebted to Louis Cotter and Brendan Kenneally for their insights into Gaelic games in the city in the 1950s and 1960s.

As with my three other case studies, I relied heavily on the resources of a number of libraries in San Francisco and the knowledge and expertise of their staff. Joan Manini, a volunteer at the library of the United Irish Cultural Centre was very helpful and I am indebted to her for allowing me free access to the library outside of regular opening hours. Thomas Carey at San Francisco Public Library was always on hand to help with my requests for information and possible sources, and Debbie Malone, periodicals librarian at the University of San Francisco's Gleeson Library, helped me track down some elusive newspaper articles. A very special word of thanks must go to Mary Ringstad and her father, Thomas J. Wrin. Over a period of years, Thomas Wrin painstakingly indexed a range of early San Francisco newspapers and made the fruits of this work available to researchers and genealogists through the 'Wrindex'. Without this database my archival research would have been akin to finding a needle in a haystack. I contacted Mary prior to leaving for San Francisco to purchase a copy of the database (available from *info@wrindex.com*) and she very kindly sent me a free copy. Beyond this gesture, Mary was constantly on hand with advice and encouragement and my research trip would not have been as productive without her help. Her father, Thomas Wrin also showed an interest in my work and on a number of occasions posted me newspaper articles that I was unable to access. Their kindness and generosity was invaluable in allowing me to uncover the history of Gaelic games in San Francisco. Any major study of the GAA would not be complete without drawing on the resources available at the Association's headquarters in Dublin. For access to minute books and for their patience I owe thanks to Joan Cooney and her colleagues at the GAA's administrative offices and to Mark Reynolds, archivist at the Association's museum.

The plates section of this book would not have been possible were it not for a number of individuals who sourced and donated photographs of GAA activity in each of the cities that form the focal point of this book. Liam Reidy kindly provided access to a digital archive of old photographs from San Francisco that he put together with the support of the local GAA. Connie Kelly also made some images of the GAA in Boston freely available to me. Kerry O'Donnell, daughter of the famous New York Gael John 'Kerry' O'Donnell, who features prominently in this book, allowed me to draw on her personal collection of New York GAA related photographs. I am grateful to Weeshie Fogarty for putting me in touch with Kerry. Finally, Eamonn Kelly and Colm Egan, Chairman of the Chicago Youth Games Development Committee helped me source images of youth Gaelic games in Chicago, while Eric Carlson, a member of the Parnells Club in Chicago and a keen chronicler of events at Chicago Gaelic Park, kindly granted permissions to use a selection of photographs from his extensive collection.

I have presented the findings of different aspects of the research for this book at conferences in places as disparate as Dublin, Pittsburgh, Derry, Texas, Manchester and Armagh, and I am grateful for the constructive comments that I received from colleagues along the way. David Hassan, at the University of Ulster, and Dean Allen, now at Northumbria University have helped in other ways and their good humour and collegiality has been much appreciated. A special thanks must go to Professor Alan Bairner also who has long supported me in my work and was always on the end of the telephone or email to offer guidance and advice. I should note that Alan is also a long time supporter of overseas branches of the GAA, particularly in Liverpool, and has endured a number of sports injuries over the years in his work to promote Gaelic games there. My final professional acknowledgement is to Barbara Mennell and Noelle Moran at University College Dublin Press for their professionalism, belief in this project and patience.

On a personal note, I am indebted to Bobby, Paul and Eamon for their friendship since my return to Belfast. Perhaps the publication of this book will convince them that I was actually working during those trips to the United States. Finally, I would like to thank Dianne for being the person that I looked forward to seeing most at the end of my bouts of fieldwork in America and the subsequent long and often frustrating days of writing. This book is dedicated to my parents, Rosaleen and Stephen (Snr).

PAUL DARBY
Belfast, March 2009

Abbreviations

AAAU	American Amateur Athletic Union
AARIR	American Association of the Recognition of the Irish Republic
ACIF	American Congress for Irish Freedom
AOH	Ancient Order of Hibernians
BGCA	Boys and Girls Clubs of America
CYC	Continental Youth Championship
DFA	Department of Foreign Affairs
FBI	Federal Bureau of Investigation
FOIF	Friends of Irish Freedom
GAA	Gaelic Athletic Association
GFA	Good Friday Agreement
GFC	Gaelic Football Club
GPA	Gaelic Players' Association
IAAC	Irish American Athletic Club
IACB	Irish Athletic Club of Boston
ICAU	Irish Counties Athletic Union
ICC	Irish Cultural Centre
IFA	Irish Football Association
IFC	Irish Freedom Committee
IFYL	Irish Football Youth League
ILIR	Irish Lobby for Immigration Reform
INC	Irish National Caucus
INS (US)	Immigration and Naturalization Service (US)
IPP	Irish Parliamentary Party
IRA	Irish Republican Army
IRB	Irish Republican Brotherhood
KRB	Knights of the Red Branch
LVF	Loyalist Volunteer Force
MTA	Metropolitan Transit Authority
NAAA	National Amateur Athletic Association
NACB	North American County Board

NAIJ	National Association for Irish Justice
NEGAA	North East Division Gaelic Athletic Association
NICRA	Northern Ireland Civil Rights Association
NORAID	Irish Northern Aid
NYGAA	New York Gaelic Athletic Association
NYU	New York University
OSSB	Order of the Star Spangled Banner
PD	People's Democracy
PIRA	Provisional Irish Republican Army
PRO	Public Relations Officer
PWC	Political Wing Committee
RHS	Red Hand Commandoes
RIGS	Randal's Island Gaelic Stadium
RUC	Royal Ulster Constabulary
SFGAA	San Francisco Gaelic Athletic Association
UICA	United Irish Counties Association
USCIS	US Citizenship and Immigration Services
WASP	White Anglo-Saxon Protestant
YMCA	Young Men's Christian Association

Introduction

In September 2000, the North American County Board (NACB), the body that has since 1959 been responsible for overseeing the development of Gaelic games in the United States,[1] held its annual play-off finals in Canton, a suburb of Boston. Although this tournament took place almost 3,000 miles west of the island of Ireland, it was, without question, a distinctively 'Irish' affair. The venue, the Irish Cultural Centre, a 47-acre facility containing three full size pitches, changing rooms, bar and function rooms, and the focal point for Irish sporting and cultural pastimes in Boston and its neighbouring suburbs and towns, would have been the pride of any club or county in Ireland. The games themselves took place amid rituals, emblems and symbols that resonated with the 'Irishness' of the occasion. For example, prior to the Gaelic football final between St Brendan's Chicago and Boston Cork, the players were led onto the field by a traditional Irish pipe band and were paraded around the pitch perimeter behind a flag bearer carrying the Irish tricolour. The Irish national anthem, Amhrán na bhFiann, was sung with great emotion and gusto, and during the trophy presentation at the end of the game the victorious captain made part of his acceptance speech in Irish.[2]

This tournament, coming as it did at the beginning of a new century and indeed, millennium, was an opportune moment to take stock of the status and profile of Gaelic games amongst the Irish diaspora in the US. In a quantitative sense, these sports appeared to be in a state of robust health. The finals were the culmination of regional championships that had taken place earlier in the summer in the 45 American towns and cities where Gaelic football and hurling are played. During the three days of competition, almost 8,000 fans watched 67 games involving over 50 teams from 16 US cities. In addition, the rapid growth and popularisation of under-age Gaelic football, particularly amongst second-generation Irish Americans resulted in these championships playing host to a record 22 games involving youth teams from Philadelphia, Chicago, San Francisco, Buffalo and, of course, Boston. Furthermore, in a press release, Eamonn Kelly, the public relations officer of the NACB, described the tournament as 'the biggest Irish sports spectacle ever held outside Ireland' (cited in NACB Press Release, 27 Sept. 2000). Although assessing the quantitative health of Gaelic games in the US at a particular point in time is a relatively easy task, quantitative measurement and, more specifically, analysis of the social, psychological, political, cultural and economic significance of these sports at various junctures in their history is a much more difficult venture. This is due in no small measure to a long-standing neglect of Gaelic games in the academic literature on the experiences of the Irish in America.

Sport, the Irish in America and the academic neglect of Gaelic games

Although Gaelic sports have been played, in an organised fashion, for over a century in the US, and as such would appear to provide a potentially revealing window into the lives and cultural dispositions of the Irish diaspora, academic research on the development and significance of these sports in America has been limited. That this is the case is hardly surprising given the relative disregard of sport in the burgeoning literature examining Irish America. Much has been written about the ways that the successes of their politicians, the efforts of their Church and the solace, identity and friendships offered by a whole range of their social, cultural, political, benevolent and charitable organisations helped the Irish adapt to life in urban America. Far less has been said though about the role of sport in allowing them to make sense of their new surroundings and deal with the rigours of adjusting to and progressing in the New World. Wilcox (1992: 177) has argued that part of the reason for this neglect can be found in 'elitist academic snobberies, harboured in the traditional halls of academe'. It should be noted at this point that historians of Irish America are not alone in their indifference to sport as a legitimate arena for 'serious' academic analysis. Sports historians around the world have also been confronted with questions from within their parent discipline about the validity of their academic endeavours. The same problem has been evident within mainstream sociology and political science, disciplines that have displayed a similar reluctance to acknowledge the growing social and cultural significance of sports (Coakley and Dunning, 2000; Bairner, 2005). Beyond such academic prejudice the dearth of sustained work on the role of sport in the lives of Irish emigrants is also due to the simple fact that the discourse on the Irish in America is at a relatively early stage in its development and as such has not yet begun to address the full range of institutions and social practices that have sustained the Irish diaspora in the New World.

Despite this neglect, intended or otherwise, the pervasive nature of sport in the modern world combined with a growing acceptance of its social, political, economic and cultural resonance has been such that social scientific and historical studies of sport have mushroomed over the last 30 years or more. Analyses of sport in the US have been central to this growth but, as noted, sport has not featured to any great degree in the research agendas of the vast majority of those who write about Irish America. This is somewhat incongruous because while involvement in sport as participants, committed spectators or casual observers may not have been as important in practical terms as politics or the Catholic Church in smoothing the transition from a slower paced and often rural existence in Ireland to frantic and noisesome urban environs in the US, the fact that it played a not insignificant role marks sport out as an institution worthy of detailed academic investigation and debate. However, a yawning chasm remains between the volume of work on the social, economic, political, cultural and religious institutions that sustained the Irish in America and that carried out on sport.

Published accounts ranging from broad surveys to partial analyses of the Irish role in a range of sports in America do exist and these have been important in helping us begin to understand the contribution and value of sport in Irish America. Of note here is the work of Wilcox (1992; 1994; 2007), Reiss (1992), Isenberg (1988), Bjarkman (1992), Peterson (2000), McCarthy (2007) and, to a lesser extent, Park (1984), McCaffrey (1992; 1997) and Ridge (1997). Their scholarly, skilful and pioneering analyses have clearly demonstrated that in the closing years of the nineteenth century and early part of the twentieth, Irish immigrants demonstrated a passion for the sports forms of the New World and drew on them to provide much needed self-esteem, ease their assimilation into their new environs and protect and preserve senses of ethnic pride and identity. This was particularly the case with baseball, America's national pastime, which was rapidly popularised amongst the Irish immigrant community in a whole range of emerging industrial metropolises. The speed at which baseball took off in Irish immigrant circles was such that Bjarkman (1992) credits the Irish with dominating the game between 1870 and 1900 whilst Reiss (1992) highlights the fact that by 1890, one-third of all Major League baseball players were believed to be Irish. The Irish in New York were amongst baseball's most ardent enthusiasts and readily embraced the game. Indeed, the names that appeared on team rosters of some of the city's highest profile teams demonstrated that the Irish regularly progressed to the higher reaches of the game in this period. For example, the Brooklyn Dodgers teams that won National League pennants in 1890, 1899 and

1900 were managed by Bill McGunnigle and Ned Hanlon and contained players whose names revealed a distinctively Irish flavour (McCaffrey, 1997).[3] This trend was also evident in the New York Giants' teams that secured the National League in 1904, the World Series in 1905 and National League pennants in 1911, 1912 and 1913.[4] New York was not the only city where baseball acquired immense popularity amongst the Irish emigrant community. The draw of the game also extended to other major urban centres, not least Boston, where there were accounts in the local press of matches involving the Hibernian Baseball Club as early as 1870 (McCaffrey, 1997).

The only sport to match baseball in terms of its appeal to the Irish in America in this period was prize fighting, which was dominated by Irish names in the nineteenth century. Chief amongst these was John L. Sullivan who was born in Boston to Irish immigrant parents and gained iconic status as world heavyweight boxing champion between 1882–92 (Isenberg, 1988). Sullivan, nicknamed 'The Boston Strongboy', lost his world title in 1892 to another Irish boxing great, 'Gentleman Jim' Corbett, who hailed from San Francisco. Beyond baseball and boxing, the Irish subsequently took an avid interest in basketball and their contribution to the development of that sport in America is exemplified in the emergence and subsequent successes of the most 'Irish' of the National Basketball Association's teams, the Boston Celtics (Bjarkman, 1992; 1999).

It is clear from the sheer weight of numbers of Irish immigrants who played American sports, particularly baseball, in the late nineteenth and early twentieth centuries that participating in or watching such activities came to represent a focal point in the social lives of those living in the myriad Irish enclaves that sprang up around the country. However, the centrality and importance of American sports for the Irish community in this period extends far beyond opportunities for enjoyment, exercise or socialising. This is a point eloquently highlighted by McCaffrey (1992: 26–7) who, in his brief assessment of the role of sport for the Irish emigrant community, commented that:

> Sports offered the Irish an ego lift as well as ways out of poverty and insignificance. Like religion and politics, sports offered possibilities to the Irish, who were excluded from business and the professions by the Anglo-Protestant establishment. And athletics provided the Irish community with badly needed heroes.

The aptitude of high profile Irish athletes in sports such as baseball, basketball, track and field and boxing undoubtedly did much to engender a healthier perception of the Irish community throughout the country, and the fact that the Irish took to these sports in such large numbers is evidence of their willingness to adapt to the cultural mores and values of their host society. However, although the adoption of American pursuits did erode cultural barriers and facilitate a degree of assimilation, the Irish drew on American sports partly to protect and preserve their ethnic pride and distinctiveness. Sporting competition allowed them to challenge and gain a modicum of superiority over America's Anglo-Protestant establishment and as such served as an arena in which they could express pride in their religion, their neighbourhood and, crucially, their Irishness. As McCaffrey (1992: 27) notes

> the Irish role in sports expressed alienation as well as assimilation. Athletic competition unleashed bottled up anger and resentment. In the games they played, the Irish were able to challenge enemies inside and outside their neighbourhoods . . . [Sport] involved competition among Catholic ethnics. They enjoyed beating each other but took even more pleasure in routing Protestant foes.

The Irish in America were by no means unusual in availing of sport as a means of both facilitating integration and marking oneself out as distinctive. Indeed, it is generally accepted that sport has served this dual purpose for a whole range of immigrant populations throughout the world (Cronin and Mayall, 1998). In much the same way as other European émigrés, Irish Catholics arriving in America during the nineteenth century were reluctant to completely discard their indigenous culture and traditions, particularly in favour of those of a society that was, as chapter 1 reveals, largely hostile towards them. Thus, they strove to come to a position of accommodation, rather than complete assimilation or acculturation. As pragmatists they absorbed those American cultural forms that would allow them to progress, socially and economically, in the New World. At the same time they sought ways to maintain their links with the 'old country' and preserve and articulate their ethnic distinctiveness. One of the key ways that sections of the Irish community attempted to do this was through the promotion of the traditional Irish sports of Gaelic football and hurling. The role of these sports and their place in the broader menu of institutions and social practices that Irish Catholics could chose from to preserve, construct and express a distinctive sense of ethnic consciousness is articulated by Miller and Wagner (1994: 110):

> In America, Irish ethnic identity flourished on many fronts. Democratic politicians waved the Green flag on election day and the Catholic clergy strove

to preserve in America the religious aspects of Ireland's heritage. Irish-American newspapers provided immigrant readers with news of the old country, giving the comforting impression that Boston or New York were merely western suburbs of Cork or Dublin. Above all, it was the Irish-American ethnic organisations that helped immigrants become reconciled to the American ways and express their abiding love for Ireland. Societies such as the Gaelic Athletic Association and the Philo-Celtic society provided numerous continuities between Irish and Irish-American life.

Elements of the relatively small body of work dealing with the Irish contribution to and involvement in sport in America listed earlier has touched on the significance of Gaelic games in preserving and promoting Irish-American identity in the late nineteenth century. Alongside this important research, there have been a number of other popular and scholarly studies that locate Gaelic games in America at the centre rather than the edges of their analyses. The academic studies include Cronin's (2007) use of the 'travel narrative' to explore the GAA's tour of America in 1888; the work of McGinn (1997) on hurling in New York in the eighteenth century; Black's (1997) unpublished doctoral dissertation on sport, gender, nationalism and the Irish diaspora in San Francisco. Brady's (2005) unpublished postgraduate thesis on Gaelic Park, the home of Gaelic games in New York and her subsequent (2007) analysis of these sports and issues of gender in Irish America. My own work on Gaelic games in Boston, New York, Chicago and San Francisco also falls into this category and has made a significant contribution to our knowledge of the origins, early history and subsequent development of the GAA in each city (Darby, 2001; 2003; 2005; 2006; 2007; 2009a; 2009b). Of the populist work on Gaelic games in the US, King's (1998) analysis of the global diffusion of hurling which includes a chapter on the game in New York, and one examining its development in the rest of North America, is the most notable. There have been also been a number of 'in-house' empirical histories of Gaelic games in America which focus on personalities and competitions. The most significant of these is undoubtedly that published by the NACB (1997). A number of those who have written more broadly on the GAA, particularly Tom Humphries (1998) and Marcus de Búrca (1999) have also commented, albeit briefly, on Gaelic games in the US. While all of this work is important and contributes in a broad sense to our understanding of the history and significance of Gaelic games in the lives of the Irish emigrant community, there has yet to be the type of sustained analysis of these games in Irish America that this book undertakes.

The book

In its most general guise, this study seeks to redress the academic neglect of the socio-economic, psychological, political and cultural import of Gaelic games for the Irish diaspora in the US. Rather than undertake a broad, and what could only be a superficial, analysis of the GAA in each of the 45 or so American towns and cities where Gaelic games are played, this book adopts a case study approach. The regions identified as case studies: Greater Boston, New York, Chicago and San Francisco were chosen largely because, historically they have not only been focal points for Irish immigration but have also been the strongest centres for Gaelic games in the US. The obvious omission in this latter regard is Philadelphia, which has at various stages been one of the healthiest divisions of Gaelic sport in America. This omission is justified on the basis that the book seeks to explore the history and significance of these sports in as geographically representative a manner as possible. Thus, the case studies chosen allow for analyses that span the breadth of the US, from the Atlantic seaboard to the Mid-West and across to the Pacific coast.

The book begins with a context setting discussion of Irish immigration to America. The Irish experience in the cities that form the cornerstones of this study are dealt with in turn and the analyses here concentrate on the period when Gaelic games began to emerge as a visible sporting practice amongst Irish immigrants. In doing so, this chapter sets out the socio-economic, political and cultural terrain within which these sports took root and as such provides the backdrop for the historical analyses of the origins and early development of the GAA that constitute chapter 2. This chapter accounts for the key individuals, organisations and groups responsible for the inception and promotion of Gaelic games in each city and begins to uncover the role that the GAA played for Irish immigrants in the US, politically, economically, socially and psychologically. Chapter 3 builds on these themes by dealing specifically with the ways in which Gaelic sports allowed the Irish in America to preserve their ethnic specificity and, in particular, identify with the Irish nationalist agenda at 'home' and lend their support to the struggle to free Ireland from British rule.

The three chapters that follow address the history of Gaelic games in the US from the turn of the century to the onset of the Great War, during the inter-war years and from the immediate post-war period until the beginning of the 1970s. The focus here is on charting the key developments, processes, agents and agencies that influenced the development of the GAA in each period. These accounts are largely empirically driven but they are cognisant of the broader experiences of the Irish diaspora in America. The narratives show the extent to which the health of Gaelic games in each period was reliant upon a combination of fluctuations in immigration flows from Ireland, the socio-economic and political conditions that the GAA found itself in each city and the resolve, initiative and dedication of a range of individuals in working towards the preservation and promotion of these sports. As these three chapters begin to reveal, the health of Gaelic games in the US across each period was also linked to the extent to which newly arrived Irish immigrants, as well as Irish Americans, felt inclined to express their ethnic heritage or for that matter, maintain more than a passing interest in Irish culture or politics. Chapter 7 picks up this theme in a more focused manner by exploring the ways in which the GAA allowed the Irish in America to articulate senses of Irishness that were rooted in an affinity for the cultural traditions of Ireland and a desire to support their compatriots in Ireland in their struggle for national independence. Particular attention is given to analysing the role of the GAA in engendering support for Irish nationalism in America in the period in and around the Easter Rising of 1916. Thereafter, the chapter concentrates on the ways in which the Association in the US became linked to militant Irish republicanism following the partition of Ireland in 1921, and remained a bulwark of irredentist sentiment in the period leading up to the outbreak of the Troubles in Northern Ireland.

The following two chapters (8 and 9) complete the historical analyses of the GAA in Boston, Chicago, San Francisco and New York by covering the period from the early 1970s to the opening years of the new millennium. As with earlier narrative chapters, the focus here is on examining the reasons behind the fluc-tuating fortunes of the GAA in this period. The socio-economic and political backdrop, continuing fluxes in immigration, not least following the terrorist attacks on America on 11 September 2001, and the enterprise of GAA admin-istrators in their efforts to preserve Gaelic games on American soil are again accorded priority. These chapters also account for the broader socio-economic and psychological functioning of Gaelic games for sections of the Irish diaspora and the role that the Association has played in providing a platform for the maintenance of strong senses of Irishness.

As in previous periods in its history, the Irishness promoted by the GAA and expressed by its members since the 1970s has been simultaneously cultural and political. The final chapter concentrates on the role of the Association in the promotion of this latter, politicised version of Irish identity in the US. It addresses, in particular, the ways in which the development of the Association as a key conduit of Irish republicanism in America was shaped by and reflective of the broader revival in Irish-American nationalism following the outbreak of the Troubles in Northern Ireland in the late 1960s. While the GAA was comprised of individuals who held a variety of political viewpoints and affiliations ranging from liberal and constitutional to republican and vehemently irredentist, this chapter examines a number of revealing examples of the ways in which more militant forms of nationalist sentiment found expression amongst the GAA fraternity in the US during the 1990s.

The book concludes by assessing the prospects for the future of Gaelic games in America in light of immigration restrictions in the post-9/11 period. Beyond examining some of the practical difficulties that the recent homeland security climate in the US has heralded for the GAA and its members, the conclusion questions the extent to which the Association, as an organisation historically linked to a relatively narrow and exclusivist form of Irishness, can continue to remain vibrant and relevant in Irish America.

Theoretical frame

Before turning to the narratives that detail the history of the GAA and account for the socio-economic, political and cultural functioning of Gaelic games in Irish America, it is important to comment on the broad theoretical framework that informs this study. In 2005, the cultural geographer, Adrian Mulligan opened an article examining transatlantic Irish nationalism in the late nineteenth century by bemoaning the lack of a spatial dimension in theorising on nationalism. Mulligan argued that this theorising has largely been 'safely corralled within the territorial boundaries of a respective nation-state' and that one of the key consequences of this was what he referred to as a 'blinkeredness' to the existence of nationalist political or cultural activity functioning beyond or across state borders (Mulligan 2005: 439–40). His own contribution to redressing this state of affairs, an analysis of Fenianism in America in the 1860s, was justified in part through his assertion that theorising the Atlantic world as a 'space of circulations, connections, transmissions and inter-relations' offered a fruitful route to overcoming state-centric analyses of nationalism (Mulligan 2005: 441).

While this book is by no means a specific response to Mulligan's thoughts on the deficiencies of analyses of nationalism, his comments chime with this study on a number of levels. Before highlighting these, it is important to qualify Mulligan's contentions and note that some, not least those who have commented on the construction and expression of Irish nationalism amongst emigrant communities as part of broader analyses of the Irish diaspora, particularly in the US, are likely to dispute his arguments. However, whether or not Mulligan is correct in what he says about analyses of nationalism is a moot point for the purposes of this book and is a debate to be taken up elsewhere. The relevance of his broad argument to this study is that his critique of theorising on nationalism applies to much of the existing scholarship on the relationship between the GAA and Irish national identities which has been overwhelmingly confined to the territorial borders of the Irish Republic and Northern Ireland (Mandle, 1987; Sugden and Bairner, 1993; Rouse, 1993; De Búrca, 1999; Cronin, 1998a and 1999; Hassan, 2003; Murphy, 2009). While in no way seeking to downplay the significance of this work here, what Mulligan's broad position does is to sensitise us to a dearth of research on the role of sport in allowing Irish emigrant communities to express their Irishness and an affinity with the land of their, or their forebears', birth.

Recently, however, there have been moves to redress this gap with the emergence of research, some of which has been detailed above, that has examined sport and the Irish beyond a state-centred territorial framework. The work of Holmes and Storey (2004: 94) on English-born soccer players representing the Republic of Ireland has been significant in this regard, not least because it recognised the need to 'move beyond a conception of national identity that is intrinsically linked to Ireland as a bounded space' and encouraged researchers to 'conceive of Irish identity in diasporic terms; an identity that is no longer place-bound or constrained by the actual borders of Ireland'. A recent co-edited collection (Darby and Hassan, 2008) sought to do this in a much more sustained way than has been the case previously, by exploring the ways in which Irish nationalism is produced, reproduced and contested through a range of sports beyond the territorial boundaries of the island of Ireland. As noted earlier, my own work on the transatlantic diffusion of Gaelic games has begun to reveal that the GAA has operated, to paraphrase Mulligan, as a space of *circulations, connections, transmissions and interrelations* in the Atlantic world within which Irish nationalist political and cultural discourses have been reproduced and can be read. This study continues in this vein, but does so in a much more focused and detailed manner, by accounting for the precise ways in which a nationalist pulse beat through the heart of the GAA in America from its formal inception in the mid 1880s through to the current day. Thus, as well as merely uncovering the history of the GAA in America, this book also seeks to advance our understanding of the relationship between sport, Irish nationalism and Irish diasporic identities.

The empirical accounts contained in this book also speak to and are underpinned by broader theorising on nationalism. Elements of the work of some of the standard bearers in this field, particularly Smith, Anderson and Hobsbawm and Ranger are particularly pertinent in this respect and their analyses inform this study, albeit loosely, in a number of ways. As the empirical evidence presented in this book shows, the versions of Irish nationalism that have been constructed and articulated around the GAA in the US, particularly in the late nineteenth century, are in many senses *imagined* and are rooted in the *invention of tradition*, concepts that lie at the core of Anderson's (1991) and Hobsbawm and Ranger's (1983) work. For example, as demonstrated in chapters 2 and 3, America's earliest Gaels drew on Gaelic games to conjure senses of Irishness that were rooted in romanticised, mythical and certainly 'invented' visions of Ireland as a rural idyll, populated by Gaelic speaking, manly and sport-loving Celts. By playing, watching or helping to organise Gaelic games, these immigrants were able to compress time and space and construct a sense of continuity between their Irish past and an American present. Consuming Gaelic sports through a growing Irish-American newspaper industry was also significant in this process. Of course, followers of Gaelic games in Irish America or the Irish emigrant community in the US more generally were not alone in availing of the print media to build an emotional connection to and unity with a much larger populace. Indeed, as Anderson (1991) notes, the evolution of 'print capitalism' throughout the industrialised world allowed vast numbers of people to think of themselves as part of much larger political communities, ones characterised by strong senses of comradeship. As revealed in chapter 2, in the late nineteenth century a whole succession of reporters and newspaper correspondents in Irish America sought to couch the playing of Gaelic games in the US as the national *duty* of Irish immigrants. In doing so, those who answered this national call and populated US branches of the GAA were able to imagine themselves as part of and reconnect with the broader Irish nationalist community.

It is important at this juncture to note that it would be erroneous to suggest that the nationalisms that became embodied in and were evoked through the GAA in the US were in some way artificial, inauthentic or that they had no material basis. Anderson's (1991: 6) work is again instructive here, particularly his criticism of Ernest Gellner whom he accuses of conflating the terms 'invented' or 'imagined' with 'fabrication' or 'falsity'. Thus, those who gleaned so much solace from the GAA by drawing on it to reinvent or imagine particular traditions, interpretations, stories or versions of Ireland and Irishness were not falsifying or fabricating senses of communal identity. Rather, an afternoon spent in the company of other Irish people focused around a distinctively Irish pastime in a physical space that was discernibly of *home* allowed them to bridge the gap, albeit temporarily but also in a very *real* sense, between Ireland and what many immigrants felt was a temporary exile in the New World. Thus, the nationalism articulated through the Gaelic football or hurling club was not only experienced psychologically but was rooted in directly observable, objective and material elements. As has been noted, of particular significance were the opportunities for interaction with fellow Irish immigrants that Gaelic games offered and the physical spaces that the GAA in America obtained and utilised to promote and preserve its sports. It is worth making a few further comments on both. In terms of the former, the narratives contained in this book reveal that much of the appeal of Gaelic games in the US was linked to the fact that they provided a setting where like-minded individuals could come together to play sport, socialise, catch up with news from home, talk about Irish politics and even simply enjoy the company of members of the opposite sex.[5] While all of this helped the Irish adjust to life in their new surrounds, it also helped them articulate their nationalism. The significance of the human interactions that the GAA facilitated between Irish immigrants in engendering nationalism can be observed in Richard English's (2006: 438) view that 'Much of the coherence and durability of nationalism has been built out of human intimacies'. As revealed throughout this book, the GAA in the US has, from the late nineteenth century to the beginning of the twenty-first, afforded Irish immigrants and their offspring opportunities to engage in and experience the sorts of *human intimacies* that English has argued are so important in the construction and fostering of nationalism.

The physicality of the GAA pitch and its environs and the sights and sounds that emanated from these spaces were also crucial in this regard. In attempting to make sense of the space within which Gaelic games in the US occurred vis-à-vis the articulation of Irish nationalism, the work of Fulton and Bairner (2007) and Bairner (2007; 2008) is instructive. Their innovative approach explores the intersections of sport, Irish nationalism and space, or more specifically, particular understandings of space. Bairner's (2007; 2008) analysis of the concept of national sports within the context of theoretical debates on nations and nationalism and more importantly for the purposes of the discussion here, readings or interpretations of national landscapes, is particularly pertinent. Bairner is drawn to the work of Lefebvre (1991) which advocates that space is accorded significance in analyses of nationalism. This allows him to argue that the landscapes, real or perceived, that are evoked through or associated with particular sports are key in allowing them to be considered national or otherwise. The importance of Bairner's analysis of notions of space and place to this study is that it helps us to view the physical spaces that the GAA has utilised in America from the late nineteenth century onwards as significant in offering immigrants and their children a material, objective and observable context in which to root their Irish nationalism. The role of these spaces is encapsulated in a poem about hurling published in *The Gael*, a New York monthly targeted at an Irish-American audience, in May 1887. The poem, entitled 'An Irish Hurling-Green: A Ballad for the Gael' opened with the following lines:

> Full many years, 'neath foreign skies,
> A stranger have I strayed,
> I've mingled in their sportive joys,
> And heard their music played;
> But still the dearest spot on earth-
> Which links me to its scene-
> For cheerful, hearty, guileless mirth,
> Is an Irish hurling-green (*The Gael*, May 1887: 705).

This poem is certainly intended to arouse an emotional, nostalgic response from the immigrant reader, one that fuses hurling with Irishness and a sense of place. It clearly seeks to remind the reader that the physical spaces within which hurling is played are distinctively Irish and offer boundless opportunities for reasserting Irish nationalist sentiment. The final line of this verse contains a certain ambiguity though, specifically its failure to reveal the geographical locale of the Irish hurling-green in question. This ambiguity may not have been intended but the fact that it exists reminds us that the Irish hurling-green or Gaelic football field in Boston, New York, Chicago or San Francisco can function as a space where the Irish immigrant can experience the sort of *cheerful, hearty, guileless mirth* and physical surrounds that links and reconnects them to Ireland and their Irishness.

Thus, while the versions of Irish nationalism that have been built and cohere around the GAA in the US are in some ways imagined and invented, they also have a tangible, material basis, one bound up with the human intimacies that engagement in Gaelic sports involves and the physical spaces where they are played. But what of the precise character of the nationalism expressed in and through the GAA in the US? Was it homogeneous or monochrome? Was it inclusive or exclusive? Was it political or cultural or both? Was it static or was it fluid and historically dynamic? The answers to these questions can be found in the narratives contained in this book, particularly those in chapters 3, 7 and 10. The analyses here are mindful of a recent trend in writing on the Irish in Canada and the US, noted by William Jenkins (2005), which has begun to deconstruct totalising notions of a 'global' or 'North American' Irish migrant identity. As such, the empirical evidence presented in this study shows that the Irishness constructed around and expressed through the GAA in America has been multifaceted, heterogeneous and has fluctuated and shifted over time according to specific circumstances both in Ireland and in the US.

In terms of capturing and framing, theoretically, the fluid, dynamic and multifaceted nature of the Irishness that coheres around and is articulated within the GAA in the US, the work of Anthony Smith, particularly the distinction that he draws between 'ethnic' and 'civic' nationalism, is especially useful. For Smith (1986; 1995), ethnic solidarity and loyalties, rooted in a common myth of descent and shared history, the possession of a distinctive shared culture and an association with and affinity for a specific territory, have been hugely instrumental in constructing the feelings of communal identity that underpin nationalism. This ethnic version of nationalism is clearly accommodated in primordial as opposed to modernist assumptions about the nation and nationalism. As a consequence, it is often viewed as closed, exclusive, regressive and intolerant. Alongside this ethnic version of nationalism though is a more civic brand, believed to have emerged in the modern age, which is more liberal and inclusive in interpreting who belongs to the nation and how that sense of belonging might be expressed. It is important to note, as many, including Smith (1995) have done, that it is erroneous to completely separate out these forms of nationalism. As English (2006: 451), recently intoned:

> There are myriad shades of national community, some more civil and relaxed and inclusive than others, some exhibiting more liberal forms of nationalism and others more illiberal varieties: But frequently one finds that civic and ethnic definitions of the nation compete, coexist and mingle with one another within the same nationalism, and that distinctions between the two tend not to be absolute in practice.

English's comments here resonate with the nature of the Irish nationalism that has been articulated within the GAA in the US from its inception up until the current day. As observed in chapter 3, in the late nineteenth-century involvement in Gaelic games allowed newly arrived Irish immigrants who had ultimately become citizens of America but who still saw themselves as Irish, to identify themselves, in ethnic terms, as part of the Irish nation. For those who joined an emergent GAA in this period, involvement in Gaelic games served as an extension of a belligerent, Anglophobic, politicised, ethnic version of Irishness, one that was fashioned by their experiences, real or imagined, of British repression in Ireland and of their experiences of exile in the US. In the opening decades of the twentieth century, participation in or consumption of Gaelic games continued to serve as a vehicle for an ethnically conceived nationalism. As revealed in chapter 7, this was very much in evidence in the period leading up to the Easter Rising in 1916 and again, as chapter 10 demonstrates, during the Troubles in Northern Ireland. That said, the extent to which America's Gaels drew on their sports specifically to express ethnic forms of nationalism fluctuated, very often according to events in Ireland and the US. While the partition of Ireland and a subsequent decline in Irish-American nationalism may have encouraged some to cling tighter to the GAA as a marker of a distinctive ethnicity, others drew on Gaelic games to retain and give vent to a relatively benign, culturally focused and ultimately liberal sense of 'Irishness'. This process of flux and the waxing and waning of nationalist discourse within the GAA in the US has been an ongoing process and one that continues apace today. Indeed, this study concludes by suggesting that while the functioning of the GAA as a reservoir of political nationalism helped to sustain Gaelic games in the US at various stages in its history, it is likely that the survival of these sports in post-9/11 America might be partly dependent on eschewing or at least downplaying the Association's long-standing linkages to ethnic versions of Irishness. Before considering the ways in which these various forms of Irishness were played out within the GAA in New York, Boston, Chicago and San Francisco, and accounting for the history of Gaelic games in these locales, it is necessary to explore the processes through which each city became so heavily populated by Irish immigrants in the first place.

CHAPTER ONE

Crossing the bowl of tears: the Irish journey to America

Introduction

Sustained Irish emigration to North America has a history that stretches back long before the American Revolution to the beginning of the seventeenth century. Initially, emigrants were made up predominantly of Irish Catholics, but during the late seventeenth century they were replaced by Protestants of Scottish and English descent as the largest grouping of Irish immigrants in the New World. This remained the case until the end of the eighteenth century, but the early decades of the nineteenth century saw a resurgence in the numbers of Irish Catholics seeking a new life in America. With the end of the Napoleonic Wars and a subsequent drop in demand for Irish agricultural products, the period between 1815 and 1845 saw around a million Irish immigrants – twice as many as in the previous two centuries combined – disembarking on American shores (Miller, 1985). Although it would be an oversimplification to view Irish emigration to the New World as simply a reactive or enforced process, the Great Famine (1845–50) was undoubtedly the most significant factor in the massive exodus of the Irish from their homeland. The impact of the famine was such that by the early 1870s the number of Irish-born people who had left Ireland had reached three million with over half of them settling in America (D'Arcy, 1999).

Beyond quantifying Irish emigration to America it is important, for the purpose of this study, to account for what the Irish encountered on disembarkation from their long, wrenching and often hazardous journeys across the Atlantic Ocean. Was the socio-economic and political lot of Irish men and

The bowl of tears: This is the name often given to the perilous and wrenching journey which millions of Irish men, women and children braved in their migrations to the New World. This phrase is also inscribed on the Famine memorial in downtown Boston.

women better in their new homes than it was in their old? How were they received and treated by America's Anglo-Protestant establishment? How did they adapt to their new environment and what institutions helped them acquire stability, respect and success in America? By addressing these questions and examining the early patterns of Irish Catholic immigration in Boston, New York, Chicago and San Francisco, this chapter provides an understanding of the socio-economic and political milieu into which Gaelic games were diffused and subsequently developed. In doing so, it sets the context for much of what is to follow.

Boston and the 'alien' Irish

Although Boston was one of America's largest eastern seaboard ports, making it an obvious location for Irish immigration, the demography of the broader Massachusetts region prior to the mid nineteenth century was such that it is somewhat surprising that it became one of the foremost Irish-American cities. As Thomas O'Connor (1995: xv), the pre-eminent historian of the Boston Irish, argued:

> If there had existed in the nineteenth century a computer able to digest all the appropriate data, it would have reported one city in the entire world where an Irish Catholic, under any circumstance, should never, ever, set foot. That city was Boston, Massachusetts.

The first settlers in the area were predominantly Anglo-Protestants many of whom possessed strong Puritan beliefs and harboured deep suspicions of Catholicism and the Irish. Indeed, it has been suggested that their sojourn to the New World in the first place was motivated in part by Anti-Irish sentiments (O'Toole, 1999).[1] In view of such attitudes, it is unsurprising that the first federal census of 1790 revealed that the number of Irish Catholics living in Boston constituted less than five per cent of the city's total population. Boston remained an Anglo-Protestant stronghold until the late 1840s. By 1850, however, approximately 35,000 – one quarter of the population – had been born in Ireland, making the Irish 'the city's most significant "alien" population practically over-night' (O'Toole, 1999: 57). The newly arrived Irish were indeed viewed as alien by Anglo-Protestant Bostonians. They had brought with them a religion that was detested and culturally, there were few, if any, areas of common ground.

For example, Boston was a city with a strong literary heritage, fostered by the Brahmin aristocratic tradition. However, enforced illiteracy through the Penal Laws introduced in Ireland by the British meant that large numbers of those emigrating in or around the famine era could not share with Bostonians their love of literature. Although prejudice against Irish Catholics was based primarily on religion, the mindset of Boston's established population towards their new Irish neighbours was also rooted in crude racial stereotypes about the Irish 'race'.

The discrimination that emanated from this religious, cultural and racist bias contributed to a growing sense of alienation and persecution amongst the Boston Irish. The Irish enclaves that sprang up predominantly around the dock areas, in the slums of the city's north end and in South Boston were home to a community which felt isolated and disenfranchised. Irish Catholics in these enclaves also experienced a range of practical, socio-economic problems. While many were able to find work, albeit as poorly paid unskilled labourers, the areas where they lived were typified by social deprivation and dire living conditions. Poor levels of sanitation and serious overcrowding contributed to the regular outbreak of diseases such as smallpox, cholera and tuberculosis resulting in high rates of infant mortality. The austerity of life in Boston's Irish communities combined with the psychological trauma caused by moving from essentially rural environs in Ireland to sprawling urban metropolises in the New World were such that Irish neighbourhoods were also often plagued by a range of social problems, particularly pauperism, drunkenness and crime.

What had once been a relatively homogeneous city soon became one that was wracked by ethnic and religious tensions with the 'Famine Irish' almost universally viewed as the primary cause. Beatty (1992: 22) paints a vivid picture of the widely held perceptions of the Irish at the time and the impact that they were believed to have had on Boston:

> The Irish had been a lump – 'undigested, undigestible,' in Oscar Handlin's words – in the throat of a city that had not asked them to come, and that regarded them as the human equivalent of locusts. Boston had been a clean and salubrious place before the arrival of the 'Famine Irish'; now it was dirty and noisome. Boston had been a unified moral community; now it was divided. Boston had stood for progress in religion and politics; now it was home to a reactionary religion.

The prejudice, animosity and discrimination emanating from such perceptions did little to ameliorate the harsh socio-economic environment encountered by Irish immigrants. Anti-Irish hostility, rooted in nativist American sentiment, had found expression in Boston since the late eighteenth century and it grew concomitantly with increasing immigration. This hostility took a variety of forms ranging from random attacks on Irish neighbourhoods by gangs of local toughs and the burning of convents and Catholic churches to discriminatory employment practices which manifested themselves most visibly in the form of the ubiquitous 'No Irish Need Apply' notices. Nativist prejudice reached its peak in Boston in 1854 with the success of the Native American Party, popularly known as the 'Know-Nothings',[2] in the Massachusetts State elections. They quickly proceeded to introduce a series of draconian reforms aimed at checking levels of immigration, restricting the vote for new arrivals and venting their enmity towards Irish Catholics by severely restricting funds to those social and religious institutions serving that community.

Despite the difficulties encountered by the Boston Irish, they were, in many ways, sustained by a range of social, political and religious institutions, not least of which was the Catholic Church which allowed them to preserve a sense of communal identity. Newspapers such as the *Boston Pilot* were also important in this respect and by carrying news from 'home' they helped to shrink the distance, psychologically at least, between Ireland and America. Irish ethnic neighbourhoods also played a role in the process of community building. Although they had functioned in many senses as 'ghettoes of mind and place' (McCaffrey, 1992), they gradually came to represent 'psychological havens . . . focused around the Catholic parish . . . preserving faith, tradition, and values, perpetuating a sense of community' (McCaffrey, 1997: 71). Despite the fact that the Irish in Boston had developed a sense of being a persecuted and excluded minority, these ethnic 'havens' did much to foster the self-sufficiency and confidence which came to underpin their gradual path to acceptance, stability and success.

Although a self-image as persecuted may have been justified, numerically the Irish were, of course, by no means a minority and this came to represent a crucial element in their slow advance within Boston. Within the context of local ward politics in the city, it was becoming increasingly unrealistic for Boston's political establishment to antagonise such a potentially politically powerful ethnic group. The tokenist patronage that resulted from this realisation allowed for a degree of social mobility for sections of the Irish emigrant community. They were aided in this regard by the fact that the Know-Nothings, unable to sustain support for their discriminatory reform policies, had effectively fallen as a political force in Boston by 1860. The Irish quest for acceptance and equality was also assisted by their contribution in the American Civil War during which the famous Ninth Massachusetts Infantry and a range of other mainly Irish regiments gave distinguished service to preserving the Union. With the conclusion of the war the Irish began to make a broader contribution to Boston society, particularly in the fields of education and business. However, it was perhaps in the domain of politics that the Irish made their biggest and most visible mark in Boston in this period.

The abilities of a range of Irishmen in local ward politics and their subsequent electoral successes in the second half of the nineteenth century provided the Irish community with a voice with which to challenge the established Protestant hegemony and gradually redress the discrimination that emanated from it. The election of Cork-born Patrick Collins to the Massachusetts State Senate in 1876, the first Irishman to achieve that feat, and the election of Hugh O'Brien as the city's first Irish Catholic Mayor in 1884 were crucial. Conscious of the primacy of patronage in local politics and skilfully manipulating ethnic and religious polarisation in the city, subsequent Irish politicians and the long line of Irish mayors of Boston who succeeded O'Brien[3] acted as advocates of the Irish community. As a consequence, opportunities, prospects and standards of living for the Boston Irish, based predominantly in areas such as South Boston, Brighton, Charlestown and the 'streetcar suburbs' of Dorchester, Jamaica Plain and Roxbury, gradually began to improve. The Boston that welcomed Irish immigrants in the second half of the nineteenth century and early years of the twentieth century was thus considerably more hospitable than that encountered by those who arrived in the city during the great waves of immigration between 1815 and 1860. It should be noted, however, that this was not the result of the efforts of a select number of successful Irish immigrants acting on behalf of a passive majority. Rather it was more a consequence of a growing confidence and resolve on the part of the broader Irish community to stand up and make their way in their new home. This is a point skilfully put across by Peter Eisinger (cited in McCaffrey, 1997: 71) who argued, 'Where their fathers and grandfathers had generally turned inward before a hostile environment, the generation of the 1880s, now reasonably well-established, held their heads high and fought back'.

The New York Irish

Following the general pattern of Irish immigration outlined at the start of this chapter, New York acquired a not inconsiderable Irish Catholic population in the decades prior to the flood of Famine Irish into the city. By the middle of the nineteenth century, over a quarter of the city's population was Irish and by the 1870s New York possessed America's largest Irish community, making it in Diner's (1997: 93) words 'the most Irish city in the Union'. Despite the presence of such large numbers of their fellow countrymen and women, New York was anything but a welcoming environment. The leaving of home and family in Ireland caused considerable anguish for the average Irish immigrant and the transition from living in essentially rural locales in Ireland to a noisome, fast-paced, urban environment created further difficulties. What they encountered in the ethnic neighbourhoods that sprang up in lower Manhattan, particularly in the Sixth Ward and the Five-Points neighbourhood, did little to ameliorate their sense of dislocation and alienation in the New World. The types of socio-economic problems experienced by those living in these neighbourhoods did not make for a comfortable existence. Social deprivation, squalor, serious over-crowding, disease, high rates of infant mortality, pauperism, drunkenness and crime were as much a part of New York's Irish enclaves as they were in Boston.

The inhospitable social environment that much of the Irish emigrant community encountered in New York was worsened by an intense anti-Irish and anti-Catholic hostility, rooted in Nativist American sentiment. Nativism had found expression in the city since the early nineteenth century, but by the 1840s it had developed into a coherent political and ideological movement, with the Nativists becoming highly visible and prominent in New York politics. More militant wings of the movement emerged and organisations such as the Order of the Star Spangled Banner gave vent to their prejudice in increasingly violent forms. The massive influx of Famine Irish did much to further fuel Nativist sentiment and, as in Massachusetts, political support for the Native American Party's anti-Irish and anti-Catholic agenda reached its peak in 1854 with successes in the State elections. Although the Know-Nothings disappeared as a political force in New York a few years later, ethnic and religious tension continued to characterise life in the city, a fact most clearly exemplified by the 12 July riots in 1871 between Irish Catholics and members of the Orange Order that left 52 dead.

Despite such harsh socio-economic and political conditions, New York's Irish community was, in much the same way as the Boston Irish, supported and sustained by various benevolent and charitable societies, Irish newspapers, Irish ethnic neighbourhoods and, of course, the Catholic Church, all of which provided them with a sense of continuity between the old country and the New World. In terms of social improvement and economic mobility, Irish involvement in the city's political machine and their relationship with the Democratic Party was crucial. Within the city's local ward politics, the Irish became the 'pawns of the urban Democratic machine' (Diner, 1997: 102), benefiting in particular from the support of William 'Boss' Tweed, the dominant figure in New York politics in the 1860s. Under Tweed, the Irish became much more visible and prominent in the city's political machine. Indeed, following Tweed's demise in 1871, the Irish assumed the leadership of the Democratic Party. The significance of this development is well summed up by Diner (ibid.), who noted, 'Now instead of crumbs and slices, the Irish had the whole loaf of New York City politics'.

Adjusting to the social, economic and political realities of life in New York was a slow and, for many Irish, a painful process. However, the city encountered by new Irish immigrants in the latter stages of the nineteenth century was a different proposition from that experienced by their predecessors. Although life could still be intensely difficult for the city's Irish, new opportunities were opening up to them and social acceptance and mobility were within reach. These were partially a result of a recognition on the part of politicians of the importance and size of the Irish vote. Equally important, though, was a confidence and determination on the part of the New York Irish, fuelled by a range of Irish social, economic, religious, political and cultural institutions that were springing up in the city, to grasp the opportunities that the city was belatedly presenting to them.

The Irish in Chicago

Until the mid 1830s, the majority of Irish immigrants in America were concentrated in the expanding cities of the north-east coast. While some did venture inland, it was not until opportunities opened up for work, albeit poorly paid and low skilled, on the Illinois and Michigan canal network between 1838 and 1848, that significant numbers of Irish Catholics made the journey to Chicago. Canal workers were joined by further waves of Irish immigrants throughout this period to take advantage of manual jobs in the city's lumber wharves, railroads, stockyards, meat packing plants, brickyards and steel mills. By 1850 the Irish constituted about one fifth of the total population of Chicago, making them, along with the Germans, the city's largest ethnic group. The Irish continued to be a numerically large grouping in the city in the second half of the century. For example, between 1860 and 1870 their number doubled from 20,000 to 40,000 and by 1890 this figure had risen to 70,000 (O'Gorman, 2001).

Because of the size of the Irish population and its presence in Chicago from the time it was formally incorporated as a city in 1837, sections of the Irish community were able to navigate a relatively rapid path to social mobility and respectability. Some Irish quickly acquired a disproportionate level of influence in the highest echelons of the Catholic Church and city government (McCaffrey et al., 1987). Despite their number and their contribution to politics, the Church and the construction of the infrastructure that allowed Chicago to transform itself from frontier outpost to thriving mid-western industrial metropolis, the Irish working classes at that time experienced the same socio-economic hardships as those endured by their countrymen and women in Boston and New York (Kelleher, 2001). The vast majority lived in impoverished conditions. They were employed on the bottom rung of the job ladder as low-paid, unskilled labourers and they lived in poor neighbourhoods such as Kilgubbin on the city's north side, Hardscrabble (renamed Bridgeport by the middle of the century), close to the south branch of Chicago River and on the west side of the city. These neighbourhoods endured similar problems to Irish enclaves elsewhere in the country. Inadequate housing, overcrowding, poor sanitation, disease, crime and poverty were all part of the lived experiences of the Irish in mid nineteenth-century Chicago. Although some continued to succeed economically and politically in the latter decades of the century, things did not improve markedly for many of the city's Irish-born inhabitants. By 1890 34 per cent of the Irish population remained in poorly paid, unskilled employment doing manual labour in difficult conditions (Miller, 1985). By the turn of the century many still lived below the poverty line and life in Irish slums continued to be marked by chronic unemployment, disease and alcoholism (Miller, 1985), circum-stances humorously lamented in the newspaper columns of Finley Peter Dunne's fictional Bridgeport based character 'Mr Dooley' (Fanning, 1999).

The lives of the Irish working class in the second half of the nineteenth century were not helped by the type of Anglo-Protestant and Nativist discrim-ination experienced by their compatriots in New York and Boston. In the

1850s, Chicago's Protestant community distanced itself from the Irish, and leading figures in this community actively discriminated against them. Joseph Medill, publisher of the *Chicago Tribune* and son of Ulster Presbyterian parents, often used the newspaper to disparage Irish Catholic Chicagoans (Skerrett, 2004). One particularly blunt editorial on the 'problem' of large numbers of Irish Catholics resident in the city commented, 'Who does not know that the most depraved, debased, worthless and irredeemable drunkards and sots which curse the community are Irish Catholics' (cited in O'Gorman, 2001: x). In 1855 this prejudice became enshrined in the position of Mayor with the appointment of the Know-Nothing candidate Levi Boone. Although Know-Nothingism soon died out as a coherent, organised political ideology, further waves of anti-Irish and anti-Catholic sentiment emerged in the city in the late 1880s and early 1890s. A number of leading Chicago Protestants lent support to anti-immigrant groups such as the American Protective Association, formed in 1887, whose prejudice manifested itself in the form of a pledge neither to vote for nor to employ Catholics (McCaffrey et al., 1987). Nativist prejudice directed against the Irish at this time was also evident in the anti-Catholicism displayed by elements of the Republican Party in the Midwest (Doyle, 1989). As will be seen in the next chapter, the discrimination that emanated from such philosophies had a negative impact on the growth of Gaelic games in the city in the early 1890s.

Although Anglo-Protestant intolerance of those Irish Catholics in their midst held sections of the Chicago Irish back, it also helped to galvanise a strong ethnic consciousness. Emerging Irish neighbourhoods and the Catholic Church had laid the foundations of a sense of communal solidarity amongst the city's Irish population during the late 1830s and 1840s. The Famine Irish that followed were sustained in a similar fashion by local parishes and their spiritual leaders. Their ethnic identity was also shaped by a strong commitment to Irish nationalism, demonstrated by the generous support in financial and human resources that Irish Chicagoans provided to the Fenians in the 1860s and later to Clan na Gael. Indeed, for a period in the 1880s, Chicago was a focal point for Clan na Gael's activities with cells existing throughout the Irish dominated Catholic parishes. Chicago's Irish also showed their support for constitutional strands of the nationalist cause by backing Parnell's parliamentary approach in the 1880s and beyond (O'Gorman, 2001). This support was galvanised in many senses by the visits of leading members of the Irish Parliamentary Party to Irish-American strongholds, including Chicago. As chapter 3 reveals, support for and involvement in Gaelic games were to provide another way in which Irish Chicagoans in this period could demonstrate commitment to the broader nationalist agenda and express politicised versions of Irishness.

Chicago's Irish community were supported and sustained socially, economically, politically and psychologically in ways other than by the Church and the Irish nationalist movement. As noted earlier, the Irish had been well represented in local politics since the incorporation of Chicago as a city and in the period following the Great Fire of 1871 they came to dominate the Democratic Party. Although there were relatively few Irish mayors in the city in this period, at least compared to other cities with high numbers of Irish immigrants,[4] the Irish propensity for and abilities in local patronage-based politics were such that sections of Irish community benefited socially and economically from the city's political machine. The Irish-dominated Catholic Church in Chicago also facilitated the provision of an expanding education system, where faith and Irishness were further preserved and nurtured. Irish newspapers, such as John F. Finnerty's strongly nationalist *New World*, also enhanced a sense of ethnic cohesion that permeated Chicago's Irish community, as did a range of social and benevolent societies, particularly the Ancient Order of Hibernians. This awareness of their ethnicity and desire to mark themselves out as distinctively Irish also manifested itself in the revival of traditional Irish culture in the city from the 1880s. Traditional music and dance featured prominently (Skerrett, 2004) and, as the next chapter highlights, this cultural revival also incorporated Gaelic games.

The Irish in San Francisco

The discovery of gold in the foothills of Sierra Nevada in 1848 was the defining moment in San Francisco's modern history, transforming it from a muddy village into a thriving mecca for prospectors and a rapidly expanding supply centre and transit town. The scale and pace of San Francisco's transformation was evident in the fact that in January 1848 there were fewer than a thousand inhabitants, but thirty years later it was the tenth largest city in the US, with a population of around 250,000 (Burchell, 1979). The Gold Rush and San Francisco's subsequent expansion also opened up the city to Irish immigrants. Although there had been an Irish presence on America's west coast (Curry, 1999), the prospect of riches and opportunities resulted in a rapid influx of Irish migrants into San Francisco. Irish Catholics soon became the largest foreign-born group in the city with their number expanding from 4,200 in 1852 to 30,000 by 1880. When second, third and fourth-generation Irish are added to these figures, San Francisco's Irish population, just thirty years after the Gold Rush, stood at one third of the city's total (Burchell, 1979).

The experiences of Irish emigrants in San Francisco were in many ways untypical of those of their counterparts elsewhere in the New World. The majority of those Irish who settled in San Francisco in the years after the Gold Rush did not arrive directly from Ireland. They came initially from already established Irish communities in Australasia and America's eastern seaboard; subsequently, the vast majority migrated from the states of New York, Massachusetts and Pennsylvania. San Francisco's burgeoning Irish community were therefore accustomed to adjusting to foreign climes, and were consequently more confident about what life in the city might have in store for them and how best to take advantage of the opportunities on offer (Clark, 1986). Their experience and confidence were augmented by their resilience, command of the English language, familiarity with American and British culture, skills and education, all of which helped them to make a success of their life in the city (O'Keefe, 2005). As Breatnac (1970: 17) observed:

> rather than arriving late and finding all the preferred places taken, the Irish were at the Golden Gate when society was still rather open and fluid. Better equipped than their eastern cousins, those Irishmen who made it all the way West possessed either greater talent or capital, or both. And their self-assurance knew no limit.

Irish settlement patterns in San Francisco also differed from those in other centres of Irish immigration elsewhere in America. The Irish who poured into Boston, New York and Chicago were tightly concentrated in particular parts of each city, forming ethnic neighbourhoods and slums. For those who travelled west to San Francisco, the settlement patterns were much more diffuse. In the years immediately following the Gold Rush, Irish immigrants took up residence in the vicinity of the Bay, but subsequently dispersed all over the city as building works and infrastructure projects were completed. Although Telegraph Hill and the area around St Patrick's on Market Street were notable for having relatively large Irish communities, these were not the heavily concentrated ethnic neighbourhoods or ghettos that were to be found on America's Atlantic coast. This trend of the Irish dispersing widely throughout the city continued into the 1870s and 1880s. By 1870 there was not a single area or ward in the city where Irish residency, as a percentage of the total ward population, exceeded 28 per cent (Burchell, 1979).

The extent to which the Irish experience in San Francisco deviated from the norm in Irish America in this period extends beyond the route of their migration and subsequent settlement patterns. The socio-economic and political environment that the Irish experienced on arrival in the city differed markedly from that found further east. Although Irish progress elsewhere in the country was undermined by anti-Catholic and anti-Irish prejudice, nativism was much less of a force in San Francisco, which resulted in fewer barriers to their socio-economic mobility and path to respectability (Kline, 2000). This is not to suggest that there was little friction between the Irish and Anglo-Americans in this period. Conflict did occur, particularly in the sphere of politics (Curry, 1999). However, nativism, as a restrictive influence on Irish progress in San Francisco, was limited by a number of factors. The lack of an established Anglo-Protestant community or a propertied, anti-Irish elite prior to the 1850s was clearly significant, as was the existence of a well-established tradition of Catholicism throughout California (O'Keefe, 2005). While sections of the city's Irish community experienced similar problems of adjustment to those found on the Atlantic coast, the Irish were not the destitute, diseased and dishevelled famine immigrants that poured into New York and Boston. Perceptions of the rapid influx of Irish immigrants were consequently characterised by greater tolerance.

The numerical strength of Irish immigrants as a proportion of the population was also important in helping them to establish themselves in San Franciscan society, not least because it made them an important electoral grouping and one whose aspirations and sensibilities needed to be indulged by those seeking political office. Their rapid advancement in the city's political machine made San Francisco the very epitome of Irish political power in late nineteenth-century America. The election of Frank McCoppin as Mayor of San Francisco in 1867, the first time an Irishman had been elected mayor of a US city, was particularly significant. As Dowling (1998: xxxi) suggests, 'The election of Irish-born Frank McCoppin as Mayor of San Francisco in 1867 rolled out the Kelly green carpet on which the Irish marched to power that lasted for well over a century'. Irish mobility, though, extended beyond politics – sections of the Irish population made a significant contribution to the city's booming business environment and became highly visible in civic life.

From the 1850s onwards, the immense variety of Irish benevolent, social, political and fraternal societies that sprang up in the city made San Francisco a more welcoming environment for the Irish who settled there (Dowling, 1998).

These ranged from the Hibernian Society, the first Irish association established in the city, which emphasised fraternity, to the St Mary's Ladies' Society, a group that brought together Irish women to celebrate social and religious bonds. Not all of the societies established by the Irish in San Francisco, however, were as benign and apolitical. By the late 1850s, support for the Irish nationalist cause found expression in the city with the establishment of a strong Fenian movement, albeit one that was undone by factionalism in the mid to late 1860s. The decline of Fenianism in the city did not, though, herald an end to the desire of the city's Irish population to meet with their compatriots and express their Irishness. The Ancient Order of Hibernians (AOH), established in San Francisco in 1869, was particularly important. Such was the success of this group in providing a focal point for the Irish community that by 1880 the AOH had ten divisions in the city (Burchell, 1979). The whole range of San Francisco's Irish associations as well as the Catholic Church nurtured and sustained the Irish community and, as they had done elsewhere, allowed for the creation and expression of a strong sense of ethnic identity. As Burchell (1979: 115) posits: 'These societies acted not only as a psychological safety net, breaking, at least, any downward fall into desperation and despair. At the same time they were the bricks that built up the public Irish community.'

None of this is to suggest that opportunities for progress and a financially secure life in San Francisco were available to all members of the Irish emigrant community. As in other parts of the country, access to all that the city had to offer – socially, economically and politically – was unequal and often determined by social class and the performance of the local economy (Burchell, 1979). As a consequence, sections of the Irish working class experienced similar failure, poverty and hardship to their counterparts on the Atlantic seaboard, exemplified by their disproportionately high numbers in the city's almshouses, correctional facilities and orphanages from the mid to late nineteenth century (O'Keefe, 2005). However, for the majority of Irish immigrants, San Francisco was a much more welcoming destination than Boston, New York or Chicago. As Riordan (cited in Dowling, 1998: xvii) has succinctly concluded, 'whatever the reasons, economic, political and social advancement was a virtual open door for the Irish in California'.

Conclusion

Although the Irish in America had experienced varying degrees of difficulty in adjusting to life in the New World, by the late 1880s they were beginning to emerge as one of the country's most confident, self reliant, politically savvy and ethnically aware immigrant groups. The transition they had made from desolate famine immigrants to a strident ethnic group was difficult and by no means complete by the close of nineteenth century. Nonetheless, the Irish had come through hard times in slum neighbourhoods. They had endured hostility, prejudice and discrimination from the Anglo-Protestant establishment and had been confronted with a welter of other social, economic and emotional difficulties. Their ability and desire to make a success of their lives in the US was fashioned in many senses by the harsh environment in which they found themselves. This environment built a strong sense of group consciousness and was one of the key building blocks on which Irish progress was built. A whole host of institutions, including the Catholic Church, political parties, benevolent and charitable organisations, county societies, nationalist groups, all played a key role here. Sports, predominantly those of the American variety, also made an important contribution. By the late 1870s and early 1880s, however, Irish versions of sport, namely Gaelic football and hurling, had emerged and began to play an important role in allowing sections of the Irish in America to adjust to their new home and preserve a strong sense of Irishness.

CHAPTER TWO

Sowing the seeds: the origins and early development of Gaelic games in America

Introduction

The largest overseas branch of the GAA can undoubtedly be found in the US. This is clearly linked to the scale of Irish immigration from the mid nineteenth century. It is also a result of the fact that, historically, Irish Catholics in the US have actively sought to preserve and project their ethnic specificity. They have done this in a range of ways. The Catholic Church, the ballot box, social organisations, the Irish-American press as well as popular cultural forms such as traditional Irish music and dance have all been highly significant. As outlined in the introduction, a range of sports such as baseball, basketball, boxing and athletics also served as mechanisms through which Irish emigrants publicly declared and celebrated their 'Irishness'. In charting the origins and early development of Gaelic games in each of the American cities that form the focal points of this study, this chapter reveals that Gaelic football and hurling were also significant in this regard. As well as identifying and examining the key agencies and individuals responsible for the inception and initial growth of organised versions of Gaelic games in the US, the historical analyses that now follow also shed light on the social, psychological, economic and political role of the GAA for Irish immigrants in late nineteenth-century America.

The origins of Gaelic sport in Boston: picnic pleasures and organised games (1879–1890)

The roots of Gaelic games in Boston can be found in the inception of the Irish Athletic Club of Boston (IACB) in September 1879 (*Boston Pilot*, 4 Oct. 1879). This club was founded by and composed of first-generation Irishmen, all of whom were members of the Boston Philo-Celtic Society, an organisation that was established six years earlier with the express purpose of preserving and promoting Irish culture throughout Boston and Massachusetts (Dineen, 1901: 292). In view of the IACB's composition, it is unsurprising to note that its central remit was to promote 'the preservation of the national games, sports, and pastimes of Ireland' amongst Boston's Irish community (*Boston Pilot*, 12 June 1886). On 29 September in its inaugural year, the club organised its first annual field sports meet or 'picnic' as it was referred to at the time. The meet took place at the Centennial Grounds in Wandem, Massachusetts, north of Boston and consisted of a varied sporting programme which included activities such as high and long jumping, a 250-yards' race, cycling, a rudimentary form of football and a number of games that were specifically Irish in their intonation. The ancient game of *Baire* or goaling, which involved the striking of a hard ball with a hurling stick, was one of the focal points of the day's proceedings. In the press reports of the afternoon's activities much was made of the Irish roots of this game:

> The occasions of playing this game in Ireland have generally been occasions of hilarity, festivity, exuberant joy, and overflowing mirthfulness to multitudes of spectators, as well as to participants in the game. It is specially an Irish game, and the etymology of its Irish name takes us back into the remotest antiquity (*Boston Pilot*, 4 Oct. 1879).

The activities on the fringes of the sporting action which included Irish dancing and music, furnished by the 23-piece Irish National Band of Boston, further reinforced the specifically Irish complexion of the afternoon's festivities. The event closed with a 'great hurling match' involving 32 players from each county in Ireland (*Boston Pilot*, 4 Oct. 1879). Of course, this game was not played according to the modern rules of hurling which were not to be formally constituted by the GAA until January 1885. From the descriptions of this game in the press, it is clear that the match was not characterised by the levels of codification and organisation that were apparent in hurling matches in Ireland and elsewhere in the post-1885 period (*Donahoe's Magazine*, Nov. 1879).[1] However, the basic elements of the 'modern' game, the use of a stick and ball, two evenly matched teams, the scoring of goals, the use of umpires and identifiable positions of play were all apparent in the match played during the IACB meet.

The precise numbers attending the event are unclear, although it was reported in the *Boston Pilot* that 'the early trains from the Eastern Depot, Boston, carried out thousands of Irish ladies and gentlemen' (*Boston Pilot*, 4 Oct. 1879).

In another report, it is estimated that 6,000 spectators lined the perimeter of the field on which the hurling match was played (*Donahoe's Magazine*, Nov. 1879: 464). Elements of Ireland's sporting heritage were thus showcased to a not inconsequential number of immigrants. Such was the appeal of the meet and the sporting activities on show that the picnic attracted participants and spectators from all sections of Boston's Irish community. The event played host to 'nearly all of the prominent Irish Americans in Boston and vicinity' and was attended by a number of clergymen of the Archdiocese of Boston (*Donahoe's Magazine*, Nov. 1879: 462). It is likely that the rest of those at the event comprised individuals hailing from Boston's emerging middle class as well as those from the city's various working-class Irish enclaves. Although the picnic was designed as a celebration of Irish sporting and cultural pastimes, it also attracted 'scores of Scotch and American visitors' (*Boston Pilot*, 4 Oct. 1879). This demonstrated that the meet was not entirely exclusive to people of Irish birth or heritage, and can be interpreted as a sign of a willingness on the part of more liberal sections of Boston's Irish community to reach out to their neighbours. The inclusion of what was described as 'a most amusing game' at two sites on the grounds, involving the throwing of wet sponges and rubber balls at a 'negro' whose head protruded from a cloth sheet, can be read as a comment on the inhospitable and racist attitudes of sections of the Irish diaspora towards African Americans (Coogan, 2000; O'Connor, 1994).[2]

During the 1880s, the IACB repeated its midsummer festivals and on each occasion the promotion of specifically Irish sporting pastimes and culture were very much to the fore. The meet held at Oak Island, north of Boston, on 17 June 1886, was celebrated as an 'Aonach', or festival, of Ancient Ireland, whilst two years later the event was reorganised in order for it to encompass 'a full representation of peculiarly Irish [games]' (*Boston Pilot*, 12 June 1886: 8). From the mid-1880s onwards, these festivals and participation in Gaelic games more generally were portrayed in the Irish-American press as being an integral part of Irish culture and quintessential to what it meant to be Irish. From the mid to late 1880s *The Gael*, a monthly New York journal devoted to the 'cultivation and preservation of the Irish language and the autonomy of the Irish nation' (*The Gael*, Jan. 1882: 1), often carried romanticised, but evocative, accounts of the place of the game of hurling in the Irish national consciousness and its significance for the Irish diaspora. The tone of newspaper reports of the formation of the GAA in 1884 and its early activities was very much in keeping with these idealised but rousing interpretations of the centrality of Gaelic games in the construction of Irish identity. For example, in an article in the

Irish Echo on the 1888 annual field sports meet at Oak Island, the GAA's activities in Ireland were reported in the following manner:

> recently the spirit of patriotism and freedom by which the Irish at home are being animated, has suggested to them that their national games and pastimes should be revived, and the result is a national association called the Gaelic Athletic Association . . . and the movement is encouraged by no less a personage than Archbishop Croke of Cashel, who is the patron of the national association (*Irish Echo*, July 1888: 4).

The programme of activities during those meets held in the second half of the 1880s continued to be made up of games that were relatively uncodified, at least according to modern standards. However, in 1886 Boston witnessed the first game of Gaelic football played outside Ireland under the new rules laid down by the GAA. The game took place on Boston Common in June when Galway and Kerry, two of the city's earliest Gaelic football clubs contested a keenly fought match (Hehir, 2000; Irish Cultural Centre, 1999). In a similar fashion to the IACB's annual field sport meets, this game served to heighten interest and increase awareness of opportunities to engage in sports which offered Irish immigrants a sense of the familiar in unfamiliar and, at times, inhospitable, surroundings. Although the IACB's picnics and one-off games such as that between Kerry and Galway were important, the most influential development in helping Gaelic sport to take root in Boston and beyond was an initiative on the part of the GAA in Ireland. This was aimed not at promoting Gaelic games in America, but rather at accumulating the finance needed to revive the ancient Tailteann games, an athletic and cultural festival which had last taken place in Ireland in the twelfth century.

The progenitor of the idea to revive the Tailteann games was Michael Cusack, the founding father of the GAA. In keeping with the *raison d'être* of the fledgling association, Cusack felt that a Gaelic athletic and cultural festival held every five years would lend support to the Irish nationalist cause. Cusack envisioned that the first edition of the revived games would take place in Dublin in the summer of 1889 and would consist of field sports and athletic contests as well as literary and musical competitions. It was optimistically anticipated that the event would attract participants and spectators from all over Ireland and from the Irish diaspora in America and Britain (De Búrca, 1999). The most pressing concern was the necessity to raise the £5,000 required to implement Cusack's ambitious vision. Michael Davitt, the Land Leaguer, and

Maurice Davin, the legendary Irish athlete and first President of the GAA, soon hit on the idea of a fund-raising tour by Irish athletes to America. In April 1888, Davin presented the concept to the GAA's Central Council, which responded favourably. Despite problems raising the requisite finance for the tour, resolved by a 'loan' of £450 from Davitt, a party of over fifty athletes, hurlers and officials departed from Cobh on the liner *Wisconsin* and arrived in New York on 25 September, on what was reported in the Irish-American press at the time as the 'Gaelic Invasion of America' (*Irish Echo*, Oct. 1888: 4).

The tour had a difficult start because of the decision of the tour manager and GAA council member, John Cullinane, to work with the Manhattan Athletic Club and the National Amateur Athletic Association (NAAA), an organisation whose activities and control were confined to the north-east of the country. In doing so, Cullinane unwittingly snubbed the more powerful, national governing body, the American Amateur Athletic Union (AAAU), thus effectively restricting the intended nationwide scope of the tour. Heavy snow also curtailed the tour and a planned two-week visit to Canada was shelved (Cronin, 2007). The touring party began their six-week visit with a series of exhibition hurling games and athletic contests in New York. Similar events were staged in a number of   other centres of Irish immigration including Brooklyn, Yonkers, Boston, Philadelphia, Trenton, Newark, Patterson, Providence and Lowell (*Donahoe's Magazine*, Nov. 1888: 474).

The 'Gaelic Invasion' has generally been written off as a failure on the basis that it failed to attract the type of interest and gate receipts that the GAA had hoped for and as a consequence did not generate sufficient funds for the Tailteann games to occur in 1889 as originally intended (De Búrca, 1999; Hanna, 1999).[3] Indeed, the whole venture left the GAA in debt to the tune of £700 (Mandle, 1987). Attendances were undoubtedly disappointing. Estimates of the number of spectators at the first exhibition in Manhattan ranged from 800 to 1,500, although the games in Philadelphia and Boston attracted more respectable attendances of 5,000 and 10,000 respectively (Byrne, 1976; *Sport*, 20 Oct. 1888, cited in Cronin, 2007). It is important to note, though, that particular circumstances militated against a larger turnout at some of the exhibition venues. For example, the games coincided with a US Presidential election year, hence publicity was directed towards domestic politics rather than the 'invading' Irish athletes. This lack of public interest was compounded by the inclement weather in some of the cities visited.

Although the 'invasion' was viewed as a failure in its inability to meet its main objective, it is difficult to classify the tour as anything other than a resounding success when considering its impact on the development of Gaelic sport in the US. Apart from the objective of fund-raising for the Tailteann games, the touring party's team manager, John Cullinane, identified as a secondary aim for the venture 'the encouragement among American Irishmen of the love of sports and pastimes peculiar to Ireland and the adoption of the Celtic rules' (cited in *Irish World and American Industrial Liberator*, 28 Sept. 1888). As a consequence of the tour the profile of Gaelic games was raised to a higher level, and a number of fledgling hurling clubs were boosted by the decision of 17 members of the touring party to remain in America rather than return to Ireland. The status of Gaelic sport in Boston, in particular, benefited greatly from the exercise. Attendances at those exhibitions hosted in Boston were the highest of the tour, and in the aftermath of the Irish athletes' departure the city's four hurling clubs (including Wolfe Tones, Emmets and Redmonds) and two Gaelic football clubs (Kerry and Galway) flourished. In 1897, the inception of the Young Ireland Hurling Club added to this healthy complement of clubs (North East GAA, 2000). It is also important to note that the 'invasion' was crucial in introducing and familiarising the official rules of the game, established by the GAA in 1885, to hurling enthusiasts in Boston and elsewhere. The hurling matches that the visiting Irish hurlers were involved in were characterised by higher levels of organisation and codification than those played at the IACB's annual picnics in the first half of the 1880s. In the various press reports of the tour, reference was made to the fact that the hurling matches were played 'very systematically according to well regulated rules and laws of the game' (*Irish Echo*, Oct. 1888: 4).

Whilst the visit of the Irish touring party was crucial to the popularisation of Gaelic games in the US in this period, the organisation and promotion of these sports were often dependent on the efforts of a range of Irish Americans who were committed to Irish sporting pursuits. The key figure in Boston was undoubtedly John Boyle O'Reilly. His involvement in these sports and the rationale behind it are worth exploring in some detail. O'Reilly was closely involved in the organisation of the IACB's first field sports meet in 1879, at which he acted as chief judge and referee. This was a role he repeated on a yearly basis until his death in 1890 (Roche, 1891). O'Reilly had a particular interest in hurling and his desire to see the game develop was such that in 1880 he presented the IACB with the John Boyle O'Reilly Hurling Cup, 'a magnificent silver cup, superbly ornamented, unique in design, and of great value', that was to be competed for by Boston's hurling clubs on an annual basis (Dineen, 1901: 292). The early practical development of Gaelic games in Boston was clearly aided by his patronage and organisational abilities. However, the ethos and philosophy underpinning the promotion of these specifically Irish pastimes were also shaped by O'Reilly's political beliefs and broader social outlook. John Boyle O'Reilly has been described by Andrew Greeley, the eminent historian of the Irish in America, as first and foremost a leader of the Irish immigrant population in Boston, but also one of Irish America's leading nationalists (Greeley, 1981). His nationalist credentials are borne out by his remarkable early life story. Born in County Meath in 1844, he worked as a journalist in Dublin before moving to England. In 1863, he returned to Ireland with the express purpose of making a practical contribution to the campaign for Irish independence. O'Reilly felt that this would be best achieved by joining both the Irish Republican Brotherhood and subsequently the 14th British Hussars, where he planned to attempt to foster a more sympathetic view of Fenianism and recruit soldiers to it. When his actions were discovered in 1866, he was hastily tried, convicted of high treason and sentenced to 20-years' penal servitude. Following short stays at four prisons in England, O'Reilly was transferred to a penal colony in western Australia. After a number of failed escape attempts, he was offered assistance by a Catholic priest, and in February 1869, on board an American whaling ship, he made what eventually proved to be a successful bid for freedom.

O'Reilly landed in Philadelphia, via Liverpool, in late November. Following a short stay in New York he finally arrived in Boston, where he almost immediately took up a position with the *Boston Pilot*, the influential weekly Catholic newspaper (*Celtic Monthly*, Aug. 1879; *Donahoe's Magazine*, Oct. 1890). He quickly gained renown amongst the Boston Irish as a talented poet and novelist and later as editor of the *Pilot*. Yet it was his 'crusading zeal and a humanitarian sympathy for the underdog' (Shannon, 1966: 197) and his undoubted status as an advocate of the Irish nationalist cause that marked him out as one of the most popular and respected Irish-American figures of this era. In the first biographical account of his life and work, published in 1891, O'Reilly was described in the following terms:

> He [O'Reilly] is one of the brightest ornaments of the Irish race abroad; he lives in exile for his service to his country; he has enriched its national literature with exquisite prose and yet more exquisite verse; he renders daily service to the national cause (Roche, 1891: 201).

O'Reilly's patronage of Gaelic games during the late 1870s and 1880s must be viewed in the context of his life history and, more specifically, as an extension of his nationalist beliefs. As well as seeking to provide recreational opportunities for working-class Irish immigrants, O'Reilly was clearly advocating participation in sports that were part of the broader cultural revival aimed at creating rallying points for Irish nationalism and separatist demands. This assertion is made on the basis that he was widely known as an enthusiastic proponent of 'any movement which promised the enfranchisement and liberty of his native land' (*Donahoe's Magazine*, Oct. 1890: 359–60).

Despite O'Reilly's clear political and ideological leanings, his use of Gaelic games for promoting the cause of Irish nationalism amongst the Irish diaspora in Boston was not without contradiction. In order to generate and encourage a revival of interest in Irish culture as part of a broader nationalist reawakening, O'Reilly and other leading members of the Irish-American community in Boston recognised the value of sport as a mobilising tool. However, O'Reilly's employment of Gaelic sports to muster Irish nationalist sentiment was juxtaposed with the fact that he was drawing on a cultural form which, although undoubtedly Irish in its origins and intonation, was organised according to British philosophies and principles. This contradiction surrounding the organisational and philosophical underpinnings of the GAA in Ireland has been well documented elsewhere. For example, in their analysis of the paradox of an organisation whose fundamental aspiration was to resist the spread of English cultural influence whilst at the same time emulating a British model of sport, Sugden and Bairner (1993: 29) have argued that 'Despite the blatant anti-Englishness which fuelled the emergence of the GAA, a characteristically British approach to sports was used by the organisation's founder members to breathe life into otherwise dormant traditional Gaelic pastimes'. John Boyle O'Reilly's stewardship of Gaelic games in Boston was rooted in the same paradox. He was clearly a firm believer in the principles that had guided the British athletic revolution in the second half of the nineteenth century. O'Reilly was very much a disciple of Muscular Christianity, believing that self-improvement amongst Boston's Irish community should occur not only through education but also through participation in codified, regulated and *rational* forms of sport and recreation. Evidence of his belief in the Muscular Christian notion of a 'healthy mind in a healthy body' and the capacity of sports to imbue the individual with a sense of moral, Christian and manly values can be found in his book, *Athletics and Manly Sport*, published in 1890.[4] The book's purpose was quite simply to extol the virtues of 'innocent sport, playful exercise and enjoyment of nature'. As O'Reilly stated in the introduction:

Its [the book] main purpose is to bring into consideration the high value, moral and intellectual as well as physical, of those exercises that develop healthy constitutions, cheerful minds, manly self-confidence, and an appreciation of the beauties of nature and natural enjoyment (O'Reilly, 1890: xi).

The inclusion of a chapter on ancient Irish athletic games, exercises and weapons reveals that his promotion of Gaelic games was very much couched in a sporting ethos that was quite clearly British in its origin. However, as in Ireland, individuals such as John Boyle O'Reilly were able to repackage and present Gaelic games in Boston in specifically Irish terms, evidently ensuring their continued popularity amongst the Irish émigrés in the late nineteenth and early twentieth centuries.

Gaelic sport in New York: from tavern pastimes to codified sports (1780–1900)

Although modern, codified forms of Gaelic football and hurling were not played in New York until the mid-1880s, there is evidence that rudimentary, unorganised versions of these games took place there as early as the American Revolutionary period. In his analysis of New York at this time, Abbott cites a form of hurling as one of the main sports played in the city (Abbott, 1929). His contention is supported by the work of McGinn (1997) who details documentary evidence of hurling in New York in the early 1780s. McGinn describes a series of advertisements placed in the *New York Gazette* in 1781 and 1782 by two New York tavern owners, Thomas McMullin and Charles Loosely, promoting the summer version of hurling or *iománaíocht*, later adopted by the GAA in 1884, as well as the winter version, *camánacht*, which was played predominantly in Ulster. These advertisements were clearly aimed at Irishmen serving in the British army in New York at that time. As might have been expected, British defeat and American independence and a desire on the part of the revolutionary leaders to develop a distinctive sense of identity saw the demise of hurling on American shores. It was not until the massive waves of emigration heralded by the Irish famine in the second half of the nineteenth century that the game began to resurface in the city in a meaningful way.

Relatively well-organised versions of football and hurling had been played in New York since the 1850s, with the city's first club, the Irish Hurling and Football Club, established in 1857 (Wilcox, 1994). New York's *Irish News* carried reports of some of this club's earliest games such as a hurling and football match against a team from Hoboken in New Jersey in 1858 (King, 1998). However, the catalyst for the introduction and development of modern, codified forms of both sports was undoubtedly the 'Gaelic invasion of America' in 1888 discussed earlier. The Irish athletes began their six-week visit to the US in New York and played a series of exhibition hurling games and athletic contests, organised and facilitated by the Manhattan Athletic Club who suspended their annual sports meets for the duration of the tour. The first exhibition took place on 29 September at Manhattan Athletic Club's home grounds before the touring party moved on to other centres of Irish immigration, predominantly around the north-eastern seaboard of the US. On completion of these legs of their tour, the athletes returned to New York for 'a grand indoor exhibition' of athletic contests at Madison Square Garden before leaving for home (*Irish World and American Industrial Liberator*, 22 Sept. 1888).

As outlined earlier, the relatively poor attendances at the exhibition games confirmed the touring party's inability to generate the funds required to revive the Tailteann games. For Gaelic sports aficionados in New York, however, the secondary objective of the tour, the desire to raise the profile of Gaelic games in America, was equally as important as a revival of the Tailteann games. This was demonstrated by the messages of support for the Irish athletes from Irish-born New Yorkers in the Irish-American press in the lead up to their arrival in the city. For example, the *Irish World and American Industrial Liberator* (15 Sept. 1888) carried a letter to the editor which expressed the hope that the exhibition would 'show the American people that hurling is qualified to be ranked in line with their dearly and deservedly prized baseball'. Although the tour did not diminish the appetite of the New York Irish for baseball, the profile of Gaelic sport was raised to a level not previously reached. Sutton, writing at the turn of the century, clearly interpreted the impact of the venture in these terms:

> Since the Gaelic Invasion of America in 1888, hurling has taken a firm root on American soil, and the present series of games at the magnificent grounds at Celtic Park for the James R. Keene Cup are certain to arouse an amount of interest and enthusiasm, and to make the Irish national pastime extremely popular with the exiled Gaels of Greater New York (Sutton, 1900: 258).

As in Boston, fledgling GAA clubs in New York received a further boost with the decision of some of the touring party not to return home. This ensured that the standard of hurling in both cities in the late 1880s was of a high level and provided the game with a solid foundation on which to build. By 1891 these foundations had given rise to 22 Gaelic football and hurling clubs in the New York metropolitan area, making it the strongest centre for Gaelic games in America at that time (Ridge, 1997).

In light of this rapidly expanding network of clubs, it soon became clear that a governing body was required to oversee and regulate Gaelic games. Thus, in September 1891, all of the clubs that existed in New York at the time agreed to the founding of the 'GAA of America' (Milkovits, 1988). However, this organisation proved to be largely ineffective in promoting Gaelic games in the city. This was largely owing to factionalist rivalries and conflict within this fledgling body, and indeed within the broader Irish community, brought about by the fall of Charles Stewart Parnell and subsequent disputes between parliamentary Irish nationalists in America and those who advocated a physical force solution to Ireland's constitutional status. Despite the demise of this body, Gaelic games in New York in the 1890s were characterised by robust health. This was due in no small measure to the actions of those involved in setting up clubs, who gave so freely of their time and finances to promote the games. Joseph P. Kennedy, honorary secretary of the Irish-American GAA club and later founder of the newspaper, the *Irish American Advocate*, was a particularly influential patron of Gaelic games in the first half of the 1890s. He argued persistently that the GAA in New York should acquire their own grounds to safeguard their future and he began to actively pursue possible venues (King, 1998). His views were shared by William Prendergast, former secretary of the GAA in Ireland, and one of the main organisers of the Gaelic 'invasion' of 1888. Prendergast returned to New York from Ireland in the early 1890s and whilst serving in the police went on to amass considerable wealth through his dealings in real estate in Long Island. He became a hugely influential figure for the GAA in the city, not least because he was more than happy to invest a proportion of his wealth in Gaelic games (Humphries, 1998).

The desire of men like Kennedy and Prendergast and early club patrons to see their sports establish a firm footing in New York was such that they were able to purchase a dedicated home for Gaelic sports at Laurel Hill in Queen's in late 1897, which subsequently became known as Celtic Park (Ridge, 1997). When the park opened in 1898 it was an almost instant success and regularly attracted large crowds. Its centrality for those Irish immigrants eager to watch or participate in sport or just experience an environment resonant of 'home' is highlighted by Seamus King (1998: 101), who argued that 'Celtic Park became a rendezvous for all lovers of manly sports and a mecca for the exiled children of the Gael'. Despite the success of Celtic Park, the demise of the GAA of America had created an administrative void in New York GAA circles. This void was soon filled by New York's Irish county societies.

As highlighted in chapter 1, many of the Irish immigrants arriving in Manhattan in the late 1840s and 1850s were ill equipped to make the transition from rural life to a sprawling industrial metropolis. But they were aided by a whole range of Irish religious, benevolent and political societies that had been in existence in the city since the late eighteenth century and which emphasised common bonds of Irishness. From 1849 onwards a number of county-based organisations were established which not only helped the Irish settle in America but also emphasised a more particularised bent of Irish identity. The first county society in New York, the Sligo Young Men's Association, was formed in 1849 and was joined in the 1850s by similar bodies from Kerry, Cavan, Galway, Monaghan and Tyrone. Although initially welcomed, these county societies were soon criticised in a number of New York Irish newspapers for promoting sectional and potentially divisive affinities rather than a unified stance on a range of more broad-based Irish issues. Although narrow factional self-interest was a feature of the relationship between the various county societies, the strength of the Ancient Order of Hibernians ensured that county-based loyalties amongst Irish immigrants did not supersede the broader socio-economic, political and religious agenda of Irish America (Ridge, 1997).

By the mid-1870s, the popularity of the AOH's agenda amongst the Irish-American working class combined with a reduction in levels of immigration from Ireland saw the county societies enter a period of decline. However, a resurgence in immigration in the early 1880s, largely as a consequence of exploitative 'landlordism' and a subsequent 'land war' in Ireland, saw a revival in the fortunes of the county societies. Their re-emergence was facilitated in no small part by the fact that the new societies formed in this period, such as the Kerrymen's Patriotic and Benevolent Society, were able to marry their sectional interests with broader national concerns. Thus, in the 1880s and 1890s, the county societies were able to come together on certain political or benevolent issues and formulate collective responses. Central to this increasingly unified sense of purpose or shared agenda was a number of attempts to unite the societies under a single umbrella organisation.[5] Although each of these ventures was ultimately undone by vestiges of factionalism, they paved the way for closer links between the county societies from the mid-1890s onwards. Arguably the key factor in this process was the decision by a number of county associations to organise Gaelic football and hurling teams.

Although some of the teams already established in New York were predominantly composed of members from particular counties,[6] it was not until 1898 and the formation of the Kilkenny Gaelic football team that a club bore a county name. Teams continued to be named after popular Irish nationalist figures, but the practice of linking them to specific Irish counties through name became more widespread in the early twentieth century, with the formation of hurling and football branches of the county societies (*Gaelic American*, 24 Oct. 1903a). In the late nineteenth century the county societies had organised a wide range of sporting and leisure activities for their members. By the turn of the century the athletic pursuits of the societies began to centre exclusively on Gaelic sports. Whilst this undoubtedly raised the profile of these sports in New York, hurling and football remained poorly organised with the existing clubs and county societies arranging games in an ad hoc fashion. With the Irish American Athletic Club, formed by the owners of Celtic Park, also involved in organising exhibition games, the promotion and development of Gaelic sport occurred in a disjointed, fragmented fashion. If these activities were to prosper in the early years of the twentieth century, a coordinated approach and the establishment of a unified governing body would clearly be required.

Gaelic games and Chicago's 'exiled' Gaels (1884–1900)

As was the case in Boston, New York and other parts of America where Irish immigrants arrived in large numbers, uncodified versions of Gaelic games were played in Chicago and elsewhere in the mid-west prior to the 1880s. However, almost as soon as the GAA in Ireland was founded in 1884 and a formalised set of rules established, more organised versions of traditional Irish sports began to appear in the city. Given the emerging linkages between Gaelic games and Irish nationalism in America, it is no surprise that the firebrand Irish nationalist newspaper publisher, John F. Finerty, was a key figure in the promotion of these games amongst Irish Chicagoans. Just like John Boyle O'Reilly in Boston, Finerty recognised the value of the revival of Irish culture as part of the drive to engender a strong political nationalism throughout Irish America. Thus, from the mid 1880s he was an energetic advocate of Gaelic games and ensured that they featured prominently at picnics organised by various Irish organisations (*Citizen*, 9 Aug. 1884).

Finerty's involvement in the GAA and the close association that developed between Gaelic games and a range of Irish nationalist organisations ensured that Gaelic football and hurling were quickly popularised amongst sections of the city's Irish emigrant community. Although the 'invading' Irish touring athletes of 1888 did not include Chicago in their itinerary, press coverage of the tour, particularly in the Irish-American weekly, the *Citizen*, reinforced a sense amongst Gaelic games enthusiasts in the city that they were not alone in their promotion of these activities (*Citizen*, 6 Oct. 1888). This gave rise to the formation of Chicago's first two Gaelic football clubs in 1888, the Emmets and the Shamrocks, both of which hailed from the Irish communities on the city's west side. In outlining the rationale behind the establishment of these clubs in a letter to the editor of the *Citizen*, one of the founders of the Emmets, Patrick Coughlin, stressed the importance of maintaining Ireland's traditional sporting heritage in America as part of the broader Irish cultural revival and struggle for Irish independence. Coughlin went on to implore other Irish Chicagoans to follow his example: 'Is it not time that the young men of our race who have settled in Chicago, should help revive and perpetuate the manly exercises in which our forefathers excelled?' (*Citizen*, 15 Mar. 1890: 1).

Similar rallying calls also emanated from leading figures within the GAA in Ireland, who were eager to see their games gain a strong foothold amongst the Irish diaspora in Chicago, and indeed throughout the US. In a letter to the *Citizen* in May 1890, the Honorary Secretary of the GAA, P. R. Cleary, reminded the 'exiled Gaels' in America that they were as Irish as those in the old country and as such it was their national duty to band together and preserve their sporting heritage. Cleary's rousing, politicised rhetoric concluded with what proved to be an overly ambitious prediction of the growth of Gaelic games in America in the opening years of the 1890s: 'The answer expected is that the clubs in America will number thousands before many months pass by, and that numerical strength of the Association in America will exceed that which is at home before a second winter comes around' (*Citizen*, 24 May 1890: 1). Although Cleary's exhortations were excessive and unrealistic some in Chicago were motivated by his and Coughlin's calls, and almost immediately established clubs. The north of the city saw its first Gaelic football club with the founding of the Columbias in 1890 (*Citizen*, 5 July 1890: 1). In the same year, the Innisfails were established, adding to the complement of teams in the city's west side. With four clubs and indications from other Gaelic games enthusiasts that they intended to establish teams, it became clear that a governing body was required to oversee the rapid expansion of Gaelic sport in the city and its neighbouring areas. By June 1891, Chicago's Gaels had not only established a governing body, the GAA of Illinois, but had also acquired its own grounds for

Gaelic games in the city with the lease of parkland at Lincoln and Polk streets. The complement of football and hurling clubs had increased to ten, comprising some 2,000 members by this time,[7] and games during the 1891 season were regularly attracting crowds of between 3,000 and 4,000 (*Citizen*, 2 May 1891: 5; *Chicago Daily Tribune*, 11 May 1891: 6).

Although this growth of Gaelic games in Chicago reflected what was occurring in Boston and New York in the same period, there were a number of nuances in the early history of these sports in Chicago. Not least of these were a series of problems that confronted Chicago's GAA fraternity on the back of a revival of anti-Irish and anti-Catholic sentiment in the city. As noted in chapter 1, the virulent strain of anti-Irish feeling associated with Know-Nothingism began to die out in Chicago and throughout the US from the mid 1850s. Despite this, vestiges of Anglo-Protestant resentment remained, albeit less openly expressed. By the late 1880s and early 1890s, prejudice towards the Irish, orchestrated largely by Henry F. Bowers secret society the American Protective Association, began to resurface. While Boston and New York experienced an increase in anti-Irish feeling, the mixed cultures of the eastern seaboard tended to protect the Irish from the more malignant forms of nativism experienced in the mid-west at this time (Doyle, 1989). This was particularly evident in the fact that while Gaelic sports grew largely unobstructed in the east in this period, prejudice, rooted in a desire to undermine Irish culture and constrain Irish Catholic advancement, restricted the activities of the GAA in Chicago. A clear example of this can be found in a major dispute between the Illinois GAA and sections of the city's Anglo-Protestant community and Presbyterian Mayor, Hempstead Washbourne, late in the summer of 1892.

The dispute arose over the GAA's use of a playing field in what was at the time a largely Protestant, upper-class part of the city. In July 1892 two well-known Gaelic sport enthusiasts, Thomas Murphy and the attorney M. E. Ames, acquired a three-year lease for a park at 37th Street and Indiana Avenue at a cost of $2,500. Prior to undertaking the work necessary to get the park into a condition suitable for hosting matches and spectators, Murphy contacted the mayor's office to confirm that there would not be any difficulties associated with using the venue on a Sunday. Murphy was clearly concerned that the movement for a revival of the city's blue laws – aimed at preserving the Sabbath for worship, which had re-emerged in Chicago in the late 1880s – might have an impact on their plans to fulfil Sunday fixtures. Murphy and his fellow Gaels were reassured by the fact that the City League of Baseball had used the same venue on Sundays earlier in the same summer. Mayor Washbourne's office duly informed them that the venue could be used as requested. However, during the course of the correspondence between Murphy and the mayor's office, someone had neglected to inform the GAA of the need for an amusement licence to host sporting events on a Sunday. When Murphy found out that a licence was required he applied to the mayor's office on behalf of the GAA. Despite Mayor Washbourne's earlier assurances that games could take place, Murphy was refused a licence because 'some of the residents . . . had an objection to Sunday Games' (*Citizen*, 24 Sept. 1892: 1). Frustrated at this lack of cooperation the GAA took the decision to go ahead with their planned programme. However, the police arrived at the venue shortly after the first match had commenced and called an immediate halt to proceedings, informing the players and some 2,000 spectators that they were acting on the orders of the mayor and should they refuse to desist from playing and disperse peacefully they would be arrested (*Chicago Daily Tribune*, 19 Sept. 1892: 3).

The actions of the police and Mayor Washbourne and the reluctance of some of the Protestant residents of the area adjacent to the park to give their approval for the games were greeted with anger by the GAA and were denounced as being underpinned by anti-Irish prejudice. This belief was rooted in the fact that baseball games, where admission fees had been charged, had taken place in the park on previous Sundays without any protest. Frank Ryan, the president of the Davitt club, made specific reference to this differential treatment in a letter to the editor of the *Citizen*: 'Are we not as much entitled to carry on our Sunday games as are the different clubs of the City League Baseball Association or is there a special city ordinance prohibiting us from playing our games, while the baseball men are allowed to play unmolested?' (*Citizen*, 24 Sept. 1892: 1). Ryan was clearly implying that some local residents whom he referred to as 'ignorant . . . Know-nothings' (*Citizen*, 24 Sept. 1892: 1) were happy to see an American sport being played, but were not prepared to countenance a sport that would bring large numbers of Irish into their neighbourhood. At a subsequent meeting of 25 members of the GAA a number of resolutions were passed, expressing in stronger terms the belief that the mayor's refusal to allow Gaelic games to take place at the park was motivated 'solely by hostility to citizens of Irish nationality' (*Chicago Daily Tribune*, 25 Sept. 1892: 5).

Such an agenda, perceived or otherwise, strengthened the resolve of the city's GAA community to meet the challenge presented to it head on and they decided to go ahead with their planned schedule of games at the park the following Sunday. As had occurred the previous week, the police arrived at the venue just as the first game of the afternoon, a hurling match between the Emmets and the Innisfails, was about to begin and informed the players and spectators, who numbered between 3,000 and 4,000, that the games could not take place. Despite the simmering anger that abounded, the assembled ranks accepted the order, but not before GAA officials organised an impromptu mass meeting during which the mayor, the city council executive and the local residents who had objected to the games taking place were 'vigorously denounced' (*Chicago Daily*, 26 Sept. 1892: 1). The response of the Chicago GAA went beyond forceful rhetoric and with legal assistance from M. E. Ames, who had originally secured the lease on the venue, they took their case to the city council before threatening action in the courts. When it became clear that city officials were likely to grant the amusement licence sought by the GAA, influential members of Chicago's legal establishment intervened on behalf of the dissenting residents and obtained a court injunction prohibiting the Association from using the venue on a Sunday (*Chicago Daily Tribune*, 9 Oct. 1892: 4). The GAA remained resolute in the face of what it perceived to be blatant prejudice and eventually the injunction was lifted and the licence granted. By Thanksgiving Day, GAA activities had resumed at the venue (*Chicago Daily*, 3 Dec. 1892: 4).

The city's refusal to allow Gaelic games to be played on a Sunday on the park at 37th and Indiana and the GAA's response to this move reveal much about the place of these sports amongst the Irish community in Chicago and the broader relationship between the Irish Catholic immigrant community and the city's established Anglo-Protestants. The political landscape in which the GAA in the city operated in the early 1890s was clearly a difficult one. Gaelic games were not immune from the broader anti-Irish sentiment that re-emerged in the mid-west and elsewhere in this period, and this affair created a feeling amongst GAA members that they were victims of Anglo-Protestant discrimination. The perception that they were being treated unfairly because of their nationality and religion was clearly not groundless paranoia. As this episode highlights, Gaelic games were treated differently from other sports in the city, which led members of the GAA to conclude that the reason for this was simply that their sports were specifically Irish, and that they allowed for a very public celebration of Irishness. For some members of the city's Anglo-Protestant establishment, this ran counter to their Anglo-Protestant sensibilities, hence the concerted campaign against the GAA's use of this venue for their activities. However, rather than weaken the resolve of the GAA to continue to promote Gaelic games, the bigotry that they felt underpinned the actions of the mayor and protesting residents actually strengthened their desire to cling to and nurture pastimes that allowed them to preserve their Irish Catholic identity.

The period between the conclusion of this episode and the turn of the century was one of relative tranquillity and stability within the GAA of Illinois. There were occasional disputes between clubs and the governing body, but generally speaking the remaining years of the 1890s was a period of consolidation, with a weekly schedule of football and hurling matches taking place each weekend between June and November (*Chicago Daily Tribune*, 27 Aug. 1894: 11). The health and stability of the GAA in this period was significantly aided by the inclusion of a Gaelic football match between the New York champions, the Barrys, and a Chicago select on the programme of the 1893 World's Fair, hosted in the city (*Chicago Daily Tribune*, 30 Sept. 1893: 3). This event helped to make Gaelic games more visible to Irish immigrants visiting the fair who may not have been aware of the opportunity to become involved with the local GAA, thus contributing to its steady growth. However, the conditions under which the game took place were less than ideal. With no designated space for field sports, an impromptu pitch was set up in the livestock pavilion. Just as the game was about to begin, it was discovered that neither of the two teams had brought a football. Rather than cancel the game, the organisers improvised and used an indoor baseball. Despite these unusual difficulties the game was a success, so much so that the *Chicago Daily Tribune* suggested that some of the facilities at Jackson Park, where the fair was held, could be put to good use by being leased to the clubs of the GAA of Illinois who, according to the paper, would 'more than furnish attractions' (*Chicago Daily Tribune*, 7 Oct. 1893: 6). Although nothing ever came of this suggestion, it is indicative of the healthy position of Gaelic games in the city at this time.

By the turn of the century the GAA of Illinois comprised 11 clubs, three hurling and seven Gaelic football, and matches continued to attract crowds of between 2,000 and 4,000 spectators. All of this demonstrates that the GAA had woven itself into the fabric of the sporting life of Irish Chicagoans. The significance of Gaelic games in the city, however, extended beyond the purely sporting. These sports helped to nourish the Irish community in a whole host of practical socio-economic ways and allowed immigrants to maintain a sense of who they were and where they came from. A number of letters written by Irish immigrants during the early 1890s to the *Citizen*, explaining the attraction of the GAA in the city, highlight these points well. One GAA enthusiast spoke about the positive role of Gaelic games in acquiring desirable moral, physical and intellectual traits, while a member of the Innisfails club wrote of the broader role of these sports as a form of social glue that allowed immigrants not only to associate with one another but also to retain an important link with Ireland (*Citizen*, 29 Mar. 1890: 2; 3 May 1890: 2). As this book reveals in later chapters, the GAA has continued to perform these same functions for Irish Chicagoans – and indeed for their compatriots in Boston, New York and San Francisco – throughout the twentieth and into the twenty-first century.

Gaelic games in San Francisco (1888–1903)

While the 'Gaelic Invasion' of 1888 did much to popularise Gaelic games on the Atlantic seaboard, the tour had no discernible influence on Gaelic games on the Pacific coast. Consequently, the diffusion of these sports amongst the Irish community in San Francisco was slower than that which occurred elsewhere in the US. That said, versions of football and hurling had been played in the city in the early years of the gold rush. Indeed, *Alta California*, one of the city's earliest newspapers, reported on the establishment of San Francisco's first hurling club in May 1853 (*Alta California*, 4 May 1853). However, games prior to the late 1880s were uncodified and took place on an irregular, ad hoc basis. It was not until 22 January 1888 that those with an interest in these sports decided to come together with a view to organising a branch of the GAA in San Francisco. This first meeting held in the Knights of the Red Branch (KRB) hall – a venue that was to become a focal point of GAA and indeed, Irish nationalist, activity in San Francisco – achieved much. Attended by Irishmen from all over the city as well as neighbouring Oakland, the meeting began with the election of a committee and the appointment of William Stokes as Chairman. Stokes, who subsequently became an highly influential figure in the fledgling San Francisco GAA, was eager to see the city's clubs match the progress of their counterparts on the east coast and immediately appointed a 'grounds committee' to locate a site suitable for hosting games (*Daily Morning Call*, 23 Jan. 1888: 2). The Presidio reserve on the northern tip of the San Francisco peninsula was quickly identified as an appropriate site. However, the prospects of acquiring a site here were undone by Sabbatarianism of the sort that undermined those of their counterparts in Chicago around the same period. Undeterred, the committee pressed on and eventually obtained grounds at 31st Street in the Mission district, where the Association subsequently hosted a series of meets which involved athletic events and Gaelic football (*Daily Morning Call*, 30 Jan. 1888: 2).

By the early 1890s, the formally constituted San Francisco GAA was organising a regular programme of league matches, typically during the winter months, at various locales around the city, including the US Army parade grounds at the Presidio and Golden Gate Park. The number of clubs involved in the Association by the start of the 1892 season was, however, comparatively modest with just five clubs in existence (Emmets, Shamrocks, Oakland Gaels, Sarsfields and Parnells). Matches between these teams were typically robust and lacking in anything resembling a 'scientific' approach to the game. As one newspaper reported:

> The ground was rough and uneven, as was the playing; and for a greater portion of the time about all that was distinguishable was a tangle of legs and a fog of dust and sand, out of which would emerge at odd intervals a . . . ball, followed by an indiscriminate mass of sweating, howling, gesticulating, red faced young men . . . who kicked and scrambled and clawed and struggled for supremacy (*Daily Morning Call*, 1 Aug. 1892: 3).

Despite, or perhaps because of, the overtly physical and frenetic nature of the play, matches regularly attracted large crowds. For example, two games between Emmets and Parnells in August and September 1892 respectively attracted a combined crowd of 4,000 spectators (*Daily Morning Call*, 1 Aug. 1892: 3; 12 Sept. 1892: 2). The popularity of Gaelic football continued to grow, and 1893 saw the addition of five new clubs, William O'Briens of Oakland, Geraldines, Sheridans, Rovers and Rangers, with the latter two teams being composed mainly of second-generation Irish born in San Francisco (*Daily Morning Call*, 13 Feb. 1893: 3). The GAA also began to expand beyond the confines of the city and soon venues in Oakland, Port Costa and San Jose featured regularly in the Association's fixture list (*Daily Morning Call*, 1 May, 1893: 2).

The profile of Gaelic sport was further bolstered by its presence on the programme of a 'Midwinter Exposition', organised in 1894 to mark and celebrate California's emergence as an important region of the US. The local GAA featured prominently at this event organising athletics contests and a Gaelic football match on St Patrick's Day, the date given over to the Irish in the city, and in doing so showcased their activities to an estimated 50,000 visitors (*Daily Morning Call*, 17 Mar. 1894: 2). The addition of a further club at the start of the 1894–5 season, the San Franciscos, brought the total number of competing clubs in the city to 11. This growing culture of Irish sport was characterised by qualitative changes in the way Gaelic football was played, with the adoption of a more orderly and scientific approach. Evidence of this can be found in newspaper coverage of games which had previously lamented the rough play on view, the lack of discernible strategy and a disrespect for match officials, but now began to congratulate teams for playing the game 'on its merits' and with due and 'prompt attention to the referee's whistle' (*Daily Morning Call*, 17 Dec. 1894: 2).

By the middle of the 1890s, Gaelic football was well established as a popular pastime for San Francisco's burgeoning Irish population. However, hurling had yet to gain any sort of foothold in the city. The fundamental reason for this was distance from Ireland and a consequent inability on the part of the GAA to obtain the requisite equipment. Shipping hurling sticks and balls (*slíothars*) to the eastern seaboard had been relatively unproblematic, but getting them out west was proving to be difficult. In early 1894 an order had been placed with a manufacturer based in Cork and the shipment was expected to arrive in time for the beginning of the winter season. By the end of December the playing equipment had yet to arrive, leading to concern that it had been embargoed by New York Customs in lieu of the payment of duty estimated at around 60 per cent (*Daily Morning Call*, 23 Dec. 1894: 4). Despite these delays, aficionados of the game pressed on and established three hurling teams, ready to begin playing as soon as the shipment of sticks landed in the city. Central to this development was Jerome Donovan, president of the San Francisco GAA at the time and Fred Palmer, widely lauded in the city's Gaelic sport circles as 'the foremost athlete on the Pacific coast' (ibid.) and a founder member and president of the Emmet club. As an influential figure in the inception and promotion of the GAA in the city, Palmer took considerable pride in announcing through the local press that the first hurling match to be played on the Pacific coast would take place in Central Park, San Francisco in early January 1895 and that the game would be included in an exhibition of Gaelic games during the St Patrick's Day celebrations in March. Despite representations to New York Customs by a delegation of influential Irish men in the city, the hurleys and slíothars failed to arrive in time for either of these dates, thus delaying the introduction of hurling to San Francisco further. In the following season, though, the game finally took off in the city with the playing of a series of exhibition matches between Wolfe Tones, the Geraldines and Columbia hurling clubs.

After this initial slow growth of hurling, by 1903 two additional clubs, Emmets and the MacBrides, based in neighbouring Crockett, had been formed. This latter club was particularly significant and took great strides in promoting the game amongst both young Irish-born immigrants and second-generation Irish. In its coverage of the establishment of this club, *The Leader* (7 Feb. 1903: 8) commended the commitment of the founders and argued that 'Their enthusiasm has aroused the entire youth of the neighbourhood', before going on to make what was a somewhat overstated claim that 'baseball has been discarded and every boy provided with a self-made caman'. The foresight of club members in promoting the game amongst the Irish youth in the neighbourhood and providing them with the requisite playing equipment bore fruit later that year when MacBrides took part in a juvenile game against the Emeralds for the Father Yorke trophy. Although an exhibition hurling game featuring boys aged between 10 and 12 had taken place in the previous month (*The Leader*, 2 May 1903), the meeting of MacBrides and the Emeralds was the first time that a competitive hurling or, for that matter, Gaelic football, match involving players under the age of 15 had taken place on the Pacific coast (*The Leader*, 13 June 1903: 8).

Despite the significance of such developments, the GAA administration in the city had fallen out of existence and by the close of the century Gaelic games were no longer controlled by a central body. As a consequence, regular league fixtures were replaced by more intermittent field days organised by individual clubs at which one-off football and hurling matches would be played between the host club and an invited team, usually alongside a programme of athletics events. Although these field meets were well attended, the lack of a governing body was not ideal for the continued development of hurling and Gaelic football in the Bay area. As a consequence, a view began to emerge that a return to the more co-ordinated approach and league system that typified the GAA's activities in the 1890s was necessary, in order to continue to popularise Gaelic games. An editorial in *The Leader* in January 1903 conveyed this sentiment well:

> To make the Athletics a permanent success, organisation is needed. Individual teams can accomplish little or nothing. All those who have at heart the honor of the Gaelic name should join forces . . . A regular program of games for the season should be outlined but this cannot be done without a central authority.

This call was quickly taken up by perhaps the most famous of Irish churchmen in San Francisco, Father Peter C. Yorke. Father Yorke was ordained for the Archdiocese of San Francisco in 1887, having arrived in the US from Galway more than twenty years earlier. He quickly gained prominence in San Francisco, founding and editing the Irish newspaper *The Leader* in 1902 and becoming heavily involved in the Gaelic League. Yorke was a leading advocate of all things Irish in the city. However, it was his actions in canvassing against the nativist American Protective Association, his efforts on behalf of the labour movement in San Francisco, and his status as a staunch proponent of Irish nationalism in particular that conferred on him almost mythic status amongst the Irish population in the city (Burchell, 1980). It was only natural then that Yorke would become involved in an organisation whose central aim was to promote the physical and cultural health of the Irish in San Francisco. Thus, in February 1903, he convened a meeting of all interested parties which concluded with the establishment of a newly constituted governing body, the Gaelic Athletic Association of California (*The Leader*, 28 Feb. 1903: 3). Father Yorke was duly installed as patron of the Association, and he was joined by two fellow churchmen: Reverend Philip O'Ryan, who was appointed president, and the Reverend Maurice Barry, who took on the role of treasurer. Involving leading priests in this way not only provided the GAA with powerful allies but also embedded the Association within the broader range of organisations that sustained the Irish in San Francisco and helped to preserve a strong sense of Irishness. This was very much in evidence a month later when the city celebrated St Patrick's Day with a mass, Gaelic speeches and 'patriotic exercises', including Gaelic football and hurling in front of an audience of 15,000 at the grounds of the Presidio (*The Monitor*, 21 Mar. 1903: 3).

Conclusion

Michael Cusack, the founding father of the GAA, wrote that in the first two years of its inception in Ireland, 'The Association swept the country like a prairie fire' (cited in De Búrca, 1999: 15). While the diffusion and development of the GAA in Boston, New York, Chicago and San Francisco may not have matched the pace and pervasiveness of the growth of Gaelic games in Ireland, the Association quickly established itself as an important sporting, cultural and socio-economic resource for those Irish immigrants who had journeyed to the New World in the latter decades of the nineteenth century. As in Ireland, the GAA in America possessed influential and tireless patrons. Men such as John Boyle O'Reilly, Joseph P. Kennedy, William Prendergast, John F. Finerty, William Stokes and Father Peter C. Yorke did more than most to promote and popularise Gaelic games, not least because they had the profile and platform to endorse Gaelic sports in a very public way. Those who worked selflessly behind the scenes were also crucial to the ability of the Association to progress in America. Just as Gaelic games in Ireland relied on volunteers, the GAA in the US was ultimately dependent on those who took on organisational, fund-raising, playing and officiating roles or merely patronised the games by attending matches and field days. The motivation of such individuals to give of their time so freely was undoubtedly rooted in the fact that their involvement in these games allowed them to experience excitement, pleasure and fun in what could otherwise be a drab and difficult existence. High skill levels as a player or organisational abilities as an administrator were likely to have con-ferred a degree of kudos on individuals, and it may have been this that encour-aged them to take part. For others, simply being outdoors and engaging in or watching robust physical endeavours may explain the appeal of hurling and Gaelic football in this period. The fact that Gaelic games were so intimately connected to and resonant of 'home' also undoubtedly piqued a primordial passion in enthusiasts and this was particularly important in cementing the place of the GAA amongst sections of the Irish diaspora in America. The specific linking of these exclusively Irish games to the broader agenda of Irish nationalism in this period was fundamental in this regard and as such it warrants further investigation.

Patriots and players: the GAA and Irish nationalism in late nineteenth-century America

Introduction

In a debate of growing international significance, it has been recognised that sport is a powerful medium for building, conveying and articulating local, regional, ethnic and national identities. Sport in Ireland has featured prominently in this debate and it is generally accepted that as well as providing opportunities for healthy exercise, sporting competition and communal bonding Gaelic games have long been a locus for the construction and reproduction of Irish national identity. Indeed, as Bairner notes, 'Ireland's Gaelic Athletic Association is frequently offered as the best example of a sporting organisation formed for the precise purpose of producing and reproducing a sense of national identity' (Bairner, 2001: 70). The historical narrative in the previous chapter gave some insight into how Gaelic games in America have also served as an arena in which senses of Irishness, cultural and political, were fostered and promoted. This chapter examines, in a more focused and sustained way, the nature of the connections between the fledgling GAA in Boston, New York, Chicago and San Francisco and the various strands of Irish nationalism that found expression in America from the middle of the nineteenth century to the beginning of the twentieth. In doing so, the chapter reveals that these were a central dynamic in the early growth and popularisation of the GAA amongst sections of the Irish diaspora across the country. Before addressing these issues, it is important to add some context, firstly by qualifying the nationalist origins of the GAA in Ireland, and secondly by commenting on the development of Irish nationalism in America in the second half of the nineteenth century.

The formation of the GAA in Ireland and Irish nationalist politics

The linkages between the GAA and Irish nationalism in Ireland have been the subject of much academic analysis (Sugden and Bairner, 1993; Cronin, 1999; Mandle, 2001; De Búrca, 1980, 1989); it is not necessary here to revisit old ground in any great detail. However, to understand fully those forces that shaped the nationalist visage of the GAA in late nineteenth-century America and rendered Gaelic games a rallying point for Irish-American nationalism, it is useful to offer a brief comment on the rationale behind the formation of the Association in Ireland. The inception of the GAA in Ireland was rooted in broader events in Irish history, specifically the problematic relations between Ireland and Britain and the response of a range of Irish individuals and groups to this relationship. Ireland had long been the subject of British political and military interference, a process advanced with the plantation of lowland English and Scottish farmers into the north-eastern corner of the country in the later Middle Ages. It was not, though, until the passing of the Act of Union in 1800 that Ireland became formally tied to Britain. In the first half of the nineteenth century various attempts were made to redress this state of affairs and the inequalities that emanated from it. For example, Daniel O'Connell harnessed growing Catholic discontent to establish the Catholic Association, an organisation committed to agitating for civil rights for Irish Catholics. O'Connell's efforts not only gave rise to the Relief Act of 1829 which addressed political discrimination against Catholics, but also began to generate broader aspirations for independence from Britain. Although his subsequent attempts to work towards the repeal of the Union were ultimately unsuccessful, his efforts heralded the Young Ireland movement which sought to generate cultural nationalism by making the Irish populace aware of Ireland's long-standing and unique cultural traditions, largely through their weekly newspaper, the *Nation*. Although these endeavours were successful in raising Irish political and cultural consciousness, they were ultimately undone by a combination of the devastating impact on Irish society of the Great Famine and the continued subordination of the Irish populace and Gaelic culture. The concomitant Anglicisation of Ireland in this period, part of a broader strategy to encourage the adoption of British values and hence lessen resistance to the formal link with Britain, left little space for the promotion of activities or institutions around which a sense of Irishness could be constructed.

Although the middle of the nineteenth century saw a revival in Irish aspirations for independence, one of the chief difficulties facing nationalist organisations such as the Fenian movement, the Irish Republican Brotherhood

(IRB) and Michael Davitt's Land League was a lack of a distinctive Irish culture and identity around which to mobilise the population. Political activists began to recognise that a drive to revive and promote Irish culture was crucial to a successful political or indeed, military campaign for Irish independence. Many traditional Irish cultural forms, including Irish music and dance, the Gaelic language and a growing literary movement formed part of this revival. Ironically, it was an understanding of the role that sport had played in generating and maintaining patriotism and loyalty to the Crown throughout the British Empire that led to a belief that sport should form one of the cornerstones of this revival. It was soon suggested, initially by the Young Ireland movement and later by the IRB, that sport could help the Irish population identify with and develop a deep affinity for the Irish 'nation'. Clearly those British forms of sports such as cricket, rugby union and football that had gained popularity in Ireland at this time could not be used to generate Irish nationalism, given the belief that any movement for an Irish Ireland should work towards the removal of all aspects of British culture. This view was increasingly shared by the Catholic Church which joined with Irish nationalists in agitating for the promotion of Ireland's ancient sporting heritage as a response to the influx of English athletic traditions.

This thinking came together at Hayes Hotel in Thurles on 1 November 1884, when a group of seven men met to form the Gaelic Athletic Association for the Preservation and Cultivation of National Pastimes. The GAA was an overtly nationalist organisation from its very beginnings. Three of those who attended the Thurles meeting were members of the IRB, while the three patrons – Archbishop Croke, Charles Stewart Parnell, leader of the Irish Parliamentary Party (IPP) and the Land Leaguer, Michael Davitt – were involved, in different ways, in the promotion of the Irish nationalist cause. Perhaps the clearest indication, though, of the centrality of an Irish nationalist agenda in the formation of the GAA can be found in the Association's charter which cites its basic aim as 'the strengthening of the National Identity in a 32-county Ireland through the preservation and promotion of Gaelic Games and pastimes' (GAA, 2002). Eoghan Corry (1989: 12) perfectly encapsulates the rationale behind the Association's formation by arguing that:

> It was a national effort to recall a national inheritance, to emancipate a people from an alien, social thraldom: to save them in the practice of their traditional amusements, in the atmosphere of active nationalism and for the ultimate achievement of national independence.

Whilst the GAA's members shared in the general philosophy underpinning its formation, the broader divisions amongst Irish nationalists about how best to achieve independence were reflected in the body's early development. The majority of members in the 1880s supported Parnell's constitutionalist agenda which sought Irish independence through parliamentary means. However, Parnell's demise as leader of the IPP, when his affair with the wife of a nationalist MP from Galway was made public, not only dented the position of constitutional nationalists in Irish politics, but also left the way open for the IRB and supporters of physical force nationalism to build on their role in the inception of the Association and play a bigger part in directing the affairs of the fledgling body. The involvement of the Catholic Church and their campaigning against the IRB's leading role intensified the factionalist conflict with the GAA and ultimately threatened its future. Following a rapid decline in the number of clubs throughout Ireland as a consequence of such disputes, some of the more open-minded members of the Association came to the fore and began to distance themselves from factionalist in-fighting, preferring instead to emphasise the broad nationalist goal that lay at the heart of their promotion of Gaelic games. It was this wider objective that also did much to shape the GAA in America in this period. Before turning to an examination of the ways in which the inception and early development of Gaelic games in the US were rooted in a broad nationalist cultural and political agenda, it is important to add further context by briefly discussing the development of Irish nationalism in America.

The emergence of Irish nationalism in America

Irish nationalism as a significant expression of Irish Catholic identity in America emerged in the first half of the nineteenth century as a result of a combination of slow social, economic and political progress for Irish Catholic immigrants and an intense sense of Anglophobia. As early as the late 1820s, nationalists in Ireland recognised the potential of the Irish diaspora as a resource that could be harnessed to bring to an end British rule in Ireland. Daniel O'Connell's Catholic agitation and Repeal Association received much support in America in this period, with Repeal clubs being established during the 1840s in strong centres of Irish immigration, and funds were regularly sent back to the old country to support his work. However, support for O'Connell amongst Irish Americans began to wane by the mid 1840s, when he alienated sections of the Irish immigrant community by criticising their support for

slavery in America (McCaffrey, 1992). The Great Famine revived Irish nationalism in America and also did much to shape its appearance and expression.
According to Miller (1985), the famine immigrants that poured into America
adopted the motif of exile and saw Britain as responsible not only for their
poverty and starvation in Ireland but also for their exodus to what was for most
of them an unwelcoming and deeply inhospitable country. From the 1850s
onwards, Irish-American nationalism became increasingly characterised not
only by a love for Ireland, or at least an 'imagined', idealised vision of Ireland,
but by a hatred of the British. Indeed, Irish nationalists in America in this
period displayed what the great Irish poet, William Butler Yeats, described as a
'fanatical heart' (cited in Miller, 1985: 94). The initial experiences of the
Famine Irish in America, blighted as it was by nativism, poverty, disease and
destitution did little neither to assuage their hatred of Britain nor to dampen
their desire to see Ireland free of British influence. Indeed, the emigrants of the
second half of the nineteenth century believed that their progress, acceptance
and recognition as fully fledged citizens of America could be won only through
the achievement of emancipation in Ireland (Ní Bhroiméil, 2003).

The revolutionary zeal of Irish Americans at this time manifested itself most
clearly in support for a physical force solution to the Irish question. Militant
Irish Americans did much to support the Young Ireland movement and,
following the failure of a military uprising against British forces in County
Tipperary in 1848, they provided shelter to some of the leaders of this movement who were forced to flee across the Atlantic (Wilson, 1995). This did much
to sustain militancy as an expression of Irishness in America in this period, but
it was the emergence of Fenianism in America in 1858 that did most to energise
the physical force movement there. The establishment of the Emmet
Monument Association in New York was of great significance. This group,
founded by two veterans of the failed Young Ireland rising of 1848, John
O'Mahony and Michael Doheny, changed its name to the Fenian Brotherhood
and it became the primary Irish revolutionary organisation in America, raising
$500,000 in 1865 alone (McCaffrey, 1997). Resistance from the Catholic Church
to Fenianism, internal dissension and the outbreak of the American Civil War
disrupted the activities of the Fenian movement. However, the formation of
Clan na Gael, a secret oath-bound organisation founded by Jerome Collins in
New York in 1867, gave the revolutionary brand of Irish nationalism a new
impetus. Following John Devoy's emergence as leader of the Clan in 1871, cells
rapidly developed throughout Irish America with membership for the rest of
the decade remaining at a constant 10,000 (Brown, 1966).

Physical-force nationalism was not the only shade of political opinion amongst Irish Americans in this period. Patrick Ford, the influential proprietor and editor of the *Irish World*, sought to combine traditional Irish-nationalist objectives with an attack on landlordism in Ireland and industrial capitalism in America. He successfully persuaded Devoy to alter the Clan's tactics to encompass these issues in the New Departure strategy. Devoy and Ford sought alliances with Home Rulers in Ireland as a way of widening the appeal of the New Departure, and in doing so opened up the possibility of Irish-American support for Parnell's parliamentary approach to the Anglo-Irish relationship. Parnell had taken over leadership of the Land League at this time with the support and encouragement of Michael Davitt and in 1880 he embarked on a tour of America to meet the leaders of Irish America and solicit funds for the Land League. His tour was successful not only in endearing the ideology of Home Rule in the hearts and minds of Irish immigrants throughout America, but also in guaranteeing an abundant flow of dollars into the coffers of parliamentary nationalism. By 1881, the 1,500 branches of the Land League that had been set up all over America had raised over half a million dollars for land reform in Ireland and Home Rule (Brundage, 1997). By the early 1880s, Parnell's parliamentary approach to Ireland's relationship with Britain had gained ground as the most popular expression of Irish nationalism in America, which was evident from the flow of dollars into Irish Parliamentary Party coffers. This is not to say that republicanism lost out to parliamentary nationalism totally in this period. In fact, Irish Americans continued to raise funds and effectively bankroll those organisations that favoured a more direct and violent approach to independence (McCaffrey, 1997).

Despite such levels of support, the development of Irish nationalism in the US in the late nineteenth century did not follow a linear, progressive path. Although a desire to see an independent Ireland remained at the forefront of the consciousness of the Irish diaspora, the ways in which Irish nationalist organisations expressed their agenda led to fluctuations in support. By the late 1880s and early 1890s, influential sections of Irish America found it increasingly difficult to reconcile their efforts to achieve respectability in the American main-stream with aspects of Irish-American nationalism. The insistence of Patrick Ford that Irish freedom should be combined with socialism worried those supporters of nationalism who had experienced the rewards and seen the benefits of free market capitalism in the US. Similarly, the violence perpetrated by Clan na Gael, particularly its dynamite attacks on a range of English cities in the early 1880s, also concerned those who felt that such a strategy did Irish nationalism few favours amongst liberal opinion in Irish America. The factionalism that dogged Irish politics in this period, caused primarily by Parnell's involvement in a divorce scandal in 1890, transferred across the Atlantic and this also led to Irish nationalism losing support in some quarters of Irish America (McCaffrey, 1992).

Regardless of this flux in levels of support, nationalism, of both the revolutionary and constitutional brands, was a key element of Irish ethnic identity in America prior to but particularly after the Great Famine. Joining revolutionary organisations, donating their dollars to parliamentary nationalism, attending political meetings dealing with the Irish question, joining Irish clubs and societies and voting for Irish politicians provided Irish Americans with an opportunity to develop and give vent to deeply politicised versions of Irishness. Taking their lead from Irish nationalist thinking in Ireland about the importance of the cultural revival, Irish-American nationalists soon recognised that any contribution to Irish separatist aspirations – politically, financially and militarily – would be much stronger and more coherent if it were built on a strong sense of cultural Irishness amongst the immigrant community. In much the same way as occurred in Ireland, Irish cultural forms, Irish literature and the Irish language were promoted in America as a way of achieving this end. The significance of sport in the British Empire and the role that American sports, particularly baseball, played in helping the Irish community to assert themselves, develop a sense of ethnic cohesion and acquire self esteem would not have been lost on the leaders of Irish-American nationalism. Thus, as it had in Ireland, Gaelic sport in America also came to represent an important cultural mechanism for building and articulating an affinity for Ireland and the nationalist agenda. Indeed, the movement to promote and preserve Gaelic games in America formed part of a deliberate strategy aimed at constructing the sort of Irishness upon which both constitutional and revolutionary brands of Irish-American nationalism could be developed throughout the country.

The GAA and Irish nationalism in late nineteenth-century America

That Gaelic games came to represent an important medium through which the Irish in America demonstrated their support for nationalism is due in no small measure to the fact that the emergence of these sports in the US coincided with the period of strength in Irish-American nationalism outlined above. The promotion of Gaelic games in the US in the late 1870s and 1880s can clearly be interpreted as part of the broader groundswell of support for Irish nationalism. As well as keeping Irish Catholics in touch with Ireland, culturally and psychologically, Gaelic games quickly provided a platform for the Irish community in a range of American cities to construct and give vent to a distinctively Irish ethnic and national identity. The use of Gaelic games in this regard was clearly not an accidental process. Rather, nationalist-minded immigrants specifically sought to use these activities in order to galvanise the Irish community in America behind the broader political goal of Irish independence from Britain.

The promotion of Gaelic games in Boston in the late 1870s and 1880s is a stark exemplar of this process. The first patrons of these games in the city, the Irish Athletic Club of Boston (IACB), were staunch nationalists who sought to bolster support for the broader struggle for Irish emancipation by encouraging and promoting a vibrant Gaelic culture in America. Other pioneering figures in the city, particularly John Boyle O'Reilly, also viewed the promotion of Irish cultural forms in America as crucial to the development of sustained support for the nationalist cause. The aims of Irish nationalism were also uppermost in the minds of the founders of Boston's earliest clubs, who articulated and celebrated their nationalism by naming them after historical and popular nationalist personalities and organisations. The work of Mike Cronin demonstrates that this trend was also widespread throughout Ireland at this time and he explains its significance in the following way:

> It is clear from the experience of GAA clubs in County Meath in the 1890s, an experience which is duplicated across Ireland, that the historical and political is embraced and championed by the Association. They are constructing an identity which stresses and publicises their links as sportsmen to the nationalist mission, the embrace of things Irish and the rejection of West Britonism (Cronin, 1998b: 96).

Whilst some clubs in Boston were named after those counties of Ireland where the majority of their members originated, the appropriation of names such as Emmets (after Robert Emmet, leader of the failed 1803 United Irishmen Rising), Redmonds (after John Redmond, leader of Irish parliamentary nationalism in the early twentieth century), Wolfe Tones (after the popular Irish nationalist figure) and Young Ireland Hurling Club (after the nationalist organisation) reveals that these clubs were embracing Irish nationalism and giving their support, in a highly visible way, to the struggle for Irish independence from Britain.

Boston was not unique as the same desire to link Gaelic games to Irish nationalism was evident elsewhere in the country. In New York, for example, Irish nationalists were clearly at the vanguard of the movement to spread Gaelic football and hurling throughout the city. This should come as no surprise given the place of New York in the broader history of Irish nationalism in America. While nationalism of either the constitutional or revolutionary brand were fundamental expressions of Irish Catholic identity in almost every American city that possessed a significant Irish immigrant population, Irish nationalism was particularly strong in New York. Two of the key pillars of Fenianism in America, the Emmet Monument Association and Clan na Gael, were formed in that city and a whole host of republican heroes and political refugees from Ireland such as O'Donovan Rossa, John Mitchel, John Devoy and John O'Mahony travelled to New York and mobilised the city's Irish community firmly behind the nationalist cause (Diner, 1997). Indeed, as Brundage has commented, 'New York remained the epicentre of the move-ment, the main locus of activities for constitutional Home Rulers and separatist revolutionaries alike' (Brundage, 1997: 322). In order to make explicit con-nections between the various teams that sprang up in the city in the 1880s and 1890s and the Irish nationalist cause, patrons followed the trend established in Boston and throughout Ireland of naming newly formed clubs after nationalist personalities and organisations. The majority of the clubs formed in this period took on appellations pregnant with nationalistic symbolism such as Wolfe Tones, Stars of Erin, Barrys, Kickhams, Mitchels, Emmets and Thomas Francis Meaghers, specifically as a way of articulating their nationalist credentials. It should be pointed out, however, that from 1898 onwards many clubs adopted county names, rather than those more readily associated with Irish nation-alism. As chapter 4 reveals, this was not a result of a decline in the extent to which the GAA community in New York was supportive of nationalism. Rather, it was a consequence of the increasing role that the county societies in the city came to play in the organisation of Gaelic football and hurling.[1]

Similar close associations between leaders of Irish nationalism and the GAA were also evident further west. In Chicago, the promotion of Gaelic football and hurling was a reflection of the broader support for both the physical force and constitutional brands of nationalism in the city at this time. Those who were directly involved in the promotion of the GAA in the city were also strong proponents of Irish independence. The nationalist newspaper publisher, John F. Finerty, was a key figure in the drive to popularise Gaelic games amongst Irish Chicagoans. His association with Gaelic games in the mid 1880s was clearly evident at a number of picnics during the summer of 1884 that were aimed at raising awareness of and support for the 'cause' in Ireland. Finerty was not only one of the leading orators at these events, but he also worked to ensure that Gaelic football was part of the programme of activities (*Citizen*, 19 July 1884; *Citizen*, 2 Aug. 1884; 9 Aug. 1884). Finerty's motivation in involving himself in the GAA in this way was underpinned by a recognition of the value of Gaelic games and Irish culture in general, in helping to engender a strong sense of political nationalism throughout Chicago and Irish America. Apart from Finerty, those who set up the city's first clubs also helped root the emerging GAA culture explicitly within the nationalist agenda, by following the pattern of naming clubs established on America's east coast. Thus, teams such as Emmets, O'Briens, Wolfe Tones, O'Connells, Davitts, Shamrocks and Emeralds were very much to the fore in the city's Gaelic games circles.

Although it took slightly longer for the GAA to become established on the Pacific Coast, San Francisco's Gaels were equally committed to publicly stating their support for the broader nationalist mission. This support was evident in the venue chosen for the inaugural meeting of the GAA in the city, the meeting hall of one of San Francisco's leading nationalist associations, the Knights of the Red Branch (KRB). The commitment of San Francisco's Gaels to Irish independence was also expressed in the same manner as their counterparts in other branches of the GAA across the country. The clubs that were formed in the years immediately following the GAA's birth adopted monikers such as Robert Emmets, Shamrocks, Sarsfields and Parnells. The emergence of Father Yorke, San Francisco's leading churchman and one of its foremost Irish nationalists, as a central figure in the GAA in the early 1900s ensured that the development of Gaelic games throughout California would continue to be rooted in the wider agenda of the movement for Irish independence.

Apart from the motivation and action of leading figures within the GAA hierarchy throughout America and the founders and patrons of the earliest clubs, the association between Gaelic games and Irish nationalism was rein-forced amongst the broader Irish community through evocative and rousing discourse on GAA activities in the Irish-American press.[2] This type of coverage was particularly evident in the *Irish Echo*'s and *The Gael*'s accounts of GAA field days in Boston in the early 1880s which were routinely described as 'patriotic', imbued with the 'spirit of freedom' and part of a practical drive for 'Irish emancipation' (*Irish Echo*, July 1888; *The Gael*, May 1887, and see chapter 2 above). This same trend was also apparent in the press narratives surrounding the establishment and development of hurling and Gaelic football in New

York, Chicago and San Francisco. Such discourse and the more general portrayal of Irish sporting pastimes as emblematic of Irish identity and aspirations for independence further reinforced the resolve of the GAA's guardians in America to persevere with their endeavours to spread and promote Gaelic games throughout their respective states and cities. Equally, if not more importantly, by conveying the philosophy and ideals of Gaelic sport in this manner, such press coverage also bolstered the desire of nationalist-minded Irish emigrants to support the games of the old country either through participation or financial investment.

The place of the GAA in the psyche of Irish nationalists in America was also broadened and cemented by a range of nationalist organisations – of both the physical force and parliamentary kind – turning to Gaelic games as a way of attracting adherents and promoting their cultural and political agendas. In Chicago for example, organisations such as the Irish National League, the Hibernian Rifles, the Advanced Irish Nationalists and the New Ireland Colonization Association organised picnics and rallies during the mid to late 1880s at which Gaelic games featured prominently (*Citizen*, 26 Sept. 1885; *Citizen*, 3 July 1886; *Citizen*, 6 Aug. 1887). Those who sought Irish-American support for Charles Stewart Parnell's parliamentary nationalism in the 1890s also drew on the medium of Gaelic games in Chicago to garner awareness and funds. William Redmond, one of Parnell's envoys, visited the GAA's grounds at Lincoln and Polk during a trip to Chicago in June 1891 to address the crowd and canvass support for Parnell's nationalist agenda (*Citizen*, 6 June 1891). Such was the support for Parnell within the GAA of Illinois, that when he died in late 1891 the various GAA clubs came together and passed a series of resolutions mourning his death and expressing sympathy for his mission for Irish Home Rule (*Chicago Daily Tribune*, 22 Oct. 1891).

This pattern was repeated on America's Pacific coast where groups such as the KRB, the Gaelic League and the Ancient Order of Hibernians all ardently got behind Gaelic games and were more than happy to be closely associated with the GAA. In Boston, too, the early picnics at which traditional Irish sports and culture featured so prominently were patronised by leading members of the city's Irish nationalist movement, who viewed such events not only as useful in encouraging a strong sense of Irishness, but also as invaluable opportunities for fund-raising. At a number of field days from the mid 1880s onwards, funds were collected from both spectators and participants for the Irish Parliamentary Fund, inaugurated by 'friends of Ireland in Boston', to enable Parnell 'to carry on the work of the redemption of Ireland to final success'

(*Donahoe's Magazine*, 1886: 180). The establishment of a more coordinated approach to Gaelic games in New York around the turn of the century heralded an increase in the use of the Gaelic games as a mechanism for raising funds for Irish nationalist causes. In this period the First Regiment of the Irish Volunteers of New York, a nationalist militia group, formed a Gaelic football team and organised field days in order to promote their cause and generate income (*Gaelic American*, 7 Nov. 1903). The Irish Republican Brotherhood Veterans did likewise and organised festivals and games to commemorate various Irish nationalist figures such as Theobold Wolfe Tone, thus keeping their memory alive in the hearts and minds of New York's Irish community (*Gaelic American*, 2 July 1904).

Of all of the nationalist groups that were associated with the GAA in the late nineteenth century, Clan na Gael had perhaps the clearest vision about how best to harness the mobilising power of Gaelic sport to generate support for their militant agenda. This is a point noted by Steven Reiss (1992: 192) who is correct in his assertion that 'Irish sport was . . . promoted by overtly political organisations, most notably the Clan na Gael (United Brotherhood), a secret revolutionary society that arranged athletic meets to gain favourable publicity, attract new adherents, and promote Irish nationalism'. This process began almost as soon as the organisation was formed. As early as 1871, just four years after its inception, Gaelic games featured prominently at the annual carnival and games of Clan na Gael in New York. Branches of the organisation in Chicago also used Gaelic games as a way of recruiting young men to physical force nationalism, demonstrated by a series of adverts that ran in *The Citizen* throughout the summers of 1885, 1886 and 1887 promoting Clan na Gael picnics and rallies at which hurling and football matches took place.

Whilst a whole host of Irish nationalist organisations and individuals benefited from the support of and connections with the GAA in the US, it should be pointed out that this relationship was symbiotic. Although Irish nationalism profited in financial, recruitment and ideological terms by incorporating Gaelic games into their social and recreational events, the GAA and its clubs benefited significantly from the patronage of organisations that were influential in Irish-American circles. This patronage not only facilitated access to finances, equipment and facilities within Irish neighbourhoods and, in some cases, beyond, but also allowed the Association to recruit politically conscious or active immigrants as players, officials, social members and spectators. In doing so this helped Gaelic games to grow and develop into a significant cultural pastime in Irish America's most populous cities.

Conclusion

By the 1890s, Gaelic sports had thrown down deep roots amongst the Irish communities of Boston, New York, Chicago and San Francisco. The connections between the GAA and Irish nationalism were clearly significant in their early development and did much to encourage politically motivated immigrants to become involved in the activities of the Association. Steven Reiss (1992: 192), in his brief assessment of the birth of traditional Irish sports in Boston, is correct in his assertion that 'Irishmen living in the United States quickly adopted these sports to show solidarity with revolutionaries'. His description of the GAA in Boston in the late nineteenth century as 'an ethnic sub-community that gave members dignity, pride, and a heightened sense of nationalism' (Reiss, 1992: 192) applies equally to the Gaels of New York, Chicago and San Francisco. However, the fact that Gaelic games continued to grow and develop in the last decade of the nineteenth century, despite the decline in support amongst Irish Americans for aspects of political nationalism, illustrates that there were other reasons why America's Irish communities engaged in and consumed these sports.

Part of the explanation for the appeal of Gaelic games can be found in the same reasons why other sports that catered for the urban working classes throughout the industrial world in the late nineteenth century were so popular. Put simply, hurling and Gaelic football provided sections of the Irish diaspora with an enjoyable and often exciting escape from the rigours of work, and allowed them to give vent to their masculinity in a boisterous and at times aggressive manner. This, however, is only part of the reason behind the popular appeal of Gaelic games in this period. Apart from the identity-forming and purely sporting functions of Gaelic games, the emerging GAA culture in some of America's main industrial metropolises performed a number of other important social, economic and psychological functions for those who engaged with it. The role of the Gaelic football or hurling club in smoothing the transition from Ireland to cities that more often than not possessed a hostile Anglo-Saxon Protestant establishment cannot be overstated. The GAA afforded Irish Catholics with opportunities to sustain themselves in the face of discrimination. It enabled them to rekindle old friendships, forge new ones, mix with their 'own' and simply be in a social and cultural setting resonant of 'home', however that was defined in the minds of individual immigrants. In doing so the Association helped to alleviate the feelings of dislocation and alienation that the Irish in America often felt. Immersion in Gaelic games also provided entrance into the social networks that allowed newly arrived immi-grants to find work and accommodation, hence supporting their first steps in the New World. By the turn of the century, the GAA had become an important political, cultural, socio-economic, psychological and sporting resource and, as the next chapter reveals, it was its ability to continue to sustain sections of the diaspora in these ways that would underpin the growth and development of Gaelic games in America for much of the first half of the twentieth century.

Preserving Ireland's sporting heritage: Gaelic games in the United States from the turn of the century to the Great War

Introduction

At the beginning of the twentieth century, the GAA had registered a significant presence in those American cities that had at first endured and subsequently embraced Irish immigrants. In the later decades of the previous century, the Irish had shown a great enthusiasm and propensity for sport. They took to baseball in large numbers and achieved the highest laurels that this game offered. They also embraced and excelled in a whole host of other sports on disembarkation on American shores. This penchant for sport extended to the games of their homeland, and although it is unlikely that they were as popular as American sports such as baseball, Gaelic games were an important element of the sports culture of sections of America's Irish Catholic population. The opportunity to combine their love of sport with the expression of a deep affinity for Ireland was readily taken up by immigrants eager to identify themselves as a distinctive ethnic group, be reminded of the homes that they had left and show a sense of solidarity with the Irish nationalist movement. The social, economic and psychological benefits of immersion in Gaelic games added further to their appeal for those immigrants, both newly arrived and established, seeking to navigate their way in the New World.

The narratives of the previous two chapters exemplify these points clearly and the analyses of the GAA's growth in New York, Boston, Chicago and San Francisco in the first two decades of the twentieth century that now follow continue in a similar vein. This chapter will demonstrate more specifically that the profile and strength of the GAA amongst the diaspora were not only closely linked to the experiences of the Irish in America but were also shaped by events in Ireland, not least the building resentment against the continued British presence in Ireland and growing support for a revolutionary response. As the previous chapter demonstrated, Gaelic games in the late nineteenth century served as a platform for politically conscious immigrants to express themselves in highly visible ways as Irish nationalists. The extent to which the GAA continued to perform this function fluctuated at various stages during the first two decades of the twentieth century, but became particularly marked in the period leading up to the Easter Rising of 1916. While a detailed analysis of the ways in which Gaelic games were linked to the Irish nationalist agenda at this time will be addressed in chapter 7, the narrative that now follows begins to account for the significance of these linkages in the growth and status of the GAA in the US in this same period.

Gaelic games and Irish county societies in New York

Although Joseph P. Kennedy, William Prendergast and others had done much to get Gaelic games off the ground in New York, the city's network of Irish county societies emerged to play a key role in the games' development in the final years of the nineteenth and the first decade of the twentieth centuries. However, as noted in chapter 2, a coordinated approach to promoting and organising hurling and football was still required. This was recognised by the city's Gaelic sports enthusiasts and gave rise to an increasingly vociferous lobby for the establishment of a governing body in New York and elsewhere. In late 1903 the *Gaelic American*, an Irish-American weekly newspaper based in New York, argued:

> That there is a necessity for a thorough reorganization of the GAA in America there is no doubt . . . The movement for the propagation of Irish athletics seems to be experiencing a revival just now, but very little progress can be made, no matter what enthusiasm may be displayed in certain sections of the country, without a systematic organisation (*Gaelic American*, 10 Oct. 1903: 4).

The setting up of boards, similar to country boards in Ireland, in every state where the game was played was specifically recommended. It was suggested that after these state boards were established, a central body could be set up to oversee the game throughout the US. Although this lobby was influential in pushing the agenda for change, the catalyst for the reorganisation of Gaelic games in New York was the announcement in October 1903 that four days of the programme for the 1904 World's Fair in St Louis would be devoted to 'distinctively Irish games' (*Gaelic American*, 24 Oct. 1903: 3). GAA enthusiasts recognised that this represented an unprecedented opportunity to popularise their games more broadly. To do this effectively it was accepted that it was necessary to change 'the present disconnected, slipshod way of doing things' in GAA circles and initiate some form of major reorganisation (*Gaelic American*, 24 Oct. 1903: 3). Although the *Gaelic American* called on James Sullivan of the Greater New York Irish Athletic Association to undertake this reorganisation, it was the county societies that came to the fore and took the lead in this venture.

Representatives from all of the county societies that had organised football clubs met on 3 June 1904 to discuss the formation of a 'council' to promote Gaelic games and regulate fixtures between teams (*Irish American Advocate*, 11 June 1904: 1).[1] This meeting was followed by similar events throughout the summer months to consider various proposals and possible structures. At a meeting organised by the Kilkenny Social and Benevolent Association attended by 24 other county societies in early September 1904, an organisational structure was agreed and the Irish Counties Athletic Union (ICAU) founded. It immediately became recognised by all county societies as the primary governing council of Gaelic games in New York. The specific purpose of the ICAU was twofold and included the propagation of Gaelic games and the fostering of 'brotherly feeling between all county organisations and more particularly among all Irish men' (*Irish American Advocate*, 10 Sept. 1904: 1). The ICAU therefore not only established a much needed organising body for Gaelic games but also provided the county societies with the common platform and focus that they had hitherto been lacking. In keeping with this latter objective, the ICAU was joined a few months later by the United Irish Counties Association (UICA), which took responsibility for a more co-ordinated approach to the social and benevolent activities of the county societies. The new governing body's regularisation of fixtures reaped almost immediate dividends with attendance figures exceeding all expectations. In a three-week period in 1904, between late May and mid June, around 20,000 spectators watched Gaelic football matches at Celtic Park (*Irish American Advocate*, 28 May 1904: 1; 4 June 1904: 1; 11 June 1904: 1).[2] In addition, from 1905 Madison Square Garden, even then one of the city's premier entertainment venues, hosted matches which generated 'intense interest' amongst both Irish-American and American spectators (*Gaelic American*, 11 Feb. 1905). Participation in Gaelic games in this period extended beyond the city's male population and around this time the seeds were sown for what was to become a thriving centre for the women's game of camogie.[3]

Although Gaelic sports had acquired a position of prominence in New York's Irish community, their development in this period was not without difficulty or controversy. The ICAU was widely recognised as the primary governing body for Gaelic games in New York, but control of the main venue for the games, Celtic Park, continued to reside in the hands of the Irish American Athletic Club (IAAC). The IAAC had a particularly close relationship with the four most prominent teams in New York at that time – Cork, Kerry, Kildare and Kilkenny. This relationship was mutually beneficial because the 'big Four' profited from preferential arrangements for splitting gate receipts while the IAAC benefited from the drawing power of these clubs. This soon led to growing resentment between the smaller counties within the ICAU and the IAAC. When repeated requests for improved financial terms for games organised at Celtic Park were not forthcoming, the smaller counties looked for alternative venues (Ridge, 1997). For example, Van Cortland Park in the Bronx was used regularly from 1906, a new pitch was opened at Ulmer Field in Brooklyn in the same year (*Irish American Advocate*, 25 May 1906) and the Cavan Young Men's Protective & Benevolent Association held its 1907 annual picnic and games at West New York Athletic Field in Weekhawken, west of Manhattan (*Irish American Advocate*, 24 Aug. 1907). It soon became clear to the ICAU that if it was to gain any sort of control of Gaelic games in the city then it would need a permanent home to rival and eventually supersede Celtic Park.

The first steps were taken in 1907 when a nine and a half acre plot in Wakefield, South-East Yonkers, was acquired by the ICAU for a fee of $70,000. The county associations were able to raise only around $30,000 and the ICAU was forced to take out a sizeable mortgage to cover the remainder of the purchase price and subsequent improvements. From the outset the venture was doomed to failure. Shortly after Wakefield Park opened in 1908, Yonkers City officials invoked its Blue Laws, which effectively outlawed any business and revenue producing events on the Sabbath. The location of the park in an area poorly served by public transport also militated against the generation of the gate receipts that were required to make the venue financially viable. In a move probably born out of desperation, the ICAU attempted to force Cork, Kerry, Kildare and Kilkenny to play at Wakefield Park by preventing its affiliated members from sending teams to Celtic Park for the 1909 season. This directive was met with hostility by the 'big Four' who were unwilling to play at a venue where they would receive lower gate receipts and they defiantly continued to play their games at Celtic Park. With Wakefield Park lacking the drawing power of New York's best teams, unable to host games on the Sabbath and being poorly served by public transport, the crowds stayed away and two years after it was opened the venue closed (Byrne, 1976).

The Gaelic Athletic Association of the United States

The failure of the Wakefield Park venue was in no way indicative of the strength of Gaelic games in New York in this period. Indeed, in the years immediately following its closure, Celtic Park continued to host very successful and well-attended events, organised predominantly by the individual county associations, at which hurling and Gaelic football featured prominently. A revival of more militant expressions of Irish nationalism in New York and other centres of Irish immigration in the US in the period leading up to the Easter Rising of 1916 also fed into the robust health of the GAA at this time. The use of Gaelic games specifically to fund-raise for organisations such as the Irish National Volunteers and Clan na Gael did much to link the GAA with the cause of Irish nationalism in the minds of Irish immigrants, many of whom were experiencing a hardening of their attitudes towards Britain's presence in Ireland. This ensured that the games were well patronised. However, despite the good health of the games in terms of attendances at Celtic Park and the number of field days held there,[4] not to mention the staging of a number of high-profile and widely publicised fund-raising field days for the Irish Volunteers, the fallout from the closure of Wakefield Park gradually began to be felt. This episode had undermined the ICAU, and in doing so had rendered it unable to oversee the longer-term health of Gaelic games in New York. It was not long before pressure began to build for the formation of a new body to administer these sports in the city.

Perhaps the key individual in the agitation for a new governing body was Martin J. Hurley, originally from Cork, who wrote a weekly column for the *Irish American Advocate* under the pseudonym Liam O'Shea. Hurley's arguments for the inception of an administrative body were broadly the same as those that had given rise to the formation of the ICAU in 1904. In particular, Hurley emphasised the widely held belief in New York Gaelic sports circles that the proprietors of Celtic Park had continued to benefit financially from organising games at that venue, very often to the detriment of the clubs that played there. In a damning critique of this practice and the individuals involved, Hurley made scathing reference to 'some ungrateful scoundrels who, years ago, played the dastardly part of the grabber' and described their actions as 'the most open-faced robbery ever rubbed into a decent race' (O'Shea, 1913: 3). In the same article, Hurley also pointed to the persistence of incidents of overly aggressive and violent behaviour on the part of both players and spectators at Celtic Park as further evidence of the need for a governing body.[5]

The presidents of a number of the county societies as well as Pat Conway, the President of the IAAC, supported Hurley's vision. However, the most significant individual in translating this lobbying into a co-ordinated attempt to organise a governing body was William Snow, manager of the Cavan Gaelic football club and one of the most prominent Gaels in the city at the time. In December 1914 he brought together interested parties to his meeting hall in the Bronx to discuss the setting up of a committee to oversee the development of Gaelic games. Representatives of 19 clubs – eight hurling and nine football – as well as two clubs from Philadelphia were represented at the meeting. By the time the discussions had closed the Gaelic Athletic Association of the United States had been formed (O'Shea, 1914a: 3). Byrne (1976: 9) has highlighted the significance of this meeting at Snow's Hall by suggesting that it 'was to New York what the Thurles meeting was to Ireland'. At a second meeting of the GAA of the US the following week, Thomas Brady of the Cavan Gaelic football club was appointed as president and all of the other administrative positions were filled thus leaving the fledgling body in a position to begin its work (O'Shea, 1914b).

The detailed reports of both meetings in the Irish-American press at the time demonstrated a shared sense of purpose on the part of the attendant delegates. On the surface at least it appeared that factionalist interests had been put to one side in the hope of promoting a common *Irish* good. This theme certainly pervaded the reports of early meetings of the new body. At a meeting in early 1915, Stephen Donleavy of the IAAC assured the members of the GAA of the US that 'before a year passes your governing body will be an honour to the Irish race' (*The Advocate*, 20 Feb. 1915: 9). However, that year did not pass without problems, and shortly after the fledgling organisation was under way it was boycotted by the 'big Four' Gaelic football clubs. These teams had historically been the main draws at Celtic Park and had enjoyed preferential financial arrangements with the proprietors of the venue. The new body, eager to preserve the amateur ethos of the GAA, decided that rather than allowing the clubs to divide the huge gate receipts generated by the field days between themselves and the owners of Celtic Park, the clubs would be limited to $50 to cover expenses. This would have seen the 'big Four' clubs' cut of gate receipts reduced by up to $1,500, which they were not prepared to countenance. Thus Cork, Kerry, Kildare and Kilkenny broke off relations with the GAA of the US, and in the spring and summer of 1915 began organising their own field days under the banner of the Gaelic League of New York.[6] Although matches involving the boycotting clubs continued to attract large crowds, it soon became clear to them that their future lay within the new structures and competitions created by the GAA of the US. It was also imperative for the long-term success of the governing body to involve the four best football teams in New York in their competitions. Thus, in early January, delegates of the GAA met with representatives of the 'big Four' with a view to their inclusion in the programme for the 1916 season. After further meetings in February, Cork, Kerry, Kildare and Kilkenny acquiesced and were persuaded to rejoin the fold (*The Advocate*, 1 Jan. 1916; 26 Feb. 1916; 1 Apr. 1916). The GAA authorities were rewarded for their efforts in bringing a successful resolution to this affair with attendances for weekly fixtures at Celtic Park during the 1916 season that regularly topped 10,000.

As this chapter will reveal shortly, America's involvement in the First World War had a negative impact on Gaelic games in many of the locales where these sports were played. In New York, however, the war had much less of an effect, at least in terms of the ability of the GAA to generate healthy attendances at matches. It is difficult to determine the precise reasons for this. Apart from the popularisation of Gaelic games resulting from their increasingly close association with Irish nationalism, part of the explanation might be found in the ways that Irish involvement in America's war effort were woven into the activities and ethos of the GAA fraternity in New York at that time. In August 1917, the city's Irish newspaper, *The Advocate*, began a campaign to raise funds to send equipment for hurling and Gaelic football to the training camp of the US Army's 69th regiment, which had traditionally been composed of Irish volunteers. The rationale behind the campaign, duly named 'The Advocate Gaelic Athletic Fund', was set out in the following terms:

> There are scores of football players and hurlers from every county in Ireland in the famous Sixty-ninth. Baseball, tennis, and other such American sports do NOT appeal to those boys, consequently they will feel the loss of the Caman and Gaelic football unless the Irishmen and women of this city get up the necessary funds to supply them (*The Advocate*, 11 Aug. 1917: 5).

The fund-raising effort was undoubtedly motivated by a genuine desire to furnish Irish soldiers in the US army with opportunities for physical activity and enjoyment amidst the rigours of war. The *Advocate*, however, was a long-established proponent of Gaelic games in the city, and it was not lost on the newspaper's publishers and editor that these sports and the organisation that governed them were likely to receive favourable publicity and exposure on the back of the campaign. This was a point specifically made in the newspaper: 'it will be a big boost for Gaelic games. When the members of this far-famed Irish regiment play those games in camp and in France, it will mean that the Irish pastimes are in for a great deal of notoriety' (*The Advocate*, 11 Aug. 1917: 5). As might have been expected, the city's Gaelic football and hurling clubs were very much to the fore in generating the requisite finances, $148 in total, and were also instrumental in procuring the consignment of hurling sticks and footballs that were delivered to Camp Mills in early September (*The Advocate*, 1 Sept. 1917: 5). It is not certain whether it was the GAA's involvement in this campaign that allowed Gaelic games in New York to remain in a relatively sound state in comparison with Boston, for example, where they were scaled down significantly following America's entry into the Great War. However, at the very least the publicity from the fund-raising contributed to keeping Gaelic sports very much in the consciousness of Irish Americans in the city during the war.

Gaelic games in Boston from 1900 to 1918

While there was less of a direct linkage between the GAA in Boston and Irish county societies than was the case in New York, the development of Gaelic games here followed a broadly similar pattern. As shown in chapter 2, by the late 1890s Gaelic sports had thrown down deep roots amongst Boston's Irish community. The work of John Boyle O'Reilly, along with those who helped administer the GAA and establish new clubs in the city and throughout Massachusetts, was fundamental in this respect. The organisation of regular competitive matches and club activity did much to maintain the profile of Gaelic games amongst the diaspora in the early years of the twentieth century. The publication of match reports and advertisements of GAA activities in Boston's Irish newspapers also helped to keep these games and the rationale behind them in the public eye. Other publications which catered for Irish Americans did likewise. The New York monthly, *The Gael*, which was also distributed in Boston carried evocative stories of the progress of Gaelic games in Ireland and on American shores. One series of articles which began in 1900 carried what were described as 'recollections of "Gaelic" days' from Ireland by Rev. James B. Dollard. Although these 'recollections' focused on the fortunes of 'The Moondharrig Hurlers', a fictionalised team from Kilkenny, they portrayed to GAA enthusiasts in Boston, New York and elsewhere a sense that they were part of a wider and long-standing community of Gaels stretching from Ireland

right across America (*The Gael*, Jan. and May 1900; July 1901). *The Gael* comple-
mented these fictional accounts with detailed articles on the history and rules
of Gaelic games in Ireland and in so doing provided a template on which
matches in America could take place (*The Gael*, Aug.–Sept. 1900; Sept. 1901).

Between 1900 and 1914 the foundations that had been laid in Boston in the
latter stages of the previous century were further strengthened with the addition
of new clubs, such as Galway hurling club, founded in 1908, and the development of formally constituted competitions. The most important competition in
this era was the Massachusetts Championship which attracted clubs from Boston
and other parts of the state. The support that these clubs received from Irish
societies such as Clan na Gael and the Ancient Order of Hibernians maintained
the link between Gaelic games and Irish nationalism. Equally as important,
though, was the fact that the patronage of these sorts of influential political and
cultural organisations ensured that access to finances, equipment and facilities
within Irish neighbourhoods in Boston proved relatively unproblematic. With
this support in place, the first decade and a half of the century found Gaelic
games in Boston in good health. A regular season of field days, organised by the
clubs, sated the appetites of those eager to play and watch hurling and football
and ensured that these games remained a part of the cultural life of those eager to
retain a link with the 'old country' and give expression to their Irish heritage.

Events outside Boston also had an impact on the place of Gaelic games in
the city. As in New York, an intensification of nationalist activity in Ireland in
the run-up to the Easter Rising in 1916 led to the GAA in Boston being utilised
by organisations such as Clan na Gael and the Irish National Volunteers to
generate funds and build broad support for a military response to Ireland's
increasingly acrimonious relationship with Britain. This strengthening of the
connections between the GAA and Irish nationalism in Boston not only
boosted nationalist organisations   but also helped further the profile of Gaelic
games amongst politically aware members of the diaspora. Despite the
development of the GAA in this period and the close association that had
developed between Gaelic games and Irish nationalism, the Great War, and
America's decision to involve itself in hostilities in 1917, brought about a virtual
halt to the development of Gaelic football and hurling in Boston. With many
Gaelic games enthusiasts volunteering for the US Army's famous 'Fighting'
69th Regiment, matches were played only on an ad hoc and infrequent basis
and it was not until the early 1920s that Gaelic sports' clubs once again began to
cater for the sporting, recreational and cultural needs of Boston's Irish
community in any kind of sustained way.

Gaelic games in early twentieth-century Chicago

As in New York and Boston, Gaelic games in Chicago were in a state of good health by the end of the nineteenth century. Sustained growth continued in the early years of the first decade of the twentieth century and by its mid point, GAA field days were regularly attracting crowds of 5,000 (*Chicago Daily Tribune*, 10 Sept. 1906). The clearest indication of the vibrancy of Gaelic games in the city manifested itself in 1907, when the local GAA acquired a long-term lease on a plot of land situated in the south-west of the city at 47th Street and California Avenue, which came to be known as Gaelic Park. Father John Fielding, a Kilkenny native, member of Chicago's Catholic clergy since 1895 and – according to newspaper reports of the time – a skilled athlete and hurler (*Chicago Daily Tribune*, 15 Aug. 1909), was a central figure in this initiative. Under his patronage and later his presidency of the GAA of Illinois, Gaelic games entered into an exciting period in their early history. Father Fielding actively sought innovative approaches to diffusing these sports across Chicago and nearby towns and cities. He was one of the main organisers of Chicago's first inter-city hurling match against St Louis in 1907, an event that was so successful that the return fixture at Chicago's Gaelic Park drew a crowd of 12,000, one of the largest to have witnessed a hurling match in the city up to that point, and raised gate receipts of almost $10,000, all of which were donated to the Good Shepherd Industrial Schools of Chicago (*Chicago Daily Tribune*, 20 Oct. 1907; 9 Nov. 1908).

With Father Fielding duly installed as President of the Chicago GAA as a result of his successful promotion of Gaelic sports, the Association began to develop more ambitious ventures designed to enhance further the profile and status of these activities. In 1909 the inter-city concept was extended to include a visit to Chicago of a New York Gaelic football select, a match that attracted 7,000 spectators and raised gate receipts in the region of $3,000 (*Chicago Daily Tribune*, 16 Dec. 1909). Fielding's most ambitious strategy was his plan to organise a tour of two leading Irish teams, one in Gaelic football and one in hurling, to play a series of challenge games against teams from a range of American cities on the north-eastern seaboard and in the mid-west (*Chicago Daily Tribune*, 16 Dec. 1909). He travelled to Ireland in late 1909 to meet with GAA officials there to discuss his plans. When he returned he announced an itinerary that would involve the Kerry footballers and Kilkenny hurlers playing exhibition games in New York, Newark, Pittsburgh, Cincinnati, St Louis and – finally – Chicago. Fielding also announced that the Association was pursuing an option to buy rather than continue to lease the grounds at Gaelic Park and that, if successful, it would build stands that would extend the seating capacity at the venue to 20,000. Most significantly he also conveyed a pledge by the GAA in Ireland to contribute half of the estimated $10,000 cost required to turn the plan into reality (*Chicago Daily Tribune*, 17 Dec. 1909). During the meeting of the Chicago GAA at which Fielding unveiled the progress that had been made on the organisation and funding of the tour, he had little difficulty in persuading his fellow Gaels to match the New York GAA's promise to contribute $2,500 to the venture (*Chicago Daily Tribune*, 17 Dec. 1909).

The immediate future of Gaelic games in the city looked to be one filled with opportunity. However, within a matter of weeks of Fielding unveiling his proposals for the tour, the GAA was thrown into disarray, blighted by a failing that had affected Gaelic games elsewhere in the US in this period. That seemingly peculiar Irish flaw, the 'split', raised its head within Chicago GAA circles in early 1910, when a grouping of members of the Clan na Gael Gaelic football team replaced their manager following a string of defeats. At the GAA's annual convention, however, the delegates present voted to recognise the deposed manager as Clan na Gael's official delegate. This prompted uproar and, dissatis-fied at their failure to acquire a position of prominence in the running of Gaelic games, the dissenting group withdrew from the GAA, immediately set up a rival body and persuaded two of the city's hurling and football clubs to join them (*Chicago Daily Tribune*, 6 Jan. 1910: 10). This move caused much embar-rassment and sullied the excellent reputation that the GAA of Illinois had built up in previous years. Perhaps of more immediate concern was the fact that the split in the GAA's ranks presented a number of more serious practical problems. Chief amongst these was the fact that one of the leading figures in the seces-sionist group, James Cahill, formerly the treasurer of the local GAA, had in his possession around $700 of the Association's funds as well as its charter and the lease of Gaelic Park (*Chicago Daily Tribune*, 12 Jan. 1910).

With a new season of fixtures due to start in May, possession of the lease was the GAA's most pressing concern, so much so that after Cahill had refused to surrender the documents, Thomas Ahern, the newly installed president of the Illinois GAA, initiated legal action (*Chicago Daily Tribune*, 13 Jan. 1910). With the Chicago courts unable to resolve the issue in the short term, what had developed into a simmering feud characterised by claim and counter claim reached crisis point when both factions chose to open their respective seasons on 8 May at Gaelic Park. On the day of the planned fixtures, the breakaway group, or 'bolters' as they were referred to by the press, entered the venue early in the morning, barricaded all the entrances and took possession of the box office. When the officers and teams of the official body arrived around noon for their programme of games, they found their entrance barred. When their demands to be allowed access to the field and box office were rebuffed, they broke down one of the fence's enclosing the park. With tensions rising, the police were called and soon arrived along with the attorney for the estate in which the ground was located. This forced the bolters to leave the venue, but not before threatening the Illinois GAA with legal action over who had rights to Gaelic Park (*Chicago Daily Tribune*, 9 May 1910). Despite the bitterness that these events caused, when it became clear to the dissenting Gaels that their claims to the lease of the park were unlikely to be upheld in court, they decided to acquiesce and following talks were permitted to rejoin the ranks of the GAA (*Chicago Daily Tribune*, 16 May 1910). Although a sense of harmony was quickly restored, this affair and the press coverage that it generated damaged the reputation of the GAA in Chicago in the eyes of their coun-terparts in Ireland. As a result, the planned tour by Kerry and Kilkenny was cancelled and a visit by an Irish county team to American shores would have to wait a further 16 years.

The club game in Chicago was not unduly affected by these internal disputes and the 1910 season, involving seven football and three hurling teams, kicked off as planned in early May and ran through to late November (*Chicago Daily Tribune*, 25 Apr. 1910). Father Fielding continued to drive Gaelic games in the city in subsequent seasons and in doing so ensured that the GAA remained relevant to Chicago's Irish neighbourhoods. Events in Ireland and the hardening of Irish nationalism in America contributed in this regard. The inclusion of hurling and football matches in the programme of broader Irish nationalist festivals ensured that the GAA were able to showcase their activities to audiences of 10,000 or more (*Chicago Daily Tribune*, 4 Aug. 1913). Despite the surge in interest in the politics, culture and sports of Ireland amongst Irish Chicagoans at this time, the involvement of American forces in the First World War had the same impact on the development of Gaelic games in Chicago as it had in Boston. Although fixtures continued to be played sporadically at Gaelic Park and other venues throughout the city, it was not until the end of the war that a full resumption of Gaelic games occurred.

San Francisco's Gaels in the first two decades of the twentieth century

As highlighted in chapter 2, the sterling work of a number of Catholic churchmen did much to set the GAA in San Francisco on a sound footing at the beginning of the twentieth century. The tireless efforts of Father Yorke particularly were significant, and his role in the establishment of a governing body to oversee Gaelic games helped to embed these pastimes firmly in the cultural life of sections of the city's Irish population. The local Irish newspapers also played an important role in helping to popularise these sports, vociferously backing the efforts of Father Yorke and publicising the work of the fledgling GAA of California. Shortly after the formation of this body in February 1903, *The Leader* implored 'every lover of the game to assist the central organization body in promoting genuine games for the Gaels of the Coast' (*The Leader*, 2 May 1903: 8). This call was well heeded and a successful first season ensued, typified by regular and well-patronised club field days. Further growth characterised the following season when the complement of hurling clubs in San Francisco was augmented by the establishment of the Independents, Young Irelands, Wolfe Tones, Emmets and Davitts (*The Leader*, 2 Apr. 1904).

Father Yorke's involvement in Gaelic games and the continued practice of naming clubs after prominent Irish political figures or with distinctively Irish appellations revealed much about the San Francisco GAA's continued nationalist credentials. This association was further strengthened by the visit of Douglas Hyde, founder of the Gaelic League, to San Francisco in February 1906 as part of a 40-city tour of the US. The aim of this tour was primarily to raise funds for the Gaelic League and gather support for Hyde's calls for the de-Anglicisation of Ireland. As a by-product, Hyde's visit and his powerful oratory raised the profile of attempts to promote Irish cultural forms and language on American shores. Specific comments on the role of the GAA as a medium for resisting the Anglicisation of Ireland and the Irish during his speech at San Francisco's Tivoli Theatre on 19 February were particularly welcomed by San Francisco's Gaelic games enthusiasts and did much to reify, in the minds of those who either listened to or read Hyde's words, the relationship between the GAA and Irish nationalism (*The San Francisco Call*, 19 Feb. 1906).

The work of Father Yorke and the impact of Hyde's visit in promoting Gaelic games in the city were ultimately undone just two months later by the devastating earthquake and subsequent fires in the city in April 1906. With the minds of San Francisco's residents focused on the recovery effort, the immediate post-Great Fire period was one that was characterised by stagnation. Although some high profile GAA meets in the year after the disaster did manage to draw crowds of up to 5,000, others struggled to attract more than 200 (*The Leader*, 2 Oct. 1909). For the city's Irish population, rebuilding their lives in practical terms clearly took on more importance than sports. This trend led to concerns being expressed in the city's Irish newspapers in the early 1910s that Gaelic games were not growing quantitatively at the rate that they were on the east coast of America. San Francisco's clubs and governing body began to think about how best they could encourage those in the local Irish community to join the Association and support its clubs. Presenting the games as wholesome, refined and exciting pastimes became central to their approach. For example, one member of the Young Irelands hurling club urged players to adhere to the rules and limit the type of overly aggressive play 'that would be liable to throw odium on the game' (*The Leader*, 20 Jan. 1912: 8). In a further effort to popularise hurling, hurleys and slíothars were made available for the first time in a number of the city's sports goods stores at the outset of the 1912 season, improving the potential accessibility of the game to a wider audience (*The Leader*, 27 Jan. 1912). Despite these measures, both hurling and football struggled to arouse much interest and what had until that point been a relatively healthy complement of clubs in San Francisco dwindled to just two in both hurling and football (*The Leader*, 26 July 1913).

By the beginning of 1913, those who retained a desire to see a strong culture of Irish sports in San Francisco recognised that the situation had reached critical point. Four clubs in one of America's foremost Irish cities was a poor return, particularly when contrasted with a number of the outlying towns such as Oakland, Richmond and Crockett which each had its own GAA club. It became clear that efforts to revive Gaelic games had to be redoubled if the GAA was to survive in the city. As had been the case at the turn of the century when Father Yorke involved himself so dynamically in the affairs of the GAA, members of the Irish Catholic clergy in the city came to the fore once again. Reverend Father M. J. Walsh was particularly influential and not only took on the role of president of the Californian GAA during the 1913 season but also helped to establish a new Gaelic football club, Sarsfields, whose members were drawn from the parishes of St Patrick's, St Rose's and St Brendan's (*The Leader*, 26 July 1913; 6 Sept. 1913). In addition to Father Walsh's efforts, the Catholic Church became involved in reviving the fortunes of the GAA in the city in other ways. In March 1913, Father John Rogers, pastor of St Patrick's church in Mission, one of the city's most prominent Catholic churches, established the St Patrick's Gaelic League Athletic Association in order to promote regular competition between the city's hurling and football clubs and thus contribute to the growth of the GAA. A tournament running from April to June was duly organised, with teams competing for the title of 'Pacific Coast Champions'. The rationale behind this venture extended beyond the athletic; Father Rogers and his colleagues recognised that Gaelic sports could be a useful medium for raising funds to help reduce the parish's debt (*The Leader*, 15 Mar. 1913). That said, St Patrick's was instrumental in helping to maintain Gaelic games in the city and elsewhere during the remainder of 1913, a fact recognised in an article in *The Leader* which acknowledged that a number of priests at the parish 'did fine work, and are to be thanked for the number of clubs in existence today' (*The Leader*, 26 July 1913: 5). St Patrick's continued to play a role in the GAA during the next few years, not least by allowing the church to be used as a venue for the Association's meetings.

While the involvement of the Catholic Church was crucial in providing the GAA with leadership, meeting rooms, resources and playing facilities,[7] the maintenance of a strong culture of Gaelic games was largely dependent on the city's Irish population coming out in numbers to patronise the various field days and meets. Despite the increase in the number of teams, albeit only in Gaelic football,[8] and the best efforts of Father Walsh, Father Rogers and a range of other Catholic priests to proselytise their clergy to Gaelic games, attendances remained low for most fixtures throughout 1914.[9] In an effort to encourage higher levels of support, *The Leader* regularly urged its readership to turn out in larger numbers. The following appeal was typical:

> These games ought to draw large audiences . . . It is now up to the people. If they will only come to the Gaelic games as they flock to the picnics and dances, we would soon have a GAA which would be second to none in the world. Let us hope that the Ocean shore grounds will be full to overflowing tomorrow to watch the Irish men who believe in being Irish and in upholding the glory and dignity of our grand old Gaelic games (*The Leader*, 13 June 1914: 7).

Urgings of this kind were aimed at resonating with nationalist-minded immigrants and reminding the city's Irish community that the GAA was part of a broader spectrum of distinctively Irish organisations that were deserving of their support. While the continued linking of Gaelic games to the nationalist agenda was very important in helping to sustain the GAA, the hosting of the Panama-Pacific International Exposition in San Francisco in 1915 proved instrumental in reviving hurling and football in the city.

When plans began to be drawn up for the content of the exposition in 1912, the GAA recognised that this event represented a unique opportunity to display its sports to a wide-ranging audience and that it should therefore be used as a catalyst for rebuilding their profile in the city. As one editorial in *The Leader* argued:

Irishmen in California should bestir themselves and prepare for the great Panama-Pacific Exposition of 1915. A strong GAA should be built up. An Association that would represent all our race on the pacific coast and that would have the backing and support of all rich and influential Irishmen and Irish Americans in the state of California (*The Leader*, 29 Nov. 1913: 3).

As noted earlier, the 1914 season did little to assuage fears about the future of Gaelic games in the city. Nonetheless, as the 1915 Exposition approached, plans to present these sports in their best possible light began to be put in place and this certainly helped to bolster their profile. In August, a judge of the California Superior Court, John J. Van Nostrand, donated a trophy for a hurling game between O'Connells and Young Irelands, organised as part of the preparations for the exposition (*The Leader*, 8 Aug. 1914). Other fund-raising events took place throughout late 1914 and early 1915, allowing the GAA to put together their programme and purchase four new uniforms for the competing teams (*The Leader*, 15 Mar. 1915). St Patrick's Day was appropriately chosen as the day to display all things Irish at the Exposition. Gaelic games featured prominently with a hurling match taking place between O'Connells and Young Irelands and a football match between two select teams involving players drawn from every club in San Francisco and its neighbouring towns (*The Leader*, 15 Mar. 1915).

It is difficult to judge with accuracy the precise nature of the impact of the Exposition on Gaelic games in San Francisco, although a number of developments demonstrated that the GAA benefited from profiling their sports at this event. The complement of hurling clubs increased from two to four for the 1916 season and a new venue, Gaelic Park, located between San Bruno and Leland Avenues, was opened in October 1916 (*The Leader*, 14 Oct. 1916). The need to provide additional transport for a number of matches during the 1917 season revealed an increase in attendances. The establishment of a committee charged with setting up camogie teams for female GAA enthusiasts in San Francisco also demonstrated that Irish sport was being opened up to a wider constituency (*The Leader*, 2 June 1917; 15 Sept. 1917). Furthermore, the establishment of Pearses hurling club in 1916, named after Patrick Pearse, the leader of the 1916 revolutionaries, and the founding of the Sinn Féin Gaelic football club a year later augmented the nationalist credentials of the Association. Although these developments were significant and could have helped to rejuvenate the GAA in the late 1910s, America's involvement in the Great War ensured that, quantitatively speaking, they were minor.

Conclusion

At the turn of the twentieth century, those with responsibility for promoting Gaelic games looked to the future with considerable optimism. The founding fathers of the GAA in America had built sound foundations. With interest in Irish affairs, politics and culture remaining high amongst the diaspora, it appeared that conditions were favourable for hurling and football to root themselves more deeply in the sporting passions of the Irish in America. While levels of immigration did not reach those of the second half of the nineteenth century, America continued to attract significant numbers of Irish immigrants in the early years of the twentieth century. Existing clubs thus had a ready supply of fresh playing talent to take over from the first wave of hurling and football playing immigrants. Although there were peaks and troughs in the development of Gaelic games, as well as various disputes within GAA circles which held back their development in this period, the general growth of these distinctively Irish sporting pursuits augured well for the future. The hardening of Irish nationalism at 'home' and in the New World also did much to bolster further the position of these games in the cultural life of athletically and politically inclined Irish immigrants. However, America's decision to enter the Great War and the involvement of sections of the Irish emigrant community in the US forces did much to diminish the GAA. Although New York's Gaels were able to continue a reasonable programme of activities, elsewhere in the country meaningful competition ceased and did not return until the early 1920s.

Fluctuating fortunes: the GAA in America from the roaring twenties through the Great Depression

Introduction

From their inception in the late 1870s and early 1880s, the development of codified versions of Gaelic games in the US had followed a relatively progressive path, one broadly characterised by quantitative growth. With the exception of New York, the onset of the Great War brought this trend to a virtual halt. There were some signs on conclusion of the war that a culture of Gaelic games was about to re-emerge, but it would not be until the early 1920s that the position of the GAA amongst the Irish diaspora would be restored to anything resembling its previous status. Although the 1920s appeared to herald a return to much more favourable conditions in which to root Ireland's traditional sporting pastimes in America, the Wall Street Crash and the resultant global depression presented potentially debilitating challenges to America's Gaels. This chapter accounts for the history of the GAA in the US in the inter-war years and demonstrates that the Association's growth and development did not follow a linear path but, rather, was reflective of the broader mixed experiences of the Irish in America. The Irish in this period were no longer the impoverished famine emigrants of the previous century; they availed themselves of the opportunities that the new century offered. Equally, though, they were also susceptible to the difficulties – social economic and political – that America faced, especially during the Depression era of the 1930s. As the analyses that now follow reveal, the place of Gaelic games in the US was intimately fused to these fluctuating fortunes of the Irish in America.

The New York GAA from 1920 to the Second World War

The 1920s saw Gaelic games become particularly vibrant in New York. By 1924, the members of the city's GAA had participated in their first officially sanctioned competition in Ireland, representing 'America' in a hurling match against an Ireland select at the 1924 Tailteann games at Croke Park, in Dublin. New York's involvement in what ultimately proved to be a misguided attempt to revive Aonach Tailteann continued in 1928 in both Gaelic football and hurling, and again at the last of these festivals in 1932. In helping to showcase the New York GAA, these events bolstered the club game in the city in this period. Indeed, by 1925 there were almost 50 clubs competing at various levels across both codes (O'Shea, 1925a: 3). Although such robust health was welcome, the presence of so many clubs created problems for the GAA, not least an acute shortage of playing fields. Celtic Park was catering for three matches each weekend during the regular season. With little remedial work being carried out on the pitch in between, the playing surface and other facilities within the complex quickly deteriorated. The poor state of Celtic Park was compounded by the fact that the relationship between the GAA and the Irish American Athletic Club (IAAC), the owners of Celtic Park, had failed to improve significantly following the Association's return to the venue in the aftermath of the failed Wakefield Park experiment. It soon became clear to the GAA that the only way to resolve the problems associated with the use of Celtic Park was to seek new grounds elsewhere in the city. This was to prove no easy task, given the lack of affordable, available and accessible land to lease.

By the beginning of 1925 the situation had reached crisis point with concern being expressed about whether a full season's fixtures could be accommodated at Celtic Park. So poor was the condition of the venue that it had come to be referred to in sections of the Irish-American press as 'old shambles' (O'Shea, 1925a: 3). A temporary solution emerged in the spring of 1925, when William Snow and Patrick Grimes, two of New York's longest standing GAA stalwarts, secured the lease on a plot of land in Westchester in the Bronx that could host Gaelic games. Innisfail Park, as it was named, opened on 30 May 1925 with much fanfare and a series of exhibition games featuring the city's finest Gaelic football and hurling teams (O'Shea, 1925b). This development was followed in the next season by the opening of another venue for Gaelic games, Steinway Park, across the East river in Astoria, which was to be used specifically by junior teams (*Gaelic American*, 11 Sept. 1926).

Apart from facilities, 1926 was a significant year for Gaelic games in New York, indeed throughout America in another important sense, because it witnessed the first visit to the US by an All-Ireland winning county team. Although the impetus for this tour came from Chicago and also took in Boston, Buffalo and San Francisco, New York was the focal point of the Tipperary hurlers' visit. The level of interest in their match against the New York champions Offaly was such that it became clear to the organisers that neither Celtic Park nor the newly opened Innisfail Park were large enough to cope with the anticipated attendance. The decision was therefore taken to host the game at the Polo Grounds, former home of the baseball franchise the New York Giants. Over 30,000 spectators, the largest attendance at any GAA match in America up to that point, watched a one-sided victory for Tipperary.[1] Despite the uncompetitive nature of the game, the hosting of the All-Ireland Champions on American soil was hugely significant. One newspaper report at the time described the fixture as 'the most successful day that Gaelic games ever had in this country', one that 'in no small way contributed to the uplift of the sport in the US' (*Gaelic American*, 5 June 1926: 7).

The other, perhaps principal, repercussion of the 1926 tour was the emergence of plans to set up a nationwide governing body for Gaelic games in the US. Although city-based or regional organisations were already in existence, some of the Association's more forward- thinking administrators quickly saw the potential of a national body. Shortly after the tour concluded, Thomas Delaney, a leading New York Gael, wrote to Liam Clifford, the GAA's president in Ireland at the time outlining plans to organise a national branch of the Association. While Delaney recognised the geographic barriers presented by such a venture, he believed that the inception of three administrative zones – an Eastern division headed by New York but also embracing New Jersey, Pennsylvania, Massachusetts and Vermont; a Western region with San Francisco as its focal point; and a Mid-western division that was concentrated around Chicago – was the best way to proceed (letter to Liam Clifford from Thomas Delaney, 11 Oct. 1926). With the nucleus of the Eastern division already formed and promising soundings emanating from Chicago and San Francisco, Delaney requested that the proposed national body be affiliated to the GAA in Ireland. Following the success of the 1926 tour, the Association's Central Council was favourably disposed to this request and this affiliation was accepted unanimously (special meeting of Central Council, 16 Oct. 1926).

Encouraged by these developments, the GAA in Ireland sanctioned a further exhibition series for 1927 between Kerry, the 1926 All-Ireland football winners, and various select teams across the US. The three games at New York's Polo Grounds in late May and early June were again well attended with an estimated aggregate attendance of almost 100,000 (New York GAA, 1964). In an indication of the quality of the Gaelic footballer talent resident in the city at that time, the New York All-Star select won each of its matches against their illustrious visitors by decisive margins (New York GAA, 1964). Not every aspect of the Kerry tour was positive though. The fact that the American sports promoter who organised and coordinated the visit disappeared without paying the Kerry touring party the monies owed to them caused much consternation and led to acrimonious exchanges between the GAA in Dublin and their counterparts in New York. Further conflict between the two bodies arose in the following year when the New York team was granted permission to play a number of exhibition games to make up a financial shortfall caused by their early exit from the 1928 Tailteann games. In their preparations for these games the visiting Gaels inadvertently broke one of the GAA's cardinal rules of the time by using the facilities of a soccer club to train.[2] Central Council immediately withdrew permission to play any further games in Ireland and the New York select departed shortly afterwards. These incidents gradually began to undermine the relationship between New York and the parent body. A growing view within Croke Park that Gaelic games across the Atlantic, and particularly the tours involving inter-county teams from Ireland, were being run professionally and in contravention of the Association's amateur ethos did little to improve what were becoming increasingly strained relations. Suspicions from Dublin that US-based players were being paid for playing Gaelic games fed into this state of affairs. On two occasions during Central Council meetings in July and August of 1929, Thomas Delaney, who by this stage had been appointed president of the Eastern division, had to provide reassurances that players in the US did not receive direct payment beyond necessary expenses (Central Council GAA Minutes, 27 July 1929 and 31 Aug. 1929). The Dublin administration remained largely unconvinced, and concerns over professionalism continued to colour its view of the development of Gaelic games across the Atlantic.

Notwithstanding these growing transatlantic fissures, a general mood of optimism prevailed in New York GAA circles at the close of the 1920s. The presence of Ireland's leading inter-county teams in New York clearly helped to stimulate further growth of Gaelic games in the city, with the number of clubs reaching 70 and 'progress' being made in encouraging young Americans to get involved in hurling and football (Central Council GAA Minutes, 27 July 1929). As a result of this growth, some local Gaels felt that the time was right to purchase a site of their own, specifically for their sports rather than continue to lease land. Thus, in 1930, a plot of land at Flushing Meadow was deemed suitable and an initial down payment of $22,000 made, with a mortgage arranged for the remaining amount. What those who made this investment could not have envisaged at this time was the depression that was to ensue in the aftermath of the Wall Street Crash of 1929. With the Great Depression having a devastating effect on those in manual and semi-skilled employment – typically the sector where much of the city's Irish community found themselves – there was a considerable drop in attendances and hence income at Innisfail Park. In the harsh economic environment, the Association began to struggle financially and this put the Flushing Meadow venture at serious risk. Indeed, after only two payments the mortgage holders foreclosed on the property and $22,000 of the essential finance disappeared in one fell swoop, not to mention the dream of sole ownership of a GAA venue in the city (Milkovits, 1988; GAA Annual Congress Minutes, 21 Apr. 1935).

Faced with mounting debts, the Eastern division, led by officials from New York, increasingly came to view the tours by All-Ireland winning inter-county teams as crucial, in terms not only of generating the sorts of funds that would allow the Association to remain financially solvent but also for maintaining interest in Gaelic games in what were increasingly difficult times. These tours were successful in both respects. Matches between the All-Ireland football champions Kerry and New York select teams at Yankee Stadium, home of the New York Yankees baseball franchise, in 1931 and 1933 drew crowds of 60,000 and 50,000 respectively (*Chicago Daily Tribune*, 18 May 1931; 8 June 1933). Elsewhere, the tours were not doing as well and, by the mid 1930s, mounting financial wrangling between visiting teams and US promoters led to discussions within the GAA's Central Council and Annual Congress about whether or not they should continue (GAA Annual Congress Minutes, 21 Apr. 1935). The main concern, expressed in some quarters as early as 1928, was that the tours were undermining the broader ethos and reputation of the GAA. Questions were increasingly asked about whether or not the tours had become too commercial and were in contravention of the Association's rules on amateurism. It was also suggested that some US-based players who were taking part in exhibition matches against their Irish visitors were in breach of the GAA's ban policy by playing soccer for local clubs (Central Council GAA Minutes, 21 Aug. 1935). Sensing growing resentment and opposition in Ireland against the continuation of the tours, Paddy Lenihan, President of the GAA's Eastern division, wrote to Central Council asking for permission to invite the 1935 All-Ireland champions in both hurling and Gaelic football to New York. In doing so, Lenihan reminded Central Council that games of this kind represented 'a wonderful opportunity for us to recover from the depression we have experienced in the last few years' (Letter from Paddy Lenihan to GAA Central

Council, 21 Aug. 1935). Central Council acquiesced and granted the required permission subject to a satisfactory resolution of outstanding financial disputes involving inter-county teams from Cavan, Galway and Limerick who had toured the US in the previous year (Central Council GAA Minutes, 21 Aug. 1935).[3] By 1937, the tours had returned to a sound footing, at least in New York, with three games involving Mayo's footballers at Yankee Stadium attracting a combined audience of over 70,000 (Canon Michael Hamilton, Report to Central Council GAA, 29 May 1937).

In light of the high levels of unemployment throughout America in this period and the fact that immigration from Ireland had come to a virtual halt,[4] it is reasonable to suggest that, without tours by visiting Irish inter-county teams, Gaelic games in New York might not have survived. The clubs struggled to generate much in the way of interest. Although regular weekly fixtures continued at Innisfail Park, they were poorly patronised, with attendances in the middle of the 1930s averaging around 200. Despite this declining interest, the quality of what was occurring on the field of play remained high. In his report to Central Council in Dublin on the visit of Mayo's footballers to New York, Boston and Philadelphia, Canon Michael Hamilton, who was to become a key advocate of the GAA in the US, commented on the high standards of play and the 'healthy and virile' condition of Gaelic games in the city, suggesting that the local teams that he watched would 'provide excellent opposition for many of our teams at home' (Hamilton Report, 29 May 1937). That this was the case was due largely to the foresight of a number of leading members of the GAA in New York who faced the challenge of plummeting levels of immigration by seeking ways to promote Gaelic football and hurling amongst American-born children. As early as 1932, Paddy Lenihan raised the issue of youth player development at a meeting of the GAA's Central Council in Dublin and spoke specifically about the possibility of introducing Gaelic football into American colleges (Central Council GAA Minutes, 25 June 1932). While this would prove difficult, it did help focus the minds of Gaels throughout the Eastern division on the need to build a youthful grassroots to compensate for falling rates of immigration.

This recognition underpinned a drive to popularise Gaelic games amongst the children of Irish immigrants which had an almost immediate impact. By 1934, the General Secretary of the GAA in Ireland, Pádraig Ó Caoimh, was able to report to Congress in Dublin that 'the extension of operations to juvenile teams is the most noteworthy feature in the new scheme of development . . . to place the Association there (New York) upon a firm and constructive foundation' (cited in GAA Annual Congress Minutes, 1 Apr. 1934). The fruits of this youth development initiative were very much in evidence in 1937, with six graduates of the programme picked to play for the New York Gaelic football select which lined out against a visiting Mayo team (*The Advocate*, 5 June 1937). In addition, as part of the same tour a team comprised solely of American-born players played a separate match against their illustrious visitors (Hamilton Report, 29 May 1937).

Despite these successes, concerns remained about the future of Gaelic games in the city. As a result, Paddy Lenihan established a committee, headed by Professor James O'Brien of Fordham University and a leading figure in the Catholic Youth Organisation, to examine ways in which the place of hurling and football might be safeguarded. Although there were at this time 12 minor hurling teams within the Eastern division and progress was reportedly being made in getting Gaelic games on to the sporting curricula of some colleges in the region (Central Council GAA Minutes, 21 Aug. 1937), O'Brien recognised the challenges that lay before the Association. As he saw it, the primary problem that confronted the GAA continued to be the dearth of 'new blood coming out from the home country' (*The Leader*, 11 Sept. 1937: 5). He felt that the only way to sustain Gaelic games in such an environment was to redouble earlier efforts to open up and popularise Gaelic games amongst a broader, American-born Irish constituency. O'Brien identified the Catholic school system in New York as the perfect medium to reach this audience and he began to work towards realising his vision. The backing of Cardinal Hayes, Archbishop of New York, was vital, and with his support the GAA was able to introduce hurling and football in several of the city's parochial schools (*The Leader*, 11 Sept. 1937: 5).

O'Brien also recognised that the support of the GAA in Ireland would be important in any plans to develop the games in New York. In August 1937 he travelled to Croke Park where he engaged in discussions with Pádraig Ó Caoimh. This visit did much to publicise the difficulties that the GAA in New York and throughout America was experiencing and helped to establish a greater spirit of solidarity between Gaels at home and those across the Atlantic. Indeed, one Dublin sports writer was moved to write a piece in *The Advocate* in January 1938, in which he called for the GAA's Central Council to do more to help overseas units of the Association (*The Advocate*, 22 Jan. 1938). The continuation of the tours were key in this respect. Despite this, a considerable lobby in Ireland saw little value in sending Irish teams to America and felt that this practice was undermining the Association's ethos. Others, though, felt more inclined to respond positively to the difficulties confronting their fellow Gaels across the Atlantic. Thus, in 1938, the New York GAA and members of the Central Council collaborated to organise what came to be dubbed, the 'goodwill tour' (*Irish Echo*, 21 May 1938), involving the beaten finalists in the 1936 and 1937 All-Ireland football series, Laois and Cavan. The game between Cavan and Laois at Yankee Stadium, the first fixture played in New York between two teams from Ireland, certainly caught the imagination of the New York public and drew a crowd of 25,000 (*Irish Echo*, 4 June 1938). However, the other two exhibition matches between Cavan, Laois and a New York select struggled to attract 10,000. The inclement weather conditions did not help and the tour finished with the New York GAA experiencing a deficit of around $10,000 (*The Advocate*, 18 Feb. 1939).[5]

Concerned that the impact of any further tours would be fleeting and would have no lasting effect on the club game in the city, prominent GAA officials in Ireland implored their New York counterparts to build on their efforts to establish junior and minor sections within clubs and continue to promote hurling and football in the city's Catholic schools. This view was articulated by Pádraig Ó Caoimh, who argued in an address to 'Gaels of the United States' published in the *Irish Echo* (4 June 1938: 11), that 'our stand should be on the younger generation of Irish Americans. Irishmen of all creeds should be rounded into our organisation so that we could have their children play the games of their ancestors, and herein I say lies your work'.

With the outbreak of the Second World War leading to the suspension of visits by touring Irish teams, Ó Caoimh's words took on added resonance. However, at the start of the 1940 season, the ability of the GAA to pay the rising rental costs of Innisfail Park in light of dwindling attendances superseded all other concerns. Recognising that 'hundreds of Gaelic fans fail to see the games at the Broadway arena because they cannot afford the price', the Association took the step of halving the admission fee to 25 cents (O'Shea, 1940a: 3). This, together with the decision of nationalist Irish societies such as Clan na Gael and the various IRA clubs to host field days at Innisfail (O'Shea, 1940b), provided the GAA with a temporary reprieve and the 1940 season was one of the more successful of the previous ten years. Liam O'Shea, *The Advocate*'s Gaelic sports correspondent, warned at the close of the season that, unless games at Innisfail were supported by local Gaelic sports enthusiasts as well as the city's network of Irish societies, 'Gaeldom will disappear from the American sports field' (O'Shea, 1940c: 3). Despite O'Shea's warning and the best efforts of Patrick Grimes and William Snow, the Association was unable to maintain payments for the lease on Innisfail Park and it was duly handed back to the city at the end of 1940 (O'Shea, 1941). Although the GAA continued to rent various public parks on a weekly basis for games, the impact of the Second World War and the continued decline in levels of emigration from Ireland placed Gaelic games in New York in a precarious, almost terminal position for much of the 1940s.

The GAA in Boston post First World War: progress and decline

The conclusion of the Great War brought renewed hope amongst Boston's Gaels that a resumption of Gaelic games in the city was not too far away. This hope was not misplaced. Aided by increased Irish immigration into the US, these sports began to resurface. However, it was not until the early 1920s that Gaelic sports clubs once again began to cater for the sporting, recreational and cultural needs of Boston's Irish community in a sustained way. The ability of the GAA to re-establish itself in Boston was helped in no small measure by Gaelic games being increasingly incorporated into the programmes of Irish dancing festivals or *feiseannas* in Boston (Cullinane, 1997). Despite signs of a return to their former levels of popularity and vibrancy, the absence of a governing body to coordinate the activities of the clubs in the region gradually came to be viewed as a major impediment. A group of long-standing Boston Gaels, including Morgan O'Connor, John Lancaster, Michael Darcy and James Galvin, began to look into the possibility of establishing a body to oversee Gaelic games. In the spring of 1923, their efforts came to fruition with the inception of the Massachusetts Gaelic Athletic Association (North East GAA, 2000). With James Galvin at the helm of this organisation, hurling and Gaelic football became more visible in the region and featured more centrally in the lives of increasing numbers of Irish immigrants. The ability of the Massachusetts GAA to set up and efficiently manage visits to Boston by the Tipperary hurlers in 1926 and the Kerry Gaelic footballers a year later, was also very important. As was the case in New York, the exploits of these touring teams generated much interest and added considerable impetus to the GAA in Boston. For the Boston select versus Kerry Gaelic football match, an estimated 22,000 spectators attended, giving the game unprecedented coverage amongst the city's Irish population. Such was the strength of Gaelic games in the city following these initiatives that, between 1927 and 1929, nine hurling and 15 football teams affiliated to the new governing body (North East GAA, 2000).

Although some of the most high profile inter-county football and hurling teams continued to play exhibition matches in Boston and Massachusetts, including the Kerry and Galway football teams in 1931 and 1935, and the Tipperary and Kilkenny hurlers in 1932 and 1936 respectively, the popularity of Gaelic games in the second half of the 1930s began to wane. The reasons for this were similar to the challenges that confronted the GAA in New York in the same period. The Great Depression, keenly felt as it was in areas of heavy industrialisation, had a devastating impact on Boston's Irish community. Given that most were employed as unskilled labour, the sector of employment that was hardest hit by the Depression, the Irish working classes were victims of the worst economic ravages of the era. Identifying ways of alleviating socio-economic hardship as opposed to seeking to preserve the sports and games of the 'old country' therefore became much more important for the Boston Irish. With the Depression also lowering rates of immigration, thereby restricting the flow of new playing resources into the Massachusetts GAA, the Association suspended its regular fixtures in 1937 (North East GAA, 2000). Even visits by touring Irish teams struggled to rouse much interest in Gaelic games or engender a desire to work towards their revival. Attendances at games involving All-Ireland winning teams within the GAA's Eastern division were typically at their lowest in Boston. For example, for the visit of Mayo's footballers in 1937, only 2,500 attended, while similar games were attracting over 30,000 more in New York (Hamilton Report, 29 May 1937). The future of the GAA in Boston looked bleak. With the outbreak of the Second World War and a continued sharp slump in Irish emigration to the US, the playing of Gaelic games in an organised fashion ceased to form a significant part of the lives of the city's Irish diaspora.

The GAA in Chicago after the Great War

Father Fielding was very much to the fore in attempts to revive Gaelic games in Chicago from 1918 onwards, as he had been before the Great War. His enthusiasm, organisational abilities and influence saw the GAA enter into a prosperous period in the early 1920s, with a further five clubs being established, three of which added to the complement of hurling teams in the city. The confidence that emanated from this growth was such that Chicago's GAA was the main instigator in the visit of All-Ireland hurling champions Tipperary in 1926. The Association also responded positively to Thomas Delaney's promptings from New York about the establishment of a divisional council to co-ordinate Gaelic games in the mid-west and organise an inter-divisional championship. However, the financial and logistical difficulties involved in travelling further afield precluded Chicago's involvement in nationwide competition. Nonetheless, the emphasis that came to be placed on institutionalising the GAA in the US in the late 1920s helped to root Gaelic games firmly amongst the local Irish community in Chicago.

While the austerity of the Depression era restricted opportunities for sporting and leisure activities throughout America's industrialised urban centres, Gaelic games continued to be played in Chicago in the first half of the 1930s. Important championship matches attracted relatively large crowds. For example, approximately 8,000 spectators watched a championship final in July 1933 between the Banner Blues and the Kickhams at Normal Park Stadium, a venue that was used by the GAA throughout the decade (*Chicago Daily Tribune*, 4 July 1933). Exhibition matches involving visiting Irish teams in this period ensured the continued enthusiasm for one-off championship matches, despite the severe economic hardship of the time. When the All-Ireland football champions Kerry, led by the legendary John Joe Sheehy, travelled to Chicago in 1931 to play against a Chicago select at Soldier Field, the home of American football in the city, 15,000 spectators attended the match (*Chicago Daily Tribune*, 25 May 1931). These visits continued throughout the 1930s and, as was the case elsewhere in America, helped to maintain some enthusiasm amongst Irish Chicagoans for traditional Irish sports. However, as the decade progressed, it became increasingly difficult for the city's Irish inhabitants to patronise domestic games on a regular basis and in large numbers. With the outbreak of the Second World War and heavy conscription, combined with what was a virtual cessation in Irish emigration to the city, the numbers playing Gaelic games dwindled to the point where Chicago's GAA hierarchy was forced to suspend the regular championship season.

San Francisco's Gaels in the inter-war period

By the conclusion of the First World War, the GAA in San Francisco was at its lowest ebb. The lull in organised games, a consequence of the war, had led to a worrying decline in interest. With too few clubs possessing adequate playing resources, the GAA in the city was unable to organise a league competition for the 1918 season. This is not to say that hurling and football ceased to be played there. GAA activity did continue, but only in the form of the occasional charity or fund-raising game. As would be expected, nationalist organisations such as St Enda's College in Dublin and the Martyrs Fund were amongst the main beneficiaries of these games (*The Leader*, 23 Aug. 1919), but the city's GAA enthusiasts also organised field days to raise funds and show their solidarity with a range of causes within San Francisco's Irish community.[6] Although attendances at these games were distinctly average, numbering at best several hundred, they did ensure that the GAA retained a presence on the Pacific coast and in doing so provided a foundation on which a post-war revival could be built.

The seeds of this revival were sown at the annual convention of the GAA of California in August 1919. This meeting, described in *The Leader* (23 Aug. 1919: 2) as 'one of the most important in the history of the GAA in California', drew a large attendance and infused the Association with renewed vigour. By early October, the GAA was able to announce the recommencement of an annual league series (*The Leader*, 11 Oct. 1919) and once games started they were well organised and patronised. The optimism that abounded in GAA circles at this time was well summed up by George Comber, a journalist with *The Leader* (1 Nov. 1919: 6), who suggested that 'it looks as if at last the right men with the right spirit are at the head of a movement that has unfortunately failed in the past in San Francisco'. The early 1920s saw continued growth within the GAA. Central to this was the support that the Association received from the city's other Irish societies, particularly the Ancient Order of Hibernians. By 1923, the AOH had three teams from its 5th, 6th and 17th divisions participating in regular competition (*The Leader*, 12 May 1923). With the GAA and other prominent Irish figures in the city continuing to link Gaelic games specifically to patriotism and a broader sense of Irishness, new clubs, such as Thomas Ashes and Yorkes, named after Father Yorke, in football and Cork and Wolfe Tones in hurling swelled the GAA's ranks in the mid 1920s.

The GAA on the Pacific coast, and more specifically in San Francisco, received a significant boost in 1926 with the decision of the All-Ireland winning Tipperary hurling team to take in the city on their tour of the US (*The Leader*, 20 Mar. 1926). Although the GAA, along with the city's Irish societies, Catholic Church and a range of civic figures including the mayor had been making arrangements for the visit of Tipperary for three months prior to the game, a fire the week before the game destroyed the stands and club rooms of Ewing Field, the proposed venue, and threw the plans for the match into disarray (*The Leader*, 11 June 1926). Kezar Stadium, then home of the American Football franchise the San Francisco 49ers, was quickly identified as an alternative venue and it proved to be more than equipped to host the game. The crowd of 15,000 which turned out to see Tipperary defeat a California select by 44 points to 17 was the largest ever to witness a hurling match in San Francisco up to that point (*The Leader*, 19 June 1926). Although the match was one-sided, Gaelic games had been presented to a large audience in a positive light.

The Tipperary tour undoubtedly had a positive impact on the popularity of hurling and football in the city and led to an intensive drive to increase the number of clubs, improve standards of play and attract new adherents. *The Leader* was firmly behind these moves and it backed the GAA by sponsoring a new championship, The Leader Cup, which was inaugurated in 1928. The fruits of these endeavours were initially highly visible. The next four years saw the founding of three new clubs in both hurling and five in Gaelic football (*The Leader*, 23 Apr. 1932).[7] Despite this growth, prominent Gaels in the Bay Area recognised that the falling levels of Irish immigration heralded by the Depression would soon have a negative impact on the health of the Association. Thus some began to agitate for a more co-ordinated approach. Thomas Delaney's proposals on the organisation of a nationwide body were positively received in San Francisco. Yet practical difficulties and growing indifference from the Eastern division meant that little of substance was done. By the early 1930s, however, there was a growing feeling in San Francisco GAA circles that the idea should be revived. According to *The Leader* (19 Mar. 1932: 5), it was believed that the inception of a nationwide body might contribute to the 'further advancement of the games in the USA, to advertise the Gaelic games and to encourage young Americans to play our games'. Following internal deliberations a letter was sent to canvass the opinion of New York's Gaels but, although the venture might have proved beneficial, the idea received little in the way of a meaningful response.

Unperturbed by New York's attitude to the idea of a national organisation, the GAA in San Francisco pursued other avenues that they felt might safeguard the future of Gaelic games locally. A key strategy was to seek to purchase land specifically for Gaelic games rather than continuing with short-term leases on Kezar Stadium, Ewing Field and St Ignatious' Stadium. Although this idea had been mooted a number of years earlier, the election of Bernard Naughton as president of the California GAA in 1933 was crucial in reviving interest in a dedicated facility for Gaelic games in the city. Naughton was an influential, well-known and highly respected figure within San Francisco's Irish community. He had formerly been President of the United Irish Societies, the St

Patrick's Day Convention, division 17 of the AOH and Director of the Irish American Hall Association, had worked with Father Yorke during his steward-ship of Gaelic games, and was noted for his enthusiasm and vigour in promoting the cause of all things Irish in the city (*The Leader*, 18 Feb. 1933). On his election he immediately established a committee charged with locating a suitable venue and raising the necessary funding to secure it. This venture ultimately proved to be futile, not least because of the broader economic climate within which the GAA was operating. However, it did demonstrate that the Association was attempting to act in a progressive manner in order to safeguard the long-term sustainability of Gaelic games in the city.

One clear example of this forward-thinking approach on the part of San Francisco's Gaels came in 1933 with the entry of a hurling team from St Mary's College in Moraga, just outside Oakland, into the local league. St Mary's, established in 1863 as a diocesan college for Catholic boys, began to develop a strong athletic reputation in the late 1920s. In the 1930s the college's American football team, nicknamed the 'Galloping Gaels' and coached by the Irish Californian, 'Slip' Madigan, achieved much success and caught the imagina-tion of the Bay Area's Irish community. As Dowling (1998: 404) notes, 'The exploits of the Galloping Gaels became the principal topic of conversation at Irish gatherings, and were argued over back fences and rehashed in Irish saloons, at Christenings, weddings and wakes'. It is thus no surprise that the establish-ment of a hurling team at St Mary's in 1933, initiated by the Tipperary-born Christian Brother and Dean of the College, Brother James Shanahan, generated much in the way of enthusiasm and interest.

The team was made up of a combination of Christian Brothers on the faculty staff as well as students, the majority of whom were of Irish descent. The inclusion in their ranks of a number of Irish-born players who had experienced hurling at home ensured that the team was able to hold its own in a number of junior games during the 1933 season. Although these games were well attended, it was their involvement at senior level hurling in 1934 that created most excitement. Their first game at this level, a victory over Cork who were then reigning Pacific Coast champions, created quite a stir and reinforced the reputation of the college as possessing a first-rate athletic programme and as an *Irish* school. St Mary's embrace of hurling was quickly viewed as an oppor-tunity to arrest the flagging fortunes of the GAA in the city. In a letter to Annual Congress in Dublin in April 1934, Donal Cummins, secretary of the Association in San Francisco, commented that they were attempting to encourage the athletic directors at the Jesuit, University of San Francisco to start a hurling team. As Cummins saw it, 'if we are successful we feel confident that hurling and football will take a firm hold and spread rapidly among other schools and colleges in California' (GAA Annual Congress Minutes, 1 Apr. 1934).

This aspiration came to an abrupt halt, however, following St Mary's decision to end their brief flirtation with the game. While the college's management were happy to bask in the kudos conferred by participation in senior-level hurling competition, the overly physical and unsporting nature of their second game of the 1934 season against Clare, which resulted in some of the Christian Brothers requiring medical attention, raised some concerns about the appropriateness of faculty staff being involved in the game. The college remained unconvinced with the representations received from Brother Shanahan, and the decision was taken to end St Mary's hurling experiment (GAA Minutes, 1 Apr. 1934). The death of hurling at St Mary's was much lamented in GAA circles in San Francisco and elsewhere because, as Dowling (1998: 408) notes, 'One can only assume that if hurling had been adopted by St Mary's on a permanent basis, other Catholic colleges would have followed, and Ireland's national game would have become an integral part of American sports'. Although it is open to question whether hurling would have established itself on California's inter-collegiate athletic programme, the decision to disband the team was clearly an opportunity missed for the GAA.

The revived interest in hurling aroused by the efforts of Brother Shanahan ultimately proved to be fleeting and the Association struggled desperately to keep the game in existence. With so few Irish immigrants coming to the city, Gaelic games were promoted to second and third-generation Irish as well as those with no lineage to Ireland. By 1934 it was estimated that more than 50 per cent of those playing Gaelic football were American born (GAA Annual Congress Minutes, 1 Apr. 1934). Increasingly, those with responsibility for safeguarding the interests of the GAA saw the introduction of Gaelic games to young Irish Americans as crucial, and in 1935 a Gaelic football league for players under the age of 18 was established (*The Leader*, 23 Mar. 1935). While this league encouraged the formation of four minor football clubs all of whom quickly affiliated to the new league,[8] it ultimately offered only a temporary reprieve. With the Depression increasingly making itself felt in San Francisco by the mid 1930s and a concomitant slowing of Irish immigration and lack of new, skilled playing talent, further curtailing the appeal of Gaelic games, the Association's traditional source of revenue – gate receipts – was barely covering the expenses of competing teams and there was nothing in the way of a surplus that could be invested in a dedicated Gaelic games facility. The GAA tried other avenues of fund-raising to provide impetus to this long-standing aspiration, including the staging of a grand ball and active canvassing of financial support from other Irish societies in the city. However, the Association's inability to attract respectable crowds to its weekly programmes at Kezar Stadium, Ewing field and elsewhere placed its finances and the future of Gaelic games in an increasingly fragile state.

With the recession continuing to bite hard, *The Leader* (3 Aug. 1935: 5) suggested that, 'It seems like Ireland's games in San Francisco are beginning to lose their appeal to our exiled Irish'. This newspaper, as it had done in the past, continued to publish pleas for the Bay Area's Irish communities to support Gaelic games, playing up their Irish origins and character and arguing that patronising the games was a 'national' duty (*The Leader*, 3 Aug. 1935: 5). However, these appeals continued to fall on deaf ears and, with the 1936 season described as 'financially disastrous' (*The Leader*, 5 June 1937: 5), plans to invest in its own grounds were finally shelved and the energies of those within the Association became focused on ensuring that hurling and football survived. A further effort was made to engage with their fellow Gaels on the east coast about the possibility of a national organising body or at least the drawing up of a uniform set of by-laws that would underpin the governance of Gaelic games across the country (*The Leader*, 2 July 1937). Ultimately, though, this idea did not get the required reaction, largely because the Depression had focused the attentions of Gaelic games enthusiasts on the Atlantic seaboard on the survival of clubs and leagues in their own locality. By 1938 regular competitive matches were replaced by occasional exhibition games which featured not only the few remaining clubs but also one-off games involving members of the St Mary's College American football squad (*The Leader*, 19 Mar. 1938), American versus Irish-born 'all-star' football teams as well as a series of challenge games in both hurling and football between San Francisco and Los Angeles (*The Leader*, 13 July 1940). While this ensured that the GAA retained a presence in the San Francisco Bay Area, a resumption of a quantitatively significant culture of Gaelic games would have to wait until the post-Second World War period.

Conclusion

The GAA recovered quickly in the immediate aftermath of the Great War and, as this chapter has demonstrated, the 1920s saw it experience a period of robust health and vibrancy. Gaelic games clearly benefited from an increase in the numbers of Irish immigrants seeking to avail themselves of economic opportunities in the US, but the recovery of these sports was also due in large part to a combination of the tireless efforts of a number of influential GAA officials and the development of closer ties between the parent organisation in Ireland and its American branches. The work of individuals such as Thomas Delaney, Father Fielding and James Galvin and the inception of tours by All-Ireland winning inter-county teams appeared to have provided a firm footing for continued expansion. However, the Wall Street Crash, which precipitated the Great Depression of the 1930s, and a subsequent virtual cessation of Irish immigration threatened to undo all that had been achieved in the previous decade.

Some units of the Association were better prepared for the challenges of Depression-era America than others. While the GAA in New York and San Francisco were progressive enough to initiate what became very successful youth programmes amongst an American- born pool of talent, the failure to do the same in Boston and Chicago quickly saw Gaelic games there go into freefall. However, even the creation of a youthful, locally based grassroots in New York and San Francisco could do little to slow the decline in interest in Gaelic games there. Once the US government took the decision to enter the Second World War it was almost inevitable that the GAA would cease to function in a meaningful way in Irish America. As chapter 7 will reveal, it is also likely that the decline in interest in Irish politics following the partition of Ireland in 1921, coupled with Irish assimilation into the American mainstream thereafter, contributed to the eventual, albeit temporary, demise of Gaelic games on American shores. With a declining sense of allegiance to Ireland typifying identity politics in much of Irish America at this time and far fewer new Irish immigrants arriving in the country, the Association's difficulties were inevitable. Irrespective of the reasons for the virtual absence of regular, organised, competitive Gaelic games by the beginning of the 1940s, it became obvious to those with aspirations to rebuild the GAA in the US that any revival of Gaelic games would need to be launched around an event of some significance.

CHAPTER SIX

Revival, 'Golden Age' and decline: Gaelic games in post-war America

Introduction

Increasing numbers of America's Irish diaspora appeared to be turning their backs on Gaelic games during the late 1930s and first half of the 1940s, yet a small corpus of dedicated Gaels remained committed to the preservation of the pastimes of the 'old country'. The immediate post-war period was clearly going to be a crucial one if these individuals were to secure any sort of future for the GAA. Indeed, if the demise of Gaelic games were not redressed, and urgently, there would be a very real danger that these sports would die out completely. This would not only have brought to an end a deep-rooted element of Irish America's rich sporting and cultural diversity, but would also have heralded the demise of a vital cultural resource for sections of the Irish emigrant community. Faced with such a possibility, a St Patrick's Day editorial in the *Irish Echo*, just prior to the end of the Second World War, attempted to rouse New York's Irish with a poignant and elegiac editorial on the role that the GAA had played in Irish-American life prior to the 1940s:

> In the heyday of Celtic Park no nationality enjoyed a social center comparable to that of the Irish people of New York. Thousands of Irishmen met and talked every Sunday at that well-known rendezvous. As a matter of fact, a high percentage of the attendance went there with no other purpose in mind than to meet their friends. And what more delightful place could there have been for freedom-loving Irish people. No formalities, just a regular Irish gathering, with warm handshakes, groups in happy mood discussing what they shared . . . all mingled with the clash of the hurley or the thud of the football (*Irish Echo*, 17 Mar. 1945).

In light of the difficulties in maintaining a culture of Irish sports in the late 1930s and first half of the 1940s, it was not going to be easy to stimulate the ambition, motivation and energy required to re-establish the GAA amongst Irish communities in the US. Fortunately, the GAA, in both America and Ireland, possessed men who had the necessary vision, organisational abilities and determination to rebuild the Association and lay firm foundations for future development. This chapter addresses what was to prove to be a remarkable post-war recovery of Gaelic games in the US. It concentrates on three core issues that were central to this revival: the hosting of the All-Ireland Gaelic football final in New York in 1947; the incorporation of American Gaels into the activities of the GAA in Ireland, particularly New York's involvement in the National League; and the establishment of a national governing body for Gaelic games in America in 1959. The inception of this body contributed much to the GAA in the 1960s, a period recognised as a golden era in the history of the Association (North American County Board, 1997). However, as was the case in the pre-war period, the fortunes of Gaelic games were largely dependent on the impact of external forces, most notably the levels of Irish immigration into the US. As well as accounting for the personalities, events and competitions that contributed to the resurgence of the GAA in America, this chapter assesses some of the ways in which the sharp downturn in Irish immigration, a consequence of the 1965 Immigration Act, impacted on Gaelic games in the late 1960s.

Early signs of recovery

The fact that Gaelic football and hurling did not completely die out on US soil during the Second World War meant that there was at least something on which to rebuild. In the immediate aftermath of the war, those who had done most to maintain what was in some cases a token GAA presence began to explore ways of initiating a rebirth of Gaelic games. In Boston, for example, the GAA of Massachusetts attempted to appeal to a wider audience by incorporating a broader range of activities such as Irish step dancing and tug of war into its field days. The organisation of representative matches between Boston and New York, in both hurling and Gaelic football, also helped to remind the city's Irish community that the GAA still existed (*Irish World and American Industrial Liberator*, 23 Aug. 1947). Interest in traditional Irish sports was also visible amongst Boston's female Irish and by the summer of 1950 there were two camogie teams, the Shamrocks and the Celtics in the GAA's ranks (*Boston Pilot*, 29 July 1950; *Boston Pilot*, 4 Nov. 1950).

In cities other than Boston, there were also palpable signs of recovery. In San Francisco, regular matches began to feature in the city's sporting calendar immediately after the war (North American County Board, 1997). The re-emergence of the GAA in Chicago was due in no small measure to the city's United Irish organisations which organised a fund-raising dance for the revival of Gaelic games and the establishment of five football and four hurling clubs. The fact that this event drew a crowd of 6,000 was clear evidence that the city's Irish community still had a strong appetite for and commitment to these sports (*Chicago Daily Tribune*, 11 Dec. 1948). As the century reached its mid-point the Association was formally reconstituted in Chicago, leases on pitches at Rockne Stadium and Shewbridge were secured and a championship initiated. After formally affiliating to Central Council in Dublin, the founders of this reinvigorated body, particularly Pat Hennessey, its first post-war chairman, also began to work with their neighbours in the mid-West with a view to setting up a governing body to coordinate Gaelic games in this region and facilitate the playing of inter city games (North American County Board, 1997).[1] The resultant Mid West GAA Board, established in 1950, immediately set about its work, and the first mid-Western championship in Gaelic football involving select teams from Connecticut, Cleveland, Hartford, Pittsburgh, Detroit and Chicago took place and was won by Chicago (*Chicago Daily Tribune*, 16 Oct. 1950).

Although these developments were significant, it was in New York that the clearest indication of the GAA's post-war revival was most evident. Even before the end of hostilities in Europe, New York Gaels were discussing the best way to revive their sporting pastimes. The impact of the decline in Irish immigration in the 1930s and early 1940s led some to argue that the key to a sustainable future was promoting hurling and Gaelic football to the country's youth (see chapter 5 above). In March 1945, the *Irish Echo* carried news of plans to introduce these sports to the city's parochial schools and to develop coaching programmes to provide opportunities for graduates to play at minor, junior and eventually at senior level. It was recognised that this would be a difficult task and one that would not bear significant fruit for at least 10 years (*Irish Echo*, 17 Mar. 1945). As it turned out, progress was much quicker. The conclusion of the war saw renewed optimism in New York GAA circles and fixtures that had lain dormant for a number of years slowly began to re-emerge. For example, the United Irish County Association's Annual *Feis* in 1945, held at the campus of the Jesuit college, Fordham University, included a hurling match between Cork and Offaly (*Irish Echo*, 26 May 1945). The success of a range of GAA mentors in initiating a parish-based minor league comprising up to 15 teams made up predominantly of American-born players was also key and added further impetus to the GAA's revival in this period (New York GAA, 1964).[2] The Association's Central Council in Dublin was also called upon to help and duly obliged by shipping out hurling sticks in September 1947 for Irish-American boys to take up the sport (*Irish World and American Industrial Liberator*, 20 Sept. 1947).

The leading figure in the GAA's revival in New York was undoubtedly John 'Kerry' O'Donnell, who was to become over the next decade one of the most influential men in New York and, indeed, US GAA circles. O'Donnell, born in County Kerry, left Ireland for Montreal in 1918 and later moved to New York, where he worked in construction. Although he lived in the city through the worst ravages of the Great Depression, by 1935 he had purchased his first saloon bar. In a clear illustration of his shrewdness as a businessman, he was able to add another four to his business portfolio over the next ten years (King, 1998). O'Donnell's involvement in the affairs of the Association in New York began in 1929, when he joined the Kerry club as a player (*Irish Echo*, 8 Feb. 1964). He acted in various administrative capacities thereafter, including president of the NYGAA in 1940. As a staunch advocate of the Association, O'Donnell would have been dismayed at the demise of Gaelic games in the early 1940s. One of the most pressing concerns of the day was clearly the situation over the lease of Innisfail Park, the chief venue for Gaelic games in the city. As outlined in chapter 5, William Snow and Patrick Grimes were struggling to raise the necessary finance to meet the rental costs on the venue. By 1942, the local GAA was no longer in a position to afford regular payments and the lease was taken up by a local soccer group and renamed. Gaelic games did still feature at the park, but only on an intermittent basis and only when the fixture was likely to cover the requisite rental costs. In November 1944, the situation worsened when some of the soccer clubs that had been using the venue sought the lease on a permanent basis.

This potentially disastrous development was averted by O'Donnell who raised the funds necessary to purchase a longer-term lease and become the sole proprietor. As Vincent O'Donoghue, the GAA president at the time, noted at a Central Council meeting almost ten years later, 'but for this fact [O'Donnell's proprietorship of Innisfail Park], there would not be any GAA in New York now' (Central Council GAA Minutes, 8 Dec. 1952). O'Donnell marked the opening of the venue by renaming it Croke Park but, following objections in the early 1950s from the Association in Dublin who felt that only one GAA field should bear the moniker of its first patron, the name was changed to Gaelic Park (New York GAA, 1964). Although O'Donnell's proprietorship of Gaelic Park was perhaps the contribution that he is best remembered for, his role in what was undoubtedly the most significant event in the history of the GAA in the US – the hosting of the 1947 All-Ireland Gaelic football final in New York – was his greatest achievement in helping to revive Gaelic games in the city and beyond.

On American soil: the 1947 All-Ireland Gaelic football final

While progress had been made in New York and elsewhere, O'Donnell recognised that Gaelic games required an event of some significance in order to revitalise their place in Irish America. Hosting an All-Ireland final on New York soil quickly became the main pillar in his ambitious plans for the GAA in the city. O'Donnell recognised an opportunity in the drawn 1946 All-Ireland football final between Roscommon and Kerry. Using his links with the GAA in Kerry, he floated the idea of bringing the replay to New York (Byrne, 1989; Puirséal, 1982). Whilst this proposal was quickly dismissed by Central Council, the idea of using the Association's showpiece event to arrest the marginalisation of Gaelic games in the US re-emerged on the GAA's agenda in the following year. The influential Clare-born Central Council delegate Canon Michael Hamilton was chief amongst those who began to canvass to turn into a reality what had seemed an outlandish proposition a year earlier. He proposed a motion at the Association's congress in 1947 to allow Central Council to consider the possibility of New York hosting the 1947 All-Ireland football final (Annual Congress GAA Minutes, 6 Apr. 1947).

That Canon Hamilton took this step on behalf of New York's Gaels was hardly surprising. He had acted as an advocate of the Association in the US since 1937 when he accompanied the Mayo Gaelic football team on their tour of New York, Boston and Philadelphia. His affection for New York's Gaels was particularly marked and was shown in a belated Christmas greeting that he sent them via *The Advocate* in January 1939. Recalling a previous visit to the city, he spoke warmly about the hospitality he had been accorded and of his impression of the city's GAA fraternity:

> I was intensely impressed with the ardour and enthusiasm with which our Irish
> exiles have preserved in the land of their adoption, the grand traditions of their
> forefathers in the matter of Gaelic pastimes, national ideals, the community of
> brotherhood of the Gael, and above all in their ardent loyalty to faith and the
> banner of St Patrick (*The Advocate*, 8 Jan. 1939).

Canon Hamilton's words reveal that he was a man sensitive to the efforts of those who had not only worked tirelessly to preserve and promote Gaelic games overseas but had also made many financial contributions to a whole range of charitable, educational, social and, of course, nationalist institutions in Ireland. This sensitivity was lacking in others within the GAA's Central Council, who were largely unmoved by the plight of the Association in the US and felt little inclination to cater for the sporting needs of the Irish abroad (De Búrca, 1999). This antipathy can be explained as part of a broader mistrust between some within the GAA's headquarters and the Association's American wing that stretched back to the controversy surrounding Kerry's tour of the US in 1927, detailed in the previous chapter. Incidents such as these and persistent concern about professionalism in the US led to 'an unwillingness [on the part of the Dublin-based GAA] to accept the Gaels in America as totally sincere about the promotion of the games' (Hanna, 1999: 353).

Thus, when Canon Hamilton took to the floor at the 1947 Congress, there was much convincing to be done. He began by stressing that the future of Gaelic games amongst the exiled Gaels in New York was dependent on the success of his motion. After detailing the decline in Gaelic games since the early 1940s, Canon Hamilton suggested that the granting of the right to host the All-Ireland final would be 'epoch-making' and akin to a 'blood transfusion to save the life of the Association'. As he continued, Canon Hamilton's address became more emotive. He appealed to the delegates' sense of shared kinship with those across the Atlantic by eulogising about what witnessing an All-Ireland final live would mean for the New York Irish:

chords will be touched in the hearts of that Irish throng that nothing else in this world could touch, tears of joy and pride will glisten in the eyes of thousands of men and women and strong hearts will throb with an emotion that only those who have been in exile can appreciate or understand.

Canon Hamilton concluded with more of the same sentiment, arguing that the gift of hosting rights for the final in the 100th anniversary of the worst year of the Great Famine would be an appropriate gesture to America's 'exiled' Gaels (Annual Congress GAA Minutes, 6 Apr. 1947). These eloquent and evocative arguments clearly touched many of the Congress delegates who duly voted in favour of the motion to allow Central Council to consider the feasibility of taking the final to New York.

Following the decision of Congress, a party that included the GAA's general secretary, Pádraig Ó Caoimh and Tom Kilcoyne, secretary of the Connaught Provincial Council, were dispatched to New York to carry out their feasibility study. During their month-long visit they met with local GAA officials, including John O'Donnell and potential sponsors. Ó Caoimh and Kilcoyne appeared to have been convinced about the logistics of moving the final to New York and of the benefits that would accrue both in terms of reviving Gaelic games in the US and bolstering the GAA's coffers at home. On their return a meeting of the GAA's Central Council was convened for 23 May to consider their report and make a final decision about where the game would be played. Stern opposition, described well by De Búrca (1999: 181), was very evident at the meeting:

> To many the idea of playing what had become the biggest national sports event of the year outside the country bordered on the unthinkable. Some also wondered if the sponsors of the idea had given any thought to the possible effects on the average Gaelic spectator, who would be deprived of the customary climax to his seasonal championship fare.

Canon Hamilton remained resolute and his persistence ultimately paid off when the motion to host the All-Ireland final in New York was carried by 20 votes to 17 (Central Council GAA Minutes, 23 May 1947). The date for the match was fixed for 14 September and the venue was to be the Polo Grounds, home to the city's baseball franchise, the New York Yankees.

There was much to be done in the months leading up to the game and it was decided that Ó Caoimh would need to move to New York to oversee preparations. The overseas hosting of the finale of the GAA's season necessitated a number of unique organisational provisions. A number of receptions and banquets had to be arranged, along with travel and hotel reservations, ticketing and radio coverage of the event for those in Ireland. An advance party of GAA officials, including the former president Pádraig MacNamee, travelled to New York to make preliminary arrangements and work closely with the local organising committee led by O'Donnell and ably assisted by the Mayo-born Mayor of New York, William O'Dwyer.[3] In a move that signalled the potential of the match to reinvigorate Gaelic games elsewhere in the US, assistance was also provided by a number of individuals from the Association in Boston, San Francisco and Los Angeles (Central Council GAA Minutes, 13 Dec. 1947). This group made good headway and Ó Caoimh's organisational contribution following his arrival in New York in late July ensured that all was in place when the Kerry and Cavan parties disembarked in New York on 9 and 10 September. Both teams were welcomed to New York with a reception, hosted by Mayor O'Dwyer at City Hall (*Gaelic American*, 13 Sept. 1947). This set the tone for a series of receptions, gala dinners and parades which did much to promote the game amongst the city's Irish. On the morning of the match, Cardinal Spellman, the Archbishop of New York, said mass for the touring party at St Patrick's Cathedral and wished both teams well (Kelly, 1997). With all of the preliminaries completed, all that was left was to play the match in front of what the organisers hoped would be a sell-out crowd of 54,000.

Despite the months of meticulous planning and promotion that went into the event, heavy rain on the evening before the final convinced many New York Irish to stay away. The actual attendance fell almost 20,000 short of the capacity of the Polo Grounds.[4] Although the turnout was disappointing, the event provided a massive boost for Gaelic games in the city and, indeed, throughout the country. The night before the game, the *Gaelic American* (13 Sept. 1947, p. 1) suggested that: 'Whatever the outcome of the game . . . the contest will mark a great victory for Irish Americans who are interested in the promotion of the Irish race'. This certainly proved to be the case and those present not only witnessed an enthralling match, won by Cavan by 17 points to 13, but also saw the next generation of New York Gaels showcasing their skills in a series of minor and intermediate level games played before the main event (*Gaelic American*, 20 Sept. 1947). Crucially for the future of Gaelic games, the 1947 final did much to improve the relationship between the GAA in America and the Association in Ireland. The manner in which the players and officials were received in New York both before and after the final and the fact that the match generated a healthy profit of just over £10,200 also proved significant in this regard (Pádraig Ó Caoimh Report to Central Council GAA, 13 Dec. 1947).

The 1947 final also encouraged the Association's grassroots membership in Ireland to view their counterparts in America with a little more empathy. While some may have remained disgruntled at missing out on their annual September 'pilgrimage' to Croke Park, Michael O'Hehir's vivid radio commentary, broadcast live on RTÉ, brought the sounds and voices of Irish America into Irish homes, reminding those in the 'old country' of the commitment of their counterparts in the New World to Ireland's sporting and cultural heritage. As Puirséal (1982: 254) observed, 'the game had cemented ties of friendship between the GAA at home and the Gaels in New York and renewed the bonds between thousands of Irish Americans and the land of their fathers'. Tangible evidence of these bonds and ties of friendship was quickly evident at the GAA's Congress the following Easter, when Central Council agreed to set aside an 'international fund' of £2,000 to facilitate closer relations with the New York GAA and institute more regular playing contact. This gesture was matched by their counterparts across the Atlantic and, just three years later, New York made the historic step into the parent body's *National* League competition (Puirséal, 1982: 254).

America's Gaels in 'transatlantic' competition

Over the course of the 1940s, Gaelic games in the US had gone from a position of virtual extinction to strident health. A revival in Irish emigration to the country in the immediate post-war period provided clubs in Boston, Chicago, San Francisco and New York with a steady flow of fresh playing talent. Teams that had lain dormant since the late 1930s were revived and new ones formed, standards of play increased, attendances were once again on the rise, with crowds frequently reaching the 5,000 mark and inter-city games peppered the GAA season (Byrne, 1969a). In New York, the force of John 'Kerry' O'Donnell's personality and his commitment to Gaelic games were central not only to the rebirth of hurling and Gaelic football in the city, but also to securing what was undoubtedly the most significant event in the GAA's history in America, the hosting of an All-Ireland final. The impact of this was immeasurable and served, more than any other development up until that point, to reignite the Irish-American appetite for the games of the 'old country'.[5] As part of this process, the GAA in Ireland gradually came to appreciate the role played by their fellow Gaels across the Atlantic in promoting Gaelic sport and relations steadily improved. Unsurprisingly, Canon Michael Hamilton was a leading figure in facilitating this and, until his death in late August 1969, he remained a staunch ally of Gaelic games in New York. Indeed, such was his advocacy of the city's Gaels that he became regarded in Ireland as the 'voice of the New York GAA' (Byrne 1969b: 22). The international fund was a further tangible manifestation of closer ties between American and Irish branches of the GAA, but it was New York's participation in the finals of the National League in 1950 that did most to cement a growing bond.

The seeds for the historic participation of an American team in a competition that was second only to the All-Ireland series were sown in the immediate aftermath of the 1947 All-Ireland final. Recognising the impact of this single event on the profile of Gaelic games in New York, officials of the GAA there began to explore ways of establishing regular contact with Ireland's finest inter-county teams. A New York delegation proposed to Central Council in early 1948 that the winners of the All-Ireland hurling final play a series of exhibition matches in the city (Central Council GAA Minutes, 25 Sept. 1948). This proposal was quickly dropped in favour of exploring whether the 1949 All-Ireland hurling final could be hosted in New York. When this appeared not to be practicable, New York's Gaels then intimated that, as the GAA's representative in America, they were planning to apply for provincial status and compete at this level (Annual Congress GAA Minutes, 17 Apr. 1949). With Central Council subsequently approving New York's application to become a fully fledged unit of the Association, the way was open for them to participate in the National League.[6] It was agreed at a Central Council meeting, prior to the Association's Annual Congress in 1950, that a motion would be submitted at Congress proposing that New York would contest the final of the 1949–50 edition of the National League. With the successful organisation of the 1947 All-Ireland final fresh in the memory, the application was accepted in principle and it was left to the New York GAA and Central Council to work out the specifics (Annual Congress GAA Minutes, 9 Apr. 1950).

A decision to play the football final at Croke Park in Dublin and the hurling equivalent at New York's Polo Grounds in September was quickly reached, and the stage was set for the series. In the football final, New York shocked the watching Croke Park crowd by defeating Cavan by two points. While the New York select lost against Tipperary in the hurling final in front of a crowd of 40,000 (*Irish Echo*, 23 Sept. 1950), the two-point margin of defeat was indicative of a more than creditable performance. The outcome of both matches guaranteed an American presence in the competition in the short term at least, and when Thomas Donlon, then president of the New York GAA, requested at Congress in Dublin the following year that both the hurling and football final's be played in New York, approval was granted. While Galway and Meath secured an 'Irish' double in hurling and football respectively, the narrow margin of victory and the competitiveness of the matches seemed set to safeguard the series in the longer term.

Despite these promising early signs, fissures soon began to appear in the relationship between New York and Central Council which threatened the future of transatlantic competition. Criticism of the handling of plans for future editions of the National League by the GAA president Michael Kehoe drew criticism from John O'Donnell. His derogatory remarks about the figurehead of the Association in Ireland were published in the Irish-American press in the aftermath of the 1951 series. This was far from appreciated at Croke Park.[7] At the GAA's Congress in Dublin in the following year, some delegates began to question whether the Association should be investing time and energy into helping Gaelic games in the US when there was much to be done to promote them in Ireland. However, a motion, presented at Congress, that international matches should continue on a 'limited' basis was passed and the matter was referred to Central Council for approval (Annual Congress Minutes, 13 Apr. 1952). What this meant in reality was that fixtures between New York and Irish inter-county teams from 1953 onwards were no longer to be considered National League deciders. At a meeting of the GAA's US Advisory Committee on 10 May 1952, New York officials reluctantly agreed to this development in order to safeguard the future of international games. In the meantime, though, Croke Park officials were already committed to a trip to Dublin by New York's footballers and hurlers to decide the 1952 National League. These fixtures added to the growing acrimony between New York's Gaels and the Association's Dublin-based hierarchy, not least because the games were scheduled by Central Council for May which left the New York teams with little time for serious preparation or match practice. Heavy defeats by Tipperary in hurling and Cork in football ensued,[8] and the tour concluded with unseemly criticism by New York officials of the parent body's organisation for the trip published in the *Irish Independent* and *Irish Press*.

An opportunity to resolve their differences presented itself in October 1952 when Cork's Gaelic football team undertook a brief tour to New York. The GAA's president at the time, Vincent O'Donoghue, travelled with Pádraig Ó Caoimh and the Cork party, to engage in discussions aimed at improving levels of understanding between Central Council and New York. These meetings also provided an opportunity to determine the nature of future 'international matches'. While the New York GAA hierarchy favoured a return to the National League, they were reminded of the decision of Congress that fixtures between New York and Irish inter-county teams would be non-title bearing (Central Council GAA Minutes, 21 Nov. 1952). A compromise, in the form of the annual St Brendan Cup between a New York select and the winners of the hurling and football National League in Ireland, was subsequently tabled at a Central Council meeting in December 1952. New York were initially reticent, suggesting that this new competition 'lacked the competitive stature to satisfy New York fans', and that it was therefore commercially unviable (New York GAA, 1964: 60). However, Central Council made it abundantly clear that this

1. John 'Kerry' O'Donnell, a leading figure in the GAA's revival in New York, with the 'Shamrock girl', an Irish airlines hostess, and Mayor John Lindsay at the St Patrick's Day celebrations, in 1970.

2. Shamrocks Senior Gaelic Football Club, New York: 1933 Champions.

3. New York Gaelic Football Team, 1969. Included in the picture is Brendan O'Donnell, John 'Kerry' O'Donnell's son.

4. The entrance to Gaelic Park, New York City, in 2003.

Redmonds Hurling Club.

F.R.J.Linehan   J.Gleason   S.Mc.Namara   C.Cuhane   S.Cuhane   E.Norton   M.Flavin   J.Scully Manager
P.E.Upperman   J.Ahearn   P.Creamer   T.Gogan,Capt.   A.Driscoll, President.   C.O'Connell, V.Capt. T.Corcoran   T.Desmond   E.Sheehan
M.Lumbardi   R.Mc Nally   D.Mc Carthy   P.Duncliffe   J.Donovan

5. Redmonds Hurling Club, Champions of New England, 1919.

6. Kerry Gaelic Football Club of Boston: 1928 US Champions.

7. Senator Ted Kennedy with members of the Cork Hurling Team of Boston, 1982: New England and North American Champions.

8. 1999 New England Gaelic Football Minor Team.

9. Waterford Ladies Gaelic Football Club 2000.

10. Billy Kelly and Bernie O'Reilly (Past Presidents of the New England GAA) at the official opening of the GAA facility at the Irish Cultural Centre in Canton, MA, October 1999.

11. Fans at Gaelic Park during the 2006 Senior Hurling Final between Harry Bolands and CuChulainns.

12. Harry Bolands *versus* CuChulainns in League Play-Off, 2006.

13. Chicago Senior Football Final, 2006: St Brendan's *versus* Wolfe Tones.

14. Chicago GAA Youth Football Match, 2006: Northside *versus* Southside.

15. Chicago Ladies Senior Football Final, 2006: Erins Rovers *versus* St Brigids.

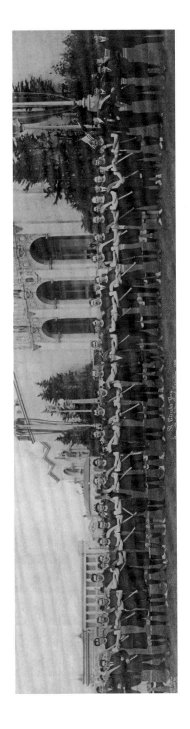

16. Young Ireland Hurling Team at the Panama Pacific International Exposition on St Patrick's Day, 1915.

17. Pearses Hurling and Gaelic Football Club, 1917: San Francisco Champions.

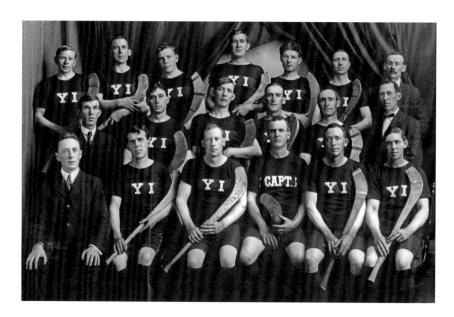

18. Young Ireland Hurling Team, 1919: San Francisco Champions.

was the only option on the table and the St Brendan Cup was eventually inaugurated in 1954 (Puirséal, 1982).

The first edition of this competition saw notable success for New York's footballers, who defeated Mayo at the Polo Grounds in mid October. The city's hurlers could not match this feat losing to Cork two weeks later. With an attendance of 25,000 for this latter game, it appeared that New York's GAA fraternity did have an appetite for the competition (King, 1998). The return trip to Dublin in the following year attracted a reasonable level of interest, but brought no success on the field of play for New York, with defeats in football by Dublin and by Tipperary in the hurling match. Despite initial concerns, it seemed that the St Brendan Cup series was putting 'international' competition between Irish and American teams back on a firm footing. Buoyed by the success of these contests, five Irish teams travelled across the Atlantic in the following year. Wexford and Cork hurling teams and Tyrone's footballers visited between May and June to play a series of exhibition games, while Tipperary's hurlers and the Galway football team played a double-header at the Polo Grounds in late October for the St Brendan Cup. Although attendances for these games matched those of the most recent tours, there were concerns that they were not drawing bigger crowds and that the costs of bringing out touring teams to New York were increasing.[9] The New York GAA nevertheless remained resolutely committed to international activities, not least because they recognised that these games not only sated the hunger of the city's Irish for top-level Gaelic sporting contests, but also provided them with an invaluable opportunity for renewing kinship ties and meeting up with old friends. As Patrick 'Wedger' Meagher, the former Tipperary hurling great and – by this time – the main chronicler of events at Gaelic Park, noted in the aftermath of the international games in 1957:

> Another tour of Irish teams has gone into the Gaelic records . . . having brought enjoyment to thousands of hurling and football fans, apart from the pleasure which relatives and friends of the players experienced while meeting and greeting them . . . Tours are like missions or retreats in the old country (*Irish Echo*, 22 June 1957: 4).

Despite the contribution that these tours were making to preserve a vibrant culture of Gaelic games throughout the US, some people in Ireland remained critical. Following the St Brendan Cup series in 1957, the official press correspondent for the touring party, writing in the *Irish Press*, criticised what he felt was a 'lack of sportsmanship' and 'rough play' exhibited by New York's footballers towards their opponents (*Irish Echo*, 1 Feb. 1958: 4). These criticisms were compounded when John Dunne, a Central Council delegate, commented that the tours, and indeed the GAA in New York more generally, were poorly organised (*Irish Echo*, 1 Feb. 1958: 4). While New York's Gaels provided a detailed response to both allegations in their Annual Report, it was felt that more needed to be done to redress such negative publicity and the potentially damaging impact that it could have for its relationship with the GAA in Ireland (*Irish Echo*, 1 Feb. 1958: 4). Thus, in May 1958, the Association established a Public Relations division aimed at 'creating an ideal understanding between the New York GAA and the public in general, but particularly the public in Ireland' (*Irish Echo*, 31 May 1958: 4).[10] A further opportunity for a riposte to Dunne's criticism and the negative publicity surrounding the New York–Galway match in 1957 presented itself and was duly taken at the 1958 edition of the St Brendan Cup, hosted at the GAA's headquarters in Dublin, when the city's hurlers defeated Wexford (New York GAA, 1964).

Lingering transatlantic resentments remained in some quarters. With steadily declining gates, questions were increasingly asked about the feasibility of continuing with transatlantic competition.[11] The Association in New York argued that the reason for this decline in interest was the fact that St Brendan's Cup was viewed by GAA fans in the city as a second-rate competition. At Annual Congress in Dublin in 1959 they put forward a motion, via Canon Hamilton, asking that the All-Ireland winning teams in hurling and football, rather than those who won the National Leagues, play off against their New York counterparts (Annual Congress GAA Minutes, 29 Mar. 1959). While such games would have provided a much bigger draw and helped revive enthusiasm for the St Brendan's Cup, those delegates who spoke in opposition to the motion were concerned that the possibility of defeat for an All-Ireland winning team in New York would serve to undermine the Association's primary competition. After much debate, sometimes heated, the motion was defeated by 86 votes to 68 (GAA Minutes, 29 Mar. 1959). This effectively sounded the death knell for the St Brendan Cup and the competition was suspended after the 1960 edition in Dublin. While county teams from Ireland continued to visit the US to play exhibition games, New York would have to wait for another three years, until their re-admittance into the National League, for the resumption of competitive action against their counterparts in Ireland.

19. Sinn Féin Gaelic Football Team, 1923–4.

20. Pearses Gaelic Football Team. Pacific Coast Champions, 1925.

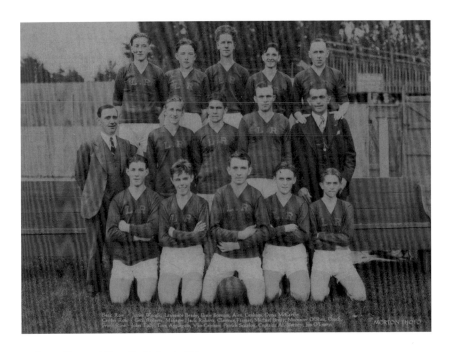

21. Laune Rangers Minor Gaelic Football Team, 1931.

22. San Francisco 1944–5 All-Star Gaelic Football Team at Ewing Field.

The institutionalisation of the GAA in the US

The impact on the revival of Gaelic games of hosting the 1947 All-Ireland football final in New York and participating in the National League and St Brendan Cup competitions extended far beyond the confines of this one city. The coverage generated by the events at New York's Polo Grounds and the subsequent contests between All-Ireland winning teams and the cream of New York's playing talent did much to rejuvenate levels of interest and enthusiasm for Gaelic games right across the country. The fact that the visiting Irish teams took part in exhibition matches beyond New York also did much to help rekindle passion for hurling and Gaelic football. The initiative and tireless efforts of those involved in promoting the games at the club level were equally significant in helping to revive these sports in America. In Boston, for example, the leading hurling club, Young Irelands, responded to the lack of hurling competition in the city, which involved only one other team (Galway), by taking the progressive decision to enter the New York junior hurling championship in the 1950 season (North Eastern GAA, 2000). This decision ultimately proved a fruitful one because it not only provided an opportunity to compete against more varied competition but also saw the Young Irelands being crowned junior champions. Interest was also evident in camogie in this period with exhibition matches involving the Shamrocks and Celtics taking place in South Boston (*Boston Pilot*, 29 July 1950; 4 Nov. 1950).

These local developments notwithstanding, if Gaelic games were to prosper and survive beyond this period, a co-ordinated, nationwide approach to the governance of the game would be required. A number of short-lived attempts had been made to institute a national governing body to oversee Gaelic games across the US. None had survived, however, which meant that the development of these games was reliant on a number of state- or city-based organisations. The GAA's revival made the immediate post-war period a particularly opportune time for the establishment of a nationwide governing body. The impetus for reviving this idea came, surprisingly, from Cleveland – not typically recognised as a hotbed of GAA activity. The key individual, according to 'official' histories, was Henry Cavanagh who was also instrumental in helping establish the Cleveland hurling club in 1949 (North East GAA, 2000). In the same year as the inception of this club, Cavanagh, along with colleagues in Chicago, helped to set up the inter-city league in the mid-West. While this regionalised approach brought benefits for Gaelic games in the mid-West, it was soon to have ramifications for the organisation of the GAA right across the country.

The visit of Tipperary to New York to contest the final of the National League in 1950 was a critical juncture in extending this coordinated approach to the administration of Gaelic games in the US, largely because of the presence in the touring party of the GAA president Michael Kehoe. Kehoe, like other high-ranking GAA officials in Ireland, was becoming favourably disposed towards his fellow Gaels across the Atlantic, a fact reflected in his comments during his stay in New York:

> We in Ireland will always remember our kith and kin who have gone abroad because whenever there was a national movement or a national emergency the generosity of the people who had sought their living elsewhere never failed the people at home (cited in *Irish Echo*, 16 Sept. 1950).

The All-Ireland final and the negotiations over New York's participation in the National League were important in encouraging this sort of outlook from the Dublin-based GAA, but so too were the efforts of the Association's membership in promoting Gaelic games in the mid-West. Kehoe gained first-hand experience of the abilities and ambitions of this grouping when he travelled from New York to meet with them in mid September 1950. At the meeting he learnt of their desire to become officially recognised as an independent county board and play against their Eastern neighbours for the right to represent the US in the National League (*Irish Echo*, 16 Sept. 1950). While Kehoe was amenable to this idea, he recognised the potentially disruptive impact of removing New York's guaranteed status as America's representative in the National League. Rather than creating divisions within the US GAA, Kehoe was keen to see a unified approach to developing Gaelic games. He, along with Henry Cavanagh, organised a conference in New York in September 1950 during which they urged GAA officials in the various cities to work towards establishing a nationwide body. The support of Central Council in Dublin was obtained in February 1951 (Central Council GAA Minutes, 9 Feb. 1951) and shortly afterwards a National Council of the GAA in the US was formed.

This new organisation divided the administration of Gaelic games into three 'zones', comprising New York which contained 36 teams; the Mid-West involving 16 football and eight hurling clubs across seven cities; and New England which had 13 football teams and three in hurling (Central Council GAA Minutes, 21 Nov. 1952). Although San Francisco and the broader Pacific region were not explicitly incorporated into this fledgling body, their officials reported to Central Council in late 1952 that they considered themselves to be under the jurisdiction of the National Council (Central Council Minutes, 8 Dec. 1952). Inter-zonal contests for the title of US champions were a feature of this new administrative set up and this competition initially proved attractive to America's GAA supporters.[12] Despite early enthusiasm, though, it became clear that the plan was overly ambitious (Central Council GAA Minutes, 13 Apr. 1952). New York soon grew disenchanted by the whole idea with its attitude towards the new body being described as 'aloof . . . hesitant . . . cold and detached' (Central Council GAA Minutes, 21 Nov. 1952). Apart from the costs and time commitment involved in fulfilling fixtures, New York's Gaels felt less reliant on other GAA units for meaningful competition, given the healthy complement of clubs and high standards of play in their city. The other factor in explaining New York's aloofness from this national governing body was a concern about the impact that the National Council was likely to have on its ability to attract visiting teams from Ireland. The city's GAA had benefited hugely from the opportunity to play against Ireland's best in competitive games. It was loath to see this threatened by being subsumed within a larger organisation composed of units that were also likely to seek to attract what was a finite number of touring teams (King, 1998). Thus, by 1956, New York took the decision to withdraw from the National Council, a move that effectively sounded the death knell on this body.

Beyond their attitude towards a national governing body, practices employed by the New York GAA in this period, most notably their use of players from other cities for weekend matches, also negatively affected the growth of Gaelic games elsewhere in the US. This was particularly the case in Boston where the success of the city's Young Irelands in the New York junior hurling championship in 1950 made New York clubs aware of the quality of the talent pool that existed there. While their recruitment of players from Boston for weekend games provided individual players with opportunities for more regular, competitive matches and did not contravene any National Council byelaws, this practice did little to aid the structural health of Gaelic games in the city. At a Central Council meeting on December 1952, one delegate suggested that the actions of recruiting New York clubs was tantamount to 'poaching' and that it was the cause of 'weakness in the Boston GAA' (Central Council GAA Minutes, 8 Dec. 1952). This practice continued during the 1950s and far beyond, but its nefarious impact was slowly negated by the influx into the city of new Irish migrants. This allowed Gaelic games in the city to grow organically. In 1958, for example, a group of players from the Galway hurling club, disgruntled at a lack of playing opportunities, broke away and formed a new club, Father Tom Burkes (North Eastern GAA, 2000). By the late 1950s Gaelic football was also well on the way to re-establishing itself in Boston, with six clubs competing at senior level and four fielding teams for junior competition.

Perhaps encouraged by this sort of local growth and despite the position of the New York GAA on the idea of a national council, a number of stalwarts of the Association elsewhere in the country still believed in the principle of a nationwide governing body.[13] In 1958, following a series of meetings, Cleveland's Henry Cavanagh published a document entitled 'The American County Board Plan', which was effectively a blueprint for a new governing body. Armed with this plan, Cavanagh and his colleagues began to lobby the clubs to seek their approval for a new divisional structure based around the main centres of Gaelic games in the country. This was not an easy process, as John Hehir, a key figure in the inception of the new body and a subsequent president, suggested: 'This plan was difficult to sell to the different cities but we were successful in doing it and eventually they came around and accepted the principle' (interview, 15 Aug. 2000). At a meeting in Philadelphia in 1959, the previous 'zonal' structure was effectively abolished and a new body, the North American County Board (NACB), initially comprising six divisions (Central, Mid-West, Western, New England, Philadelphia and Northern/ Canada), was formed. In a statement of intent, the NACB almost immediately sought, and subsequently was granted, county-board status within the parent body (North Eastern GAA, 2000; King, 1998).[14] In keeping with its earlier approach to national governance, New York continued with a policy of separatism and jurisdiction over the New York and New Jersey region, outside the remit of the NACB, as it does to this day.

The New York GAA's 'Golden Age'

New York's decision to remain separate from the NACB did not detract from the health of Gaelic games in the city. With emigration continuing apace during the late 1950s and early 1960s GAA culture was once again vibrant. Regular visits by Ireland's finest teams to compete for the St Brendan Cup were important, but outside of New York's international activities, the local club game was thriving. A regular championship series enraptured large crowds at Gaelic Park, while field days in support of Irish nationalism and a range of benevolent causes in both Ireland and New York also attracted healthy attendances.[15] John 'Kerry' O'Donnell remained a central figure. Gaelic Park, dubbed at this time by some in the Irish-American press as the 'O'Donnell Arena' (*Irish Echo*, 30 Mar. 1957), had become not only the focal point for GAA activity in the city, but also an important hub for Irish culture with banquets, meetings and music featuring prominently at the venue. O'Donnell's influence in New York's GAA was cemented in 1958 when he was voted president, a position he held for three years.[16] When he stood down as president in 1960, O'Donnell continued to play a major role in directing the affairs of the GAA in the city, adopting a range of roles with the Association. Crucially, he was instrumental in securing New York's readmittance to the National League series following discussions in Dublin in 1963 with Pádraig Ó Caoimh and other GAA officials.

The New York GAA could not have been stronger as it entered its Golden Jubilee year in 1964. The local club game had just experienced what was reported in the *Irish Echo* (21 Dec. 1963: 4) as its 'most successful year',[17] and international competition was about to return to the city. Excitement at the arrival of Tipperary hurlers to contest the National League final in May was augmented by the Central Council also sanctioning a visit by Kilkenny, winners of the All-Ireland hurling title in 1963, to play a series of games to mark the New York Association's Golden Jubilee and help to bolster the profile of the sport elsewhere in the US (Byrne, 1976). In some ways, the New York–Tipperary game was incidental to the contest between Tipperary and Kilkenny for what was described as the 'World Hurling Cup' (Byrne, 1976: 12).[18] In August, a New York select football team embarked on a 'good-will . . . round the world tour', that took in America's west coast, New Zealand, Australia and England before finishing in Ireland in September with a famous victory over Offaly (*Irish Echo*, 7 Dec. 1963).[19] After the completion of the domestic season, all that remained in the Jubilee year was the National League final between the city's footballers and those from Dublin. Buoyed by their successes on the round the world tour, New York went on to capture their second National League title, winning the game by 2–12 to 1–13. This was a fitting end to what had undoubtedly been a year of high points in New York GAA history. The future of Gaelic games in the city seemed set to go from strength to strength.

The New York Board, or for that matter the NACB, could not have envisaged the introduction of a piece of legislation in the following year that was to seriously curtail Irish immigration to the US and, in doing so, threaten the progress that had been made in the late 1950s and early 1960s. The Immigration Act of 1965, passed through Congress with little opposition, abolished the national quota system which had operated in the country since 1921.[20] Under the new provisions preference was given to those potential immigrants with immediate family ties to US citizens and beyond this to those with skill sets required in the American economy (Keely 1971). Given that many Irish had lost their immediate generational connection to American citizens, rates of immigration decreased to levels last seen during the Depression era (Lobo and Salvo, 1998). These tighter regulations were not the only reason behind plummeting Irish immigration. The appointment of Seán Lemass as Irish Taoiseach in 1959 and his role in Ireland's economic recovery, one built on expansionist policies and membership of the European Economic Community, brought about a sharp reduction in Irish emigration (Reimers, 1997; Cochrane, 2007). By 1969 the effect of these developments on the GAA was already being felt. In noting a significant drop in attendance for regular season matches at Gaelic Park and a perceived decline in playing standards, Byrne (1969c: 22) pointed specifically to the 1965 Immigration Act as the chief cause and suggested that the New York GAA should support the American Irish Immigration Committee, a pressure group set up in 1967 to agitate for the repeal or amendment of the legislation:

> This legislation is a major factor in the decline of playing standards and paying patrons at Gaelic Park. It would seem to me that a greater effort and concerted support for the American Irish Immigration Committee and others are urgently required and unquestionably necessary if the present laws are to be repealed to permit resumption of normal immigration from Ireland. The Gaelic Athletic Association and the Irish societies will continue to lose ground under the present unfair immigration law.

The GAA in New York, and indeed throughout the US, in addition to encouraging its membership to support the American Irish Immigration Committee, responded to the reduced levels of new adherents coming into the country by approaching players in Ireland on a more sustained basis to travel across the Atlantic and play for teams on a weekend basis. Although the system that facilitates this movement of players today is heavily regulated by a closely monitored transfer or sanction system, in the mid 1960s the GAA's rule book did not include provisions for this transatlantic movement of players. There were moves towards stricter regulation as concerns began to grow in Ireland about the impact that this process was having on club and county teams. For example, a motion by the Monaghan county board, passed by Congress in

1969, required players to obtain an official transfer from their club or county before travelling to New York (Annual Congress GAA Minutes, 6 Apr. 1969; *The Advocate*, 24 Oct. 1970). This transient flow of players from Ireland was far from ideal. By the late 1960s, the broader decline in more permanent Irish immigration to New York and further afield began to seriously undermine the vigour of the GAA.

Apart from the decline in immigration, New York was confronted with some other pressing concerns. Relations with the Association in Ireland had gradually soured during the second half of the 1960s; by the end of the decade they were essentially unworkable. By the mid 1960s the international series was beginning to struggle financially and the international fund had plummeted into the red by £6,000 (McAllister, 1965).[21] This led to terse exchanges between New York and Dublin about how best to arrest the haemorrhaging of finance that increasingly typified international matches played in Ireland. Worse was to come, though, during New York's visit to Ireland to contest the 1966 National League finals. While the hurling game was won convincingly by Kilkenny without incident, the second leg of the football final against Longford at Croke Park descended into chaos when members of the crowd encroached on to the field of play and attacked some of the New York players and the referee (Byrne, 1976).

Although these incidents and the financial difficulties surrounding the tours had raised questions about the value of international games, the National League series went ahead in the following year and saw New York's footballers win their third title, defeating Galway over two legs. Further success ensued in the following year with a victory over Down, the reigning All-Ireland Champions. This two-leg series generated a profit of $16,000 which gave the International Fund a healthier complexion (Byrne, 1969c). Financial anxieties remained, though, and the fact that the majority of the funds required to maintain the international series were being generated by the New York GAA began to fuel resentment. Indeed, in January 1969, John O'Donnell took the decision to freeze the profit generated from Down's visit of the previous year. In outlining his rationale, O'Donnell pointed to what he described as a failure on the part of the Dublin administration to live up to 'contractual obligations' surrounding visits to Dublin by the New York hurlers and footballers in 1968.[22] His criticism of what he saw as the *laissez-faire* approach of the GAA to the 1968 series and persistent sniping about the physicality of the return fixtures in New York was scathing and did little to engender relations that might bode well for the future of international fixtures:

The Central Council should shake itself up. There are far too many incompetents in it; too many people keeping seats warm. What is needed is people who are prepared to think and plan to do something for the players . . . Let the Central Council ease off with the talk of authority and discipline and give us cooperation and understanding and a desire to do things in harmony. (*The Advocate*, 25 Jan. 1969: 6)

Despite these acrimonious exchanges, 1969 was a high point of international competition, not only because of New York's hurlers' two-legged victory over Kilkenny at Gaelic Park to claim their first National League title, but also because of a record ten teams from Ireland playing at Gaelic Park during the course of the season (Byrne, 1969d; 1969e; *The Advocate*, 8 Feb. 1969).[23] While some in New York expressed concern that the level of transatlantic competition was reducing interest in the local club game (*Irish Echo*, 8 Nov. 1969), generally speaking fixtures against teams from Ireland were doing much to promote Gaelic games in the city and ensured that Gaelic Park continued to function, psychologically at least, as an authentically Irish space.

The NACB and Gaelic games in Boston, Chicago and San Francisco

While New York was clearly the leading division in the US during the late 1950s and 1960s, Gaelic games in Boston, Chicago and San Francisco had been built on the firm foundations laid in the immediate post-war period. GAA officials in each city ensured that they were able to benefit from New York's participation in international fixtures by inviting the touring teams to play against select sides, a move that bolstered the profile of the game there in much the same way as it had in New York. The inception of the NACB in 1959 was the key development in this period, and was instrumental in improving the health of the GAA across the US, not least because it provided an end of season nationwide championship competition for the country's leading clubs. The successes of clubs from Boston, San Francisco and Chicago in the first decade of the tournament's history revealed much about the strength of these clubs, with the senior hurling and football accolades regularly being won by teams from these cities.[24]

By the beginning of the 1960s, the complement of clubs in each city was relatively healthy and the more structured approach to championship football in each of the NACB's divisions ensured that these clubs had regular, competitive fixtures. While the number of teams in Boston was not on a par with that of earlier periods, the ranks of the New England division swelled from four Gaelic football and three hurling clubs at the end of the 1950s to ten in football and four in hurling by the middle of the following decade (North American County Board, 1997).[25] This growth was clearly aided by the increase in Irish immigration to the US evident during the 1950s and early 1960s. The changes to the immigration legislation in 1965, as noted earlier, did not have an immediate impact on the status of Gaelic games in the city; but, by the beginning of the 1970s, the number of football clubs in existence had halved while the complement of hurling clubs was reduced to three (North American County Board, 1997). As the Boston GAA looked to the 1970s and beyond, they were faced with an uncertain future.

For those with responsibility for promoting Gaelic games in Chicago, the same could equally be said. Hurling and football quickly re-emerged after the war, albeit not on the same scale as occured on the north-east seaboard. Much of the emphasis in Gaelic games in the late 1940s and early 1950s was on inter- rather than intra-city competition. This intra-city competition was serviced by an increasingly healthy culture of Gaelic games within Chicago. In much the same way that increased immigration had bolstered the GAA further east, the number of clubs in the city grew as the 1950s progressed. One significant example of this was the re-establishment of Harry Bolands hurling club in 1952. This club, based in the city's South Side, originally came into existence in 1925; but, as with many other clubs throughout America, it struggled during the depression years of the 1930s before folding in the early 1940s. Once re-established, Harry Bolands were hugely influential in rejuvenating the game in Chicago. Their promotion of visits by teams from New York, many of which included players of great renown who had excelled against Ireland's finest talents in the 1950s and 1960s, was significant and ensured that Chicago's GAA fraternity were able to enjoy the highest standards of hurling (Byrne, 1970).

The presence in the Harry Boland ranks of Pat Hennessey, first chairman of the reformed Chicago GAA, was critical in the promotion of Gaelic games throughout the city. As a hurler, Hennessey was a big draw, not least because he had captained the Kilkenny minor team in 1938. He was also skilled as an administrator and proponent of Gaelic games in foreign climes. During a spell in Nottingham prior to his arrival in Chicago, he had helped to organise a unit of the GAA and acted as its first president (Byrne, 1970). It seemed inevitable that he would be at the forefront of the revival of hurling in Chicago, and his involvement in Harry Bolands, as one of the founders and its first president, allowed him to influence the future of the game there. With Hennessey at the helm, the club dominated the local hurling scene in the city, winning 14 Chicago titles in the period up to 1968 (Byrne, 1970). This is not to suggest that Harry Bolands were the only significant hurling or GAA club in the city. By 1959 and the inception of the NACB, the city possessed four teams in both hurling and football.[26] The complement of clubs remained consistent during the 1960s, and regular visits by leading Irish county teams, such as the Down and Galway All-Ireland winning footballers in 1962 and 1965 respectively, ensured that interest remained relatively high. Although the number of affiliated GAA clubs did not dip below seven in the second half of the 1960s, the slowing of Irish immigration to the city as a result of changes in the legislation governing immigrant entry into the US meant that the city's GAA fraternity were faced with an continuing struggle to ensure the survival of Gaelic sport into the next decade and beyond.

The status of the GAA amongst Irish Chicagoans in this period was clearly reliant on the efforts of individuals clubs, the work of particular administrators and high profile visits by Ireland's finest Gaelic games talent. However, the ability of these sports to achieve a foothold in the city was also dependent on the fact that, as it had in the era before the Second World War, the GAA continued to fulfil a whole range of socio-economic, political and cultural functions for the Irish. The role of the Association in helping those who arrived in Chicago as part of the post-war wave of Irish immigration to settle into their new environs and fraternise with people from their own ethnic group was crucial in enabling the city's clubs to attract new adherents. The ability of the GAA to satisfy what was a deep-seated psychological need to feel part of an Irish ethnic community was particularly important for those immigrants who arrived from rural parts of Ireland and were unaccustomed to life in a large, sprawling metropolis. This was a point made explicit by one Gaelic sport-playing migrant who left Dublin for Chicago in 1958:

> what I found too when I first came here in the late 1950s was that there were other lads who were coming out in droves . . . In my club, St Vincents, I was maybe the only city guy who had emigrated and I found myself settling in a lot quicker than my country (rural) colleagues. They were very lonely for a long period of time and I think it was because a lot of them came from rural areas and farms and had a real tough time settling in. Had they not been a hurler or a footballer, I think many of them would have gone back home (interview with Eamonn Kelly, 29 July 2005).

The same view was repeated by others within the GAA fraternity in Chicago (interview with Tommy Dolan, 30 July 2005). The ability of the Association to continue to fulfil this role for the Irish community was crucial in the continuation of the city's long-standing tradition of Gaelic games for the remainder of the 1960s.

In San Francisco, the preservation of Gaelic games amongst the Irish diaspora in the immediate post-war period was largely dependent on links with Los Angeles' Gaels and annual two-legged inter-city fixtures played on 4 July and Labour Day weekend (interview with Brendan Keneally, 5 Sept. 2006). A strong rivalry rapidly emerged and the intensity and physicality of these games did much to encourage the Irish community in both cities to patronise Gaelic sports (North American County Board, 1997). The inception of regular fixtures between San Francisco select teams and their counterparts from New York in 1951 helped further to popularise hurling and Gaelic football, but it was the influx of new Irish immigrants from Ireland and from elsewhere in the US after Second World War that did most to re-establish these sports as important pillars in the lives of sections of the city's Irish community (North American County Board, 1997). Edward Farley, a native of San Francisco with Irish-born parents, was a key figure in the emergence of the club game in the city in this period. According to the NACB's official history, Farley was inspired by the sight of hundreds of emigrants from Ireland playing casual games of hurling and football and decided to begin the process of starting up clubs to cater for more organised versions of these sports (North American County Board, 1997). By the year of the NACB's founding, four Gaelic football and two hurling clubs were in existence and the main venues for matches, Beach Chalet and Balboa Stadium, were regularly attracting crowds in excess of 1,000 (interview with Louis Cotter, 3 Sept. 2006; interview with Mike Moriarity, 27 Aug. 2006). Thanks to such popularity, the numbers of GAA clubs had increased to seven in football and four in hurling for the start of the 1961 season.[27]

The strength of Gaelic games in the city in the early 1960s was very much in evidence in the first three editions of the NACB championships, with San Francisco winning the inaugural hurling crown and the footballers claiming back-to-back titles in 1960 and 1961. The visit of All-Ireland football winners Down to play a San Francisco 'All-Star' select team in front of a crowd of 4,000 in June 1962 as part of their US tour was a further highlight in the history of Gaelic games on America's West coast at this time (interview with Louis Cotter, 3 Sept. 2006). In summarising the health of the GAA in the city by the end of 1962, John Duffy, then president of the Ulster Gaelic football club, painted an optimistic picture for the future:

The local competitions are very keenly contested. The standard of football is of very high calibre, and with the influx of new young players from Ireland and some Eastern cities, the future of Gaelic football indeed looks bright for the Irish and non-Irish fans in the Bay Area (cited in *Emerald Echo*, Sept. 1962: 6).

In his assessment of what the future might hold for the Association, Duffy went on to thank the proprietor of the *Emerald Echo* for their support in the promotion of Gaelic games via the print media. However, the San Francisco GAA's use of the media extended beyond newspapers, and they took every opportunity to ensure coverage in a range of Irish radio programmes including, 'Bits from Blarney', 'Innisfree Hour' and 'Irish Hour', which were broadcast through the Bay Area (*Emerald Echo*, Sept. 1962: 6; *Irish Herald*, Dec. 1964). This not only allowed the Association to remind long-standing Irish immigrants of the existence of a thriving GAA culture but also made newly arrived migrants, and potential new recruits, aware of the presence of Gaelic games in San Francisco. Progress continued to the mid-point of the decade, with 1964 being described by the then president of the San Francisco GAA, Mike Howard, as 'a tremendous success', in financial terms (cited in *Irish Herald*, Dec. 1964: 6). This success was built upon and at the start of the 1965 season two new clubs were established – Cork in hurling and Donegal in football (*Irish Herald*, Apr. 1965).[28]

Despite what appeared to be solid foundations, the passing of the 1965 Immigration Act completely reversed the fortunes of the city's GAA almost overnight. With the quota of immigrant slots being quickly taken up by other nationalities with easier access to the city, Irish emigration, and the flow of new GAA adherents, virtually dried up. By 1967 many of the established clubs in the city could not field a team and quickly folded. This left the few remaining clubs with limited opportunities for expending their competitive energies beyond playing frequently against one another. This brought its own problems, with the tensions that invariably built up between players often spilling over into acrimony in the city's Irish bars. This, according to Brendan Keneally, who was involved with the Sarsfields club when it was formed in 1957, combined with the slowing of emigration, was instrumental in the decline of the San Francisco GAA as the decade reached a close:

then the problems with immigration kicked in and all of a sudden there was nobody coming to town. It changed the whole thing. The other problem was that because there were too few teams, the same teams were playing each other too often and the rivalry was carrying over into bars. A lot of us got embarrassed by this and thought, 'to heck with it'. Then it died out altogether for a few years, maybe around 1968 (interview, 5 Sept. 2006).

Although some clubs persisted in this period, the city's participation in the NACB championship ceased. Anxious about a future without Gaelic games, some of the city's GAA stalwarts examined a range of avenues to redress what was a potentially terminal decline. Danny Boyle emerged as a key innovator and his idea to establish a minor programme that encouraged participation from all ethnic groups found within San Francisco was quickly adopted. This was a plan that required time to come to fruition; for the rest of the 1960s only occasional games between the surviving club sides and a number of matches featuring San Francisco select teams remained of GAA culture in the city (NACB, 1997).

Conclusion

According to Kieran Conway, journalist and long-time observer of the GAA in America, the profile and development of Gaelic games in the US has been in many senses dependent on 'the pendulum of migration' (interview, 25 July 2000). In the period between the end of the Second World War and the early 1970s, this pendulum swung in both directions. In the post-war era, the influx of Irish immigrants seeking to escape from the austerity of life in Ireland and avail themselves of economic opportunities in America did much to revitalise and enrich a whole range of Irish social, political and cultural organisations. The GAA was no different and it underwent the sort of revival that seemed set to secure its future for many years to come. The Immigration Act in 1965 sent the pendulum in the opposite direction, turning off the flow of fresh blood into the Association. In doing so, it created an exceptionally difficult climate in which to grow and nurture these distinctively Irish pastimes. In the past, those seeking to preserve and promote Gaelic games in the US had risen to the challenges presented to them and had ensured that the GAA maintained a meaningful presence in Irish America. The assistance of the Association's Central Council in Ireland, particularly the decision to afford New York the honour of hosting the All-Ireland Gaelic football final in 1947, had been crucial in the re-emergence of Gaelic football and hurling in post-war America. However, as the GAA in New York, Boston, Chicago and San Francisco entered into an uncertain future, it seemed unlikely that the parent body would be as inclined to help their siblings across the Atlantic, given the splintering of relations between the New York GAA Board and Central Council in the late 1960s. For as long as this remained the case, and with Irish immigration set to continue its downward spiral, organised Gaelic games seemed unlikely to survive far beyond the generation of players and administrators who had preserved these sports up to the early 1970s. The remaining decades of the twentieth century were set to provide the GAA in America with its sternest challenge yet.

CHAPTER SEVEN

Lest we forget: Gaelic games and Irish-American nationalism, 1900–68

Introduction

The history of the GAA in the US was anything but one of linear progress as the narrative of the previous three chapters has revealed. The fortunes of the Association waxed and waned according to fluctuations in levels of Irish emigration as well as broader social and political developments on both sides of the Atlantic. That Gaelic games survived what were, in the first half of the twentieth century, extremely trying conditions and managed to maintain a presence in the sporting and cultural landscape of Irish America in the post-war era is testament to the appeal of these games and the resilience of those who took responsibility for preserving and promoting them on American shores. A passion and enthusiasm for sport was only one of the reasons for the survival and progress of Gaelic games following the conclusion of the Second World War. The fact that these sports continued to perform a whole host of social, psychological and economic functions for sections of the Irish-American populace was significant. The preservation of the GAA in America was also rooted in the role that the Association played in allowing Irish immigrants in places like Boston, New York, Chicago and San Francisco to reconnect, at least temporarily, with Ireland and senses of Irishness. This is not to say that the Irishness the GAA did so much to encourage amongst Gaelic sport-playing immigrants was monolithic or remained static through time. At various junctures during the twentieth century, the Association provided a platform on which some engaged in what they saw as a predominantly cultural act, one that allowed them to keep in touch with the traditions and heritage of their homeland. At other points, though, membership of the GAA and involvement in Gaelic games provided sections of the emigrant community with an opportunity to express themselves politically and in ways concomitant with their broader desire for and commitment to an Ireland free of British influence. This chapter concentrates on the role of the GAA in this latter sense and examines the ways in which the Association acted as a conduit for the expression of politicised versions of Irish-American nationalism in the period from 1900 to the beginning of the troubles in Northern Ireland.

The GAA and Irish-American nationalism from the turn of the century to 1920

Those who took up the baton of developing the GAA in America at the outset of the twentieth century were well aware of the significance of Gaelic sports as important markers of Irish ethnic identity. However, they did not seek to link their activities to the physical force tradition of Irish nationalism to the same degree as had their predecessors at various stages during the late nineteenth century. This was largely a consequence of developments in nationalist politics in Ireland. The reunification of the Irish Parliamentary Party at the turn of the century, after years of infighting following the death of Parnell in 1891, did much to restore confidence and a sense of solidarity in constitutional Irish nationalism in Ireland and America (McCaffrey, 1997). Almost as soon as John Redmond became leader of the party in 1900, he sought to re-galvanise Irish America behind the constitutionalist position and helped to establish the United Irish League of Ireland to raise funds from the diaspora and generate support from US politicians (Wilson, 1995). The GAA espoused financial and political support for Redmond's brand of nationalism in the opening years of the twentieth century; but, as hopes for Irish independence grew following the introduction of the third Home Rule Bill to the British Parliament in 1912, there was less evidence in the Irish-American press of Gaelic games being used specifically to further this agenda. Instead, sporting rivalries, often rooted in county affiliations, and a desire to preserve what was on the whole a benign, culturally-oriented Irish identity replaced more politicised expressions of nationalism for a time as the key driving forces behind the GAA's growth in America.

This is not to say that the political was completely absent from Gaelic games in the opening years of the new century. Indeed, at this time a range of Irish nationalist organisations followed the precedent set in the late 1870s of incorporating these sports into their annual picnics and field days. In a clear example of this, the programme of activities at the United Irish Societies of Chicago's celebration of Hugh O'Donnell's late sixteenth-century victory over the army of Queen Elizabeth featured a number of 'championship' matches between the city's leading teams (*Chicago Daily Tribune*, 9 Aug. 1903: 5), thus allowing the connections between the nationalist agenda and the GAA there to be publicly expressed. This trend continued intermittently into the early 1910s, when a number of Gaelic Feis's organised by the Gaelic League at various venues in the US, but particularly in New York, included hurling and football matches in their programme together with speeches by various Gaelic orators, some of whom spoke specifically, in Gaelic, about the 'Irish question' (*Gaelic American*, 23 Mar. 1912; *Gaelic American*, 7 June 1913).

While a thin thread of nationalist sentiment continued to weave its way loosely through the fabric of the GAA in the opening years of the century, by 1914 the association between Gaelic games in America and more anti-British, belligerent expressions of Irish nationalism once again began to gather strength and become more centrally incorporated into the affairs and activities of its members. This was largely a response to events in Ireland. The slowdown in the progress of parliamentary nationalism, particularly the political procrastination surrounding the passage of the third Home Rule Bill, quickly increased levels of popular support for militant separatism in Ireland. The formation of the Irish National Volunteers in 1913, in response to the signing of the Ulster Covenant and the formation of the Ulster Volunteers by Unionists in the north-east corner of Ireland,[1] was the clearest manifestation of a growing feeling that force was the only solution to Ireland's fractured relationship with Britain (Coogan, 1995). Although funds continued to flow across the Atlantic to support the constitutional platform, this more combative position increasingly found currency in Irish-American circles. With the possibility of Civil War in Ireland between nationalist and unionist looming, concrete plans were put in place for a military uprising against British control and Irish Americans were only too willing to demonstrate their support politically and financially. Redmond's decision to support Britain at the outset of the Great War and his encouragement to Irishmen to enlist in the British Army hardened this willingness and added further impetus to Irish-American backing of militant irredentism.

This support became very apparent within US branches of the GAA, whose members sought to demonstrate their patriotism by sending money back across the Atlantic to arm and equip the National Volunteers. With a long-standing tradition of engaging in fund-raising efforts for various nationalist causes behind them, supporters of the GAA in New York, a city historically positioned at the centre of Irish-American nationalism, began to urge local hurling and football clubs to respond to appeals coming from Ireland for financial support. A letter to the editor of the New York Irish newspaper, *The Advocate*, in July 1914, implored the city's most prominent clubs to organise a series of fund-raising matches at Celtic Park with the following emotive and evocative plea: 'We ought to do it, if not for Ireland's sake, at least for shame-sake. Ireland when in need always looks to America, and New York in particular for aid. Let us not be found wanting in this crisis' (*The Advocate*, 25 July 1914). Although the clubs had responded positively to these appeals and had continued to back other nationalist organisations and causes such as Clan na Gael and St Enda's College in Dublin,[2] there was agreement that additional support was entirely appropriate. Thus there was unanimous support when the Irish National Volunteer Committee of New York approached ten leading clubs with a view to organising a fund-raising day at Celtic Park on 7 September 1914.[3] The clubs' agreement to offer their services gratis and the decision of the Irish American Athletic Club (IAAC), the leaseholders of Celtic Park, to provide the venue free of charge were further evidence of the commitment and unity of purpose in GAA circles on the Irish 'question' (*Gaelic American*, 29 Aug. 1914; 5 Sept. 1914). In their promotion of the event, *The Advocate* made explicit the politicisation that the GAA in New York was undergoing at this time:

> The Gaelic athlete here never forgets his national honour. He was ever in the van when Ireland called for arms or money. Today Ireland is undergoing a trying ordeal. Thousands of Irishmen have volunteered to defend IRELAND FOR IRELAND, and in this way they must be armed. The Irishmen of Greater New York can show their appreciation of Ireland's National Volunteers by turning out in their thousands at Celtic Park on Labor Day . . . It's an occasion that the Gael should make the most of and show the hated Saxon that at least there are a few Irishmen in New York who are not willing to 'hold Ireland for England'. Monday next will be a great day for Ireland, a great day for the games of the Gael and a greater day for the Irish National Volunteers of Ireland, the savers of the Irish nation (*The Advocate*, 3 Sept. 1914).

Rallied by this call, the event was attended by over 10,000 spectators, each paying 25 cents admission. Further funds were solicited through the selling of volunteer's tags, subscriptions and a programme which contained articles on the Irish Volunteer movement as well as the words and music of patriotic Irish songs. The radical tone of the event was further highlighted when a group of supporters of Redmond's parliamentary nationalism attempted to raise 'three cheers' during a break between games. The result, described in the *Gaelic American* as 'melancholy and weak as the death rattle in the throat of a dying call', illustrates that a more militant brand of Irish nationalism was the position most favoured by the majority of New York's Gaels (*Gaelic American*, 12 Sept. 1914).

Fund-raising for the Irish National Volunteers was not specific to the New York GAA. Three thousand miles away on the Pacific coast of America, the Association's members in San Francisco were engaged in similar activities. In December 1914, MacBrides Gaelic football club organised a tournament at St Ignatius stadium to raise finances for the Volunteers. In advertising this event in the local Irish press, the organising committee employed the same sort of rousing, nationalistic rhetoric as their counterparts in New York:

> No individual or club of men claiming to be Irish should at this critical moment refuse to aid . . . the young men at home who will have to fight for the freedom of their native land. Wake up you indifferent Gaels! . . . The blood of the patriots and martyrs of your ancestors must not be shed in vain, while you are alive today to take up the cause of freedom for which they died (*The Leader*, 5 Dec. 1914: 5).

The use of this kind of language was not new in San Francisco's Irish newspapers in this period, nor was it entirely motivated by Irish politics. Members and supporters of the Association recognised that linking involvement in Gaelic games with a sense of belonging to the 'old country' as well as the ongoing struggle for independence from Britain could be useful in helping to bolster the flagging ranks of the GAA. Thus, 'a spectator' wrote to the editor of *The Leader* in April 1913, imploring the city's Irish community to 'be either a Gael or a "shoneen"',[4] before going on to challenge them by saying that 'no Irish man or woman can afford to be called the latter' (*The Leader*, 19 Apr. 1913: 7). With a more militant version of Irish nationalism re-establishing itself on American soil and the Easter Rising looming, Gaelic games in San Francisco continued to be closely intertwined with the Irish nationalist agenda and senses of Irishness that were intensely ethnic, hostile to the British presence in Ireland and supportive of a solution by physical force. This continued to be the case in the aftermath of the failed 1916 Rising. Leading figures in the city's GAA emphasised that involvement in Gaelic games should be considered the 'duty' of those who called themselves Irish, while individual clubs donated money and organised benefit matches for a fund for 'the widows and orphans of the Irish Martyrs' (*The Leader*, 26 Aug. 1916: 1; *The Leader*, 22 July 1916: 7).[5]

The GAA and the post-partition decline of Irish-American nationalism

While the response of Irish Americans in joining the US army in such large numbers – following President Woodrow Wilson's decision to enter the First World World War in 1917 – revealed a growing sense of patriotism towards America (McCaffrey, 1997), a commitment to Irish revolutionary nationalism continued to colour large swathes of Irish-American opinion. The work of the Friends of Irish Freedom (FOIF) and the American Association for the Recognition of the Irish Republic (AARIR) established in 1916 and 1920 respectively, coupled with Eamon de Valera's tour of America in 1919 to generate finances for the Irish Republican Army (IRA) and gain US recognition for the Irish government, did much to keep the struggle for Irish independence at the centre of the consciousness of Irish Americans (Wilson, 1995; Davis, 2006). During the War of Independence in Ireland of 1919–21, financial and political support flowed freely for Sinn Féin and the IRA from sections of the Irish diaspora (McCaffrey, 1992). However, the outcome of this war and political negotiations with the British government, which ultimately led to the partition of Ireland in 1921 and the establishment of the Irish Free State, effectively resolved the Irish question for much of Irish America (McCaffrey, 1992). Despite some lingering resentment at the failure to achieve independence for the whole island of Ireland, most viewed partition – with the possibility of full sovereignty further down the line – as a reasonable outcome and therefore felt little need to continue to donate their dollars or to agitate for total Irish independence.

The Irish Civil War of 1922–3 hastened a declining interest in Irish political affairs, not least because most Irish Americans struggled to comprehend what was driving Irishmen at 'home' to kill their compatriots. Many were also bemused and felt increasingly alienated by some dimensions of post-partition Irish nationalism, particularly its isolationist Gaelic and socialist leanings. Other factors in the first half of the century, including the Depression of the 1930s and a shift in the focus of Irish emigration towards Great Britain, further lessened the inclination of Irish Americans to express their Irishness with the same intensity and vigour as they had in the late nineteenth century and in the period leading up to the Easter Rising. While there remained some support for a campaign for complete reunification in Ireland, events in Ireland combined with greater levels of social mobility and cultural assimilation into American society ultimately led to less of a preoccupation with the affairs of the 'old country', hence a more general decline in Irish nationalism as an expression of Irish Catholic identity. As McCaffrey (1992: 154) succinctly put it: 'As the Irish achieved success and respectability in the United States, they became more American and less Irish.'

Dire economic conditions and reduced levels of Irish immigration, as well as this Americanisation of the Irish diaspora and a diminishing concern for Irish politics, undoubtedly fed into the decline of the GAA in Depression-era America. Conversely, those who remained committed during the lean years of the Association, especially from the 1930s through to the 1940s, did so not only because of their love of hurling and Gaelic football, but also because of their politics and their continued aspirations for an Ireland free of British influence. In Chicago, for example, for much of the 1920s, the AARIR sponsored organised Gaelic football and hurling matches, thereby helping to develop a close relationship with the GAA (North American County Board, 1997). The establishment of a GAA club in 1925, named after Harry Boland, the prominent republican and Easter Rising veteran who had been shot dead by members of the Irish Free State National Army three years previously, was a further indication of the political inclinations of the city's Gaels. Chicago was not alone in this regard, and despite the broader waning of Irish-American nationalism in this period, leading figures elsewhere within the GAA remained vociferous and steadfast in their support for physical force nationalism and were only too eager to use Gaelic games as a way of encouraging others within the diaspora to revive what had become a largely dormant element of their identity.

This support for the physical-force tradition within the GAA, and in pockets of Irish America more generally, was aided by the presence, particularly in New York, of Irish republicans who had fought on the anti-Treaty side in the Irish Civil War (Hanna, 1999). This did much to ensure that, from the mid 1920s until well into the 1950s, the GAA in New York and elsewhere in the US was favourably predisposed to lending support for political and military agitation for a united Ireland. One particularly revealing example of this was evident during the visit of the County Laois and Cavan footballers to play a series of exhibition matches in New York in 1938. Right at the outset of the visit, Lar Brady, manager of the Laois team and chairman of the Laois county board, set a militant nationalist tone when, during a radio broadcast, he sought to remind the 'exiles of our race in the United States' that 'we will continue the national struggle until the aspirations and hopes of our people are realized and Pearse's dream comes true: Ireland our love, one and indivisible, Gaelic and forever free' (cited in *Irish Echo*, 21 May 1938: 4). Roused by such sentiments and eager to express the nationalist credentials of the GAA in New York, the *Irish Echo* responded by calling on the city's Gaels to show their solidarity with the continued struggle for Irish freedom by attending in 'great numbers' the matches featuring the touring teams:

> At the remaining All-Ireland games . . . show to Britain and the world that all Ireland-in-America is in arms to bring at last, to a swift end, the sassenach's presence: show your loyalty to Ireland's cause and the warmth of your American welcome to Ireland's fighting sons! (*Irish Echo*, 21 May 1938: 1).

Along with engendering support for an overtly republican agenda, the tours by inter-county teams from Ireland during the 1930s also did much to preserve a strong sense of cultural Irishness which often laid the foundations for more politicised expressions of identity. In his report to Central Council in Dublin on the visit of Mayo's footballers to New York, Boston and Philadelphia in 1937, Canon Michael Hamilton described the setting in which the games took place as one that was visibly Irish, infused with an 'atmosphere of Gaeldom' and underpinned by an 'evident self-consciousness of our historic past' (Canon Michael Hamilton, Report to Central Council GAA, 29 May 1937). Even within the context of this seemingly benign, culturally focused celebration of Ireland and Irishness, expressions of an identity built on a sense of injustice and Anglophobia were also visible, most prominently so in the presence of a banner at one match in New York which depicted a mountain mass during the penal days under the words 'Let Erin Remember' (Hamilton Report to GAA, 29 May 1937). Although the suspension of tours involving visiting Irish teams provided one less avenue for America's Gaels to display their nationalistic fervour, the relationship during the early 1940s between Gaelic games in the US and republican politics continued to be in evidence. In New York, for example, organisations such as Clan na Gael and the various IRA clubs regularly hosted field days at Innisfail Park (O'Shea, 1940b). Elsewhere in the US, however, the decline in the visibility and popularity of Gaelic games during the Second World War made these activities much less attractive for republican groups and their propensity to draw on them to recruit or promote their agenda dipped.

The New York GAA and post-war Irish-American republicanism

Irish nationalism in America reached a low ebb during the Second World War. Ireland's neutrality throughout the war was the key cause here, not least because influential emigrant leaders had long stressed that an independent

Ireland would be an ally of the US. However, at a time when American soldiers, including Irish Americans, were losing their lives on the battlefields of Europe, de Valera remained immovable on the issue of neutrality. His message of condolence to the German ambassador following Hitler's death further angered Irish-American opinion and led to many turning away from Ireland and its politics (Wilson, 1995). Continued social mobility and the slow decline of old ethnic neighbourhoods in America's major 'Irish' cities further hastened this process of waning nationalism amongst established Irish Americans. Nonetheless, pockets of support for militant republicanism remained and, as occured in the 1930s, the GAA became a key arena for the expression of what was, in this period, a residual form of Irishness in America.

The linkages between the GAA and Irish republicanism in New York prior to America's involvement in the Second World War and the city's status as a popular destination for former anti-Treaty militia in the 1920s were such that, when the GAA experienced a revival from the late 1940s, its association with the movement for a united Ireland was also reignited. At one field day at Croke Park, later renamed Gaelic Park, Clan na Gael and the IRA clubs of New York staged a series of Gaelic football and hurling matches in order to raise funds for the republican cause. The character and purpose of this event was made explicit in *The Irish World and American Industrial Liberator* (20 Sept. 1947: 8):

> The guest speakers of the day will be Joe Sheehy, famous All-Ireland footballer and true soldier of Erin; Peter Campbell who was recently just released after spending a 10 year term in a British prison. . . . The Chairman of arrangements is Jim Brisbane, noted Cork IRA rebel and other staunch believers in a 32-county Irish Republic. The proceeds will go towards the promotion and ideals of the Clan na Gael and the IRA.

Leading figures within the Association in Ireland also began to publicly promote the cause of a united Ireland amongst Gaels in the US, contrary to the stance adopted by the GAA's Central Council in the immediate aftermath of the establishment of the Irish Free State, when they stated their support for the Treaty and fell in behind the newly installed Provisional Government (De Búrca, 1999). The hosting of the All-Ireland Gaelic football final in New York in 1947 was very important in this sense, functioning as it did as a vehicle for the articulation of politicised nationalist rhetoric. In his attempt to gain support from delegates at the GAA's 1947 Congress in Dublin for his motion to stage the 1947 All-Ireland Gaelic football final in New York, Father Michael

Hamilton linked this event to a planned convention in the city on the issue of partition in Ireland. For Father Hamilton, the success of this convention in helping to build Irish-American pressure for the reunification of Ireland would be assisted by the hosting of an All-Ireland final on American soil:

> The Football Final would help immensely to focus attention on that Convention and I have the opinion of a distinguished American statesman that a packed stadium would be more effective as a demonstration than a few thousand delegates in an Assembly Hall in the City (cited in GAA Annual Congress Minutes, 6 Apr. 1947).

This linking of the 1947 All-Ireland football final with Irish nationalist politics was again very much in evidence following the game when Dan O'Rourke, then president of the GAA, used the occasion of the post-match banquet to encourage 'Irish Americans to join forces with their kinsfolk in Ireland so that the partition of the Irish nation may be ended in our generation' (cited in Report of Pádraig Ó Caoimh to Central Council, 13 Dec. 1947).

New York's Gaels certainly responded to O'Rourke's promptings. Throughout the early 1950s they lent their support to a range of field days and fund-raisers organised by nationalist groupings such as Sean Óglaigh na h-Éireann (IRA Veterans), Undivided Ireland and Clan na Gael (*Irish Echo*, 22 July 1950; 23 Dec. 1950). Such was the strength of the nexus between the GAA and agitation for a united Ireland that Vincent O'Donoghue and Pádraig Ó Caoimh, then president and general secretary of the GAA in Ireland, noted in a report to Central Council on their visit to New York with the touring Cork Gaelic football team in 1952, that the Association was 'the chief rallying ground, and the spearhead of National thought and action among the Irish of New York' (Central Council GAA Minutes, 21 Nov. 1952). That this was the case was due largely to the presence in the New York GAA's ranks of a number of prominent Irish republicans, particularly John 'Kerry' O'Donnell[6] and former members of the IRA. The central involvement of Matthew Higgins, then president of the United Irish Counties Association (UICA) and a former IRA soldier, in the promotion of Gaelic games in the early 1950s was also noteworthy. His decision to play a more active role in the GAA not only meant that the Association benefited from a closer relationship with the UICA but also ensured that an explicitly political agenda remained close to the heart of its affairs (*Irish Echo*, 19 May 1951). Indeed, by 1957, the UICA was using Gaelic games to support its Full Freedom for All Ireland Committee, which was established specifically to raise funds for the 'fight against the British Army occupation in north-east Ireland (*Irish Echo*, 16 Feb. 1957: 5).

While Higgins was influential, it was the involvement of Michael Flannery in the city's GAA that perhaps did most to underscore and reinforce its republican persona at this time. Born in Tipperary, Flannery had joined the Irish Volunteers at 14 before joining the Tipperary Brigade No. 1 of the IRA. He was a veteran of the Irish Civil War and in 1927, like so many others on the republican side, he emigrated to the US. He settled in Queen's and quickly immersed himself in the city's Irish community, joining and subsequently attaining high office in a range of cultural and political organisations including: the Tipperary Men's Association, Clan na Gael, the Ancient Order of Hibernians, the UICA, the American-Irish Action Committee, the American Congress for Irish Freedom and of course, the GAA (Rohan, 1994a). Flannery was perhaps most widely known for his role in the establishment of Irish Northern Aid, or Noraid as it came to be popularly known, in 1970.[7] Such were his republican credentials that his obituary in *The New York Times* noted that 'The fight of the Irish against the British was the great theme of Mr Flannery's life' (Martin, 1994: 64).[8]

For Flannery, involvement in the GAA was an extension of his politics and he clearly felt that Gaelic games should play a role in the promotion of the republican movement in New York. He was elected president of the New York board in 1957 and during his tenure he, along with other republican sympathisers within the GAA's ranks, including Higgins, John 'Kerry' O'Donnell, George Harrison, Liam Cotter and John English, ensured that the Association was at the vanguard of fund-raising efforts for a variety of nationalist organisations and events. This was evident almost as soon as Flannery became president of the New York board. In late March of his first year in office, a field day held under the auspices of the Irish Freedom Committee took place at Gaelic Park to 'support the Irish Republican Army' and the healthy attendance at the event revealed how well disposed he as well as New York's broader GAA fraternity was to this mixing of sport with republican politics (Meagher, 1957; *Irish Echo*, 6 Apr. 1957). As well as being backed by the Association's rank and file membership, Flannery's use of the GAA to lend political and financial support to the IRA was supported by prominent Irish Americans in New York, perhaps most notably Paul O'Dwyer, the famous New York City Counsellor, civil rights lawyer and brother of former mayor of New York, William O'Dwyer.[9] Buoyed by such support, the Association's leadership in New York continued to sponsor and promote a range of other republican events including those organised by the Northern Republican Society, Clan na Gael and the IRA Veterans (*Irish Echo*, 27 Apr. 1957).

The GAA continued to publicise and promote the republican agenda throughout the late 1950s and 1960s, with Flannery remaining centrally involved. He was not alone in influencing the Association in this way. Sean Maxwell was another IRA veteran who almost immediately sought out the GAA on his arrival in New York from County Leitrim in 1949 and, following a playing career with Leitrim football club, he took up a number of administrative positions, including secretary of the city's GAA in 1962 and 1963. The extent to which the Association in New York was dominated by republican-minded immigrants was made clear by John Byrne, the Gaelic games columnist for the *Irish Echo*, who recalled on Maxwell's death in 1970, that it was at the GAA's administrative headquarters in Kelly's in upper Manhattan, and later at Gaelic Park, that Maxwell met 'his kind of people'. Byrne acknowledged that the symbiosis between the GAA and the nationalist movement in New York was such that it was inevitable that Maxwell should seek involvement in Gaelic games:

> Because Sean knew the important role of the Gaelic Athletic Association in resurrecting Ireland's national aspirations and keeping them inviolate through the years of war and persecution, it was natural that he became wholeheartedly associated with the Gaelic Athletic Association in New York (Byrne, 7 Mar. 1970: 22).

This same symbiosis was evident elsewhere in the US in the 1950s and early 1960s and did much to ensure that, at a time when Irish America had lost much of its interest in Ireland, its politics and its culture, Gaelic games was able to survive and prosper.

Conclusion

In many senses, the continued support that emanated from US branches of the GAA for militant nationalism in the period between the partition of Ireland and the late 1960s was somewhat out of step with the broader cultural and political shift in Irish America, which saw declining levels of interest in the Irish nationalist agenda. Paradoxically, the survival of the Association and its growth in the 1950s were partially rooted in the fact that, at a time when opportunities to give expression to a more politicised, militant form of Irishness were shrinking, the GAA provided a platform where those Irish Americans who remained disgruntled and angry at the continued partition of Ireland could give vent to revolutionary nationalism. While the aspirations of Irish nation-alists rarely registered in a significant way in the political antennae of the majority of Irish Americans from the late 1920s through to the mid 1960s, the onset of serious civil unrest in Northern Ireland in the late 1960s and the start of the Troubles did much to reignite concerns around the Irish question within a large proportion of the diaspora. Indeed, in the space of a few short years, marginal, politicised versions of Irishness, of the type championed by the GAA's influential republican element during the 1950s and 1960s, began to be realigned with broader swathes of popular Irish-American political opinion. This will be further explored in chapter 10. It is first necessary, however, to account for the fortunes of Gaelic games in Boston, Chicago, San Francisco and New York between 1970 and the beginning of the new millennium, in order to complete the historical narrative of the GAA's development in the US.

...g to survive: the North American County Board in the late twentieth century

Introduction

If the playing of organised, codified versions of Gaelic games in America was to reach the milestone of 100 years, the NACB would require all of the resolve and resilience that had seen it survive the bleak years of the 1930s and 1940s. The challenges that confronted the Association at the beginning of the 1970s were as significant as any that it had faced previously. The 1965 Immigration Act and economic progress in Ireland had severely dented the number of Irish disembarking in the US; with those who had emigrated in the 1950s and early 1960s retiring from active participation, the GAA's ranks were becoming increasingly depleted. Little support was to be found in the existing Irish-American population, most of whom had fully assimilated into the US and retained, at best, only a transient, residual Irishness. There did not appear to be an easy remedy and, perhaps for the first time since the conclusion of the Second World War, the NACB was forced to think about how best to preserve a meaningful presence. This chapter addresses the fortunes of the GAA in Boston, Chicago and San Francisco in the last three decades of the twentieth century and, in doing so, charts the ways that the Association in each locale negotiated the difficulties that beset it, as it sought to remain relevant, both quantitatively and qualitatively, in Irish America.

A 'bright jewel': the Boston GAA since 1970

As was observed in chapter 6, with a well co-ordinated centralised body directing developments, steady growth characterised the development of Gaelic games in Boston during the late 1950s and first half of the 1960s, with an increasing number of clubs from the city and New England region affiliating to the NACB.[1] Visits from county teams including Down, Kerry and Roscommon, amongst others, as well as exhibition matches involving the Connaught Railway Cup footballers and All-Star select teams, did much to maintain the profile of Gaelic football and hurling in this period. Tours by club teams from various counties in Ireland also contributed, not least a visit in 1966 by the Cork hurling team Glen Rovers, captained by one of the GAA's most famous personalities, Christy Ring (NACB, 1997). Despite this progress, the 1965 Immigration Act and the subsequent slowing in rates of immigration threatened this steady progress. The clearest signs of this were fluctuations in the number of clubs competing for the New England championship in the late 1960s and early 1970s. While nine football and four hurling clubs took part in the 1965 season, by 1972 these numbers had decreased to four in football and three in hurling (NACB, 1997).

This quantitative decline in GAA clubs in the Boston area was the cause of serious concern; the city's Gaels quickly sought ways to arrest its slump and re-establish interest and ultimately a healthy complement of clubs. Together with the increased practice of bringing out players from Ireland to play for the city's clubs, one of the earliest innovations was the first live closed-circuit telecasting of the All-Ireland Gaelic football and hurling finals from Ireland to Boston. This development, occurring for the first time in 1973 but repeated every year thereafter, helped to regenerate flagging levels of interest in Gaelic games. More importantly, the New England board also began to give sustained thought to the promotion of a youthful grassroots for the game and the provision of opportunities for second and third-generation Irish Americans to continue the sporting traditions of their parents and grandparents. This gave rise to the establishment of a number of under-age clubs in the early 1970s (North East Gaelic Athletic Association, 2000), and by the middle of the decade there were enough teams to inaugurate a youth league which operated under the steward-ship of the Kerry-born GAA stalwart and former chairman of the New England divisional GAA board, Jimmy Maunsell (*Irish Emigrant*, 30 Nov. 1998: 64–5).[2] The effect of these developments was such that by the end of the 1970s the complement of Gaelic football clubs had returned to a healthier position – totalling ten. Significantly for the level of sporting provision for Boston's female Irish community in this period, three camogie clubs were established and by the early 1980s they were competing in regular competition against one another.[3]

The live airing of the final of the All-Ireland series in Boston, the inception of minor football and an emerging culture of camogie were clearly crucial in ensuring that the city's clubs were less dependent on immigration and that a long-standing GAA tradition was able to survive and prosper through the 1970s. Of equal significance was the broader practical role that the Association continued to play for sections of the Irish community in Boston and its immediate surrounds. As it had from its inception in the late 1870s and early 1880s, the GAA here remained an invaluable socio-economic, political and cultural resource for post-war migrants. It allowed those who felt so inclined to reconnect with their Irishness on a regular basis and helped to satisfy their yearnings for Ireland and its cultural and sporting traditions. In articulating the role of the Association in this sense, John Hehir, a highly respected figure in Boston GAA circles and former president of the NACB, argued that 'The GAA is our heritage, our tradition, it is what we are all about. It defines us better than any Irish organisation that I know of' (interview, 15 Aug. 2000). The fact that the GAA club was instantly recognisable as a distinctively Irish sporting and cultural space was clearly central to its appeal as was the fact that immersion in Gaelic games helped to provide Irish immigrants with a sense of the familiar and a continuity with their lived experiences in the cities, towns, villages and parishes that they had left behind. John Hehir again encapsulates the significance of the Association in this respect:

> The GAA is very important especially for newcomers because on the day you arrive here you may have left home for the first time. So you meet some friends and they take you down to Dilboy (former home of the GAA in Boston). Well, you are immediately in an environment that you recognise quickly as being a friendly one. It took some of the edge and roughness of being 3,000 miles from home (interview, 15 Aug. 2000).

This was a view shared by Connie Kelly, former Public Relations Officer for the North Eastern GAA Board, who described the role of the GAA in Boston in this period as 'an extended family' which 'helped people settle into life over here straight away' (interview, 30 July 2000).

Apart from providing this general sense of communal belonging and easing the transition into their new home, immersion in GAA activities in Boston also afforded sections of Irish Americans with opportunities to express very specific elements of their identity. Up to the late 1960s, Gaelic games allowed the city's migrants to give vent to a combination of largely benign, culturally centred versions of Irishness as well as more militant expressions of their Irish identity. With the onset of the Troubles in Northern Ireland in the late 1960s, the GAA in Boston came to represent one of a number of focal points for the expression of politicised Irish nationalist sentiment (see chapter 10). This is not to suggest that the identities articulated by the city's Gaels from the late 1960s onwards were shaped entirely by political events in Northern Ireland. The GAA in Boston also continued to allow for more regionalised, county-based forms of identity. This was because clubs, since the inception of Gaelic games in Boston, had often been formed around county-based affiliations and matches between such clubs provided players, administrators, benefactors and spectators with opportunities to renew the intense county rivalry upon which elite-level Gaelic sport in Ireland was based. This came very much to the fore in the post-war period and was accentuated by the establishment of the NACB and the inauguration of regional competition. Although clubs such as Cork, Kerry, Mayo, Donegal and the many others that were formed with county loyalties in mind were not always composed solely of players and officials from one county, they still permitted sections of the Irish diaspora to identify themselves not only as Irish but also as belonging to a particular county in Ireland. One member of the Boston Kerry club put into words the significance of membership of GAA clubs in allowing individuals the opportunity to express a sense of allegiance and belonging to 'their' county:

> I find it very hard if a person comes over from Kerry and he plays for another county. I actually feel offended . . . At our banquets we would have 400 people attend and 90 per cent of them would be from Kerry. So people from the same county do support each other. Most of the other clubs would be the same. For example, Cork are very clannish and they support each other 100 per cent (interview, 30 July 2000).[4]

The solace and support provided by the GAA for the city's Irish population in the 1970s extended beyond the psychological and the affirmation of particular identities. While there were far fewer Gaelic sport-playing Irish immigrants coming into the city, involvement in a GAA club or attendance at a match in Boston continued to provide networking opportunities that helped with what could be transient employment opportunities. As John Hehir notes: 'The GAA also did its bit to welcome them (Irish immigrants). If you went down to Dilboy Stadium on a Sunday and you had no job, you would very likely have one going home. Somebody would know if there was a day's work or a day's pay available' (interview, 15 Aug. 2000).

The long-standing tradition of the Irish in Boston benefiting economically from an association with the GAA carried on after the 1970s. The Association proved to be invaluable for the new waves of immigrants who arrived in the 1980s following a downturn in the Irish economy and soaring levels of unemployment which encouraged tens of thousands to emigrate to the US. Most of those who took the decision to leave Ireland for the US in this period failed to meet the stringent requirements of the 1965 Immigration Act but they came nonetheless, staying on to live and work illegally when their visas expired. For these migrants, the cultivation of ethnic contacts and ties was essential if they were to find regular work in the informal economy, particularly with an employer who was unlikely to ask awkward questions about legal status or official documentation (Corcoran, 1997). The GAA in Boston offered a fruitful route into the sorts of ethnic networks that helped in this process and provided access to established figures in the Irish community who were in a position to make job offers. With most GAA clubs supported by a range of entrepreneurial Irish businessmen, self-made building contractors and those who owned other more small-scale blue collar enterprises, employment and the sense of security that came with working for someone from your own ethnic community were readily available for those who became involved in Gaelic games in the city. All parties benefited. Immigrant Gaels secured gainful employment; Irish businesses had a ready-made pool of relatively cheap and hard-working employees and the promise of work from those with connections to particular clubs ensured that new arrivals saw the value in ingratiating themselves into the local GAA.

It was not only those whose stay was either long-term or permanent that benefited from the economic incentives attached to participation in Gaelic games in Boston in this period. As noted in chapter 6 various GAA clubs in the US made financial provision for players coming over from Ireland, either for specific matches or for full seasons from as early as the 1950s. The post-war influx of new Irish immigrants and fresh talent for the GAA ensured that this trend was relatively limited. However, it began to increase through the late 1980s and particularly into the 1990s when the strengthening economic climate in Ireland persuaded increasing numbers of Irish immigrants, including those who played Gaelic games, to return home. This rendered clubs increasingly dependent on bringing players over from Ireland in order to compete for honours, sustain their reputations and win bragging rights. The clubs organised fund-raisers, sold raffle tickets and drew on wealthy benefactors to raise the finances necessary to offer the sorts of inducement packages that would attract the best talent from Ireland. This made the prospect of a summer playing for a club in Boston or any of the other major NACB divisions an attractive proposition for prospective players. In many cases, the opportunity to reside in the US cheaply or free of charge and have a guaranteed job through involvement with one of the city's GAA clubs became a central factor in enticing new and often highly skilled playing talent into the city during the summer months.[5] This was, and remains, the case for those Gaelic sport playing third-level students who acquire J1 visas that allow them to live and work in the US during their summer vacation period.

The incentive package offered at this time to elite-level players – those who were playing or who had played at inter-county level – also included direct payment for playing.[6] This practice, denied by some GAA officials in the US and openly acknowledged by others, has historically caused considerable acrimony between the NACB and GAA Central Council in Dublin, largely because it contravenes the strictly amateur ethos of the Association.[7] Croke Park has been relatively powerless in halting this practice, because the only penalty that it has open to it – the suspension of a player receiving payment for playing and the suspension of the club making such payments – can only be imposed with irrefutable proof. With both clubs and players publicly denying that this practice goes on, it has been difficult for the Association to gather the requisite evidence and act accordingly (interview with John Hehir, 15 Aug. 2000). Thus, in their quest for divisional and national honours, clubs in Boston and throughout the US have overlooked the amateur cornerstone of GAA activities and have paid and continue to pay top-level players for their services.

The practice of offering attractive incentives to some of Ireland's most talented footballers and hurlers allowed the standard of Gaelic games to remain high throughout the 1990s, ensuring that quantitative growth characterised the GAA's development in Boston. By the middle of the decade, the addition of three new clubs – Boston Mayo, Notre Dame and Aiden McAnespies – brought the total number of clubs in the greater Boston area to 24. As a reflection of the rapid popularisation of ladies' Gaelic football in Ireland during the 1990s, four of these clubs – Boston Shamrocks, Tír na nÓg, Roscommon and Waterford – were established in order to provide sporting opportunities for Boston's female Irish community (Gaughran, 1999). While this growth was welcome and established the North Eastern board as the strongest of the NACB's divisions, the fact that it was rooted in the ability of Boston's clubs to offer attractive incentive packages increasingly polarised views and led to a debate about how best to protect and preserve Gaelic games in the longer term. Some, particularly those involved with Boston's more prominent clubs, saw no difficulty in continuing to import and pay for quality talent from Ireland. As they saw it, they were able to generate the funds necessary to bring over high-profile players and, for as long as this remained the case, there was no reason not to continue to do so. Others within the North Eastern division, and more generally in the NACB, were less convinced about the long-term value of this strategy. They argued that while it was always entertaining for GAA followers to watch high-profile players from Ireland displaying their abilities, this approach concentrated too much on the short term. They suggested that the money that was being used to pay these players would be better invested in the sort of youth infrastructures that would help secure the longer-term health of Gaelic games. This debate continued throughout the 1990s and, as will be demonstrated in the conclusion to this book, it became much more divisive in the aftermath of the terrorist attacks on New York on 11 September 2001 and the subsequent tightening of immigration into the US.

Provision for youth Gaelic sport was not being totally neglected in late 1980s and 1990s. Some worked diligently to promote Gaelic football to second- and third-generation Irish-American children and by 1985 a total of 13 teams were playing at various age ranges including under-18, under-16, under-14 and under-12 (NACB, 1997). By the middle of the following decade, under-age football in Boston received a significant boost with the formation of the New England minor football board in 1996. The positive response to the activities organised by this board was such that, in 1998, it was renamed the Irish Sports Youth League of New England to reflect the broadening of its target age range to accommodate children as young as six (*The Boston Irish Reporter*, 1 July 1999: 35). This programme brought almost immediate results at under-age level, with a New England select team capturing its first national under-18 title in 1998. Of equal significance, the playing talent that came through the Youth League helped to swell the ranks of a number of junior clubs in Boston with the result that, by the end of the decade, most of the clubs competing at this level had at least one American-born player whilst some had as many as four (Breslin, 2000a).[8]

The century ended with what was undoubtedly one of the most influential developments in the history of Gaelic sports in Boston. In terms of playing facilities, participants and spectators had enjoyed their 'national' games in a variety of leased venues throughout Boston and New England.[9] The renting of facilities was not ideal, and as early as 1974 Gaelic games enthusiasts sought opportunities for the purchase of a site to construct their own playing field. Connie Kelly, then secretary of the Kerry Gaelic football club, took the lead, approaching the city's mayor, governor and local building contractors, but his efforts ultimately came to nothing (*Boston News*, 3 Mar. 1974). The construction of purpose-built facilities in Chicago at Gaelic Park in 1984 revived interest in this idea, and in the late 1980s a strong lobby emerged in support of plans to construct a permanent home for Gaelic sports in Boston. Mike O'Connor, a native of County Galway, who had been involved in the administration of Gaelic games in Boston and also a former treasurer of the NACB, was particularly influential. In 1990, after deciding that such a venture should encompass other elements of Irish culture such as music, dance and language, he, along with some of his Irish friends and colleagues, established the Irish Cultural Centre (ICC), a non-profit corporation (*Irish Voice*, 5 Oct. 1999). After a series of annual festivals and other fund-raising initiatives the ICC was able to purchase 47 acres of land in 1996 in the Boston suburb of Canton. Three years later, Phase I of the project was complete and, as part of an agreement which guaranteed GAA clubs exclusive use of the playing fields, the North Eastern division of the NACB made a $200,000 contribution to the ICC (*Boston Irish Reporter*, Apr. 1999: 3). As a sign of the Canton facility's status as the new focal point for Irish sporting and cultural pastimes in Boston and its neighbouring suburbs and towns, the opening was marked with an exhibition match featuring the All-Ireland hurling champions Cork and the 1998 All-Star select team, as well as a rematch of the 1999 All-Ireland football final between Cork and Meath (*Irish Voice*, 5 Oct. 1999). Dermot Ahern, the then Irish minister for Social, Community and Family Affairs, and the GAA president at the time, Joe McDonagh, were also in attendance for the opening. In his dedication of the new facility, McDonagh commended the vibrancy of the North Eastern GAA board and referred to Boston as 'a bright jewel in the crown of the GAA's growth outside Ireland' (*Boston Irish Reporter*, Oct. 1999: 20).

Gaelic games in late twentieth-century Chicago

At the beginning of the 1970s, the GAA appeared to be in better health in Chicago than in Boston. While a combination of the 1965 Immigration Act and the subsequent slowing of Irish immigration led to Boston shedding some of its clubs, the complement of teams in Chicago remained steady. By 1970 there were eight clubs in existence, playing either hurling or Gaelic football (NACB, 1997).[10] This figure remained constant for the first half of the decade revealing that the Immigration Act had little impact, quantitatively at least, on Gaelic games in the city. There were three main reasons for this. The first was linked to the fact that the Association had made provision for minors to become involved in Gaelic football from as early as 1972,[11] and in doing so helped to ensure that the clubs had an emerging pool of playing talent to draw on. The willingness of the city's teams to open themselves up to anyone, irrespective of nationality, who was eager to play, was another reason why the GAA was able to survive despite immigration restrictions. Liam O'Brien, a former chairman of the Chicago central divisional board, commenting at the time, acknowledged that the significant slowing of Irish immigrants into the city had forced the clubs to go down this more cosmopolitan recruitment route: 'The whole thing (slowing of immigration) is hastening the Americanization of these sports. Some clubs now have Germans, Italians, anybody who wants to play' (cited in Husar, 1976: G4). The final, and undoubtedly most significant strategy adopted by the clubs to survive in an era of severely restricted immigration was to recruit, by means of attractive incentives, a proportion of their players from Ireland for the duration of the summer season. As Husar noted at the time:

> Now that the mainstays of these demanding Gaelic games are getting on in years, new blood must be sought – any way it can be found . . . Each year, some 20 to 30 young, husky Irishmen arrive in Chicago to spend the summer with relatives or 'friends'. Often, they will find jobs, no matter what their visa limitations say. Sometimes, even their air fare will have been paid by one of the clubs with a hectic fund-raising campaign (Husar, 1976: G4).

While this strategy was employed by both football and hurling teams, the city's hurling clubs were more reliant on this source of playing talent because of the pedagogical difficulties, perceived or otherwise, involved in coaching what is a highly technical and skilled sport to the young children of Irish immigrant parents (Pridmore, 1983). Nonetheless, this three-fold approach to the challenge presented by the 1965 Immigration Act allowed the Association in Chicago to survive in this period and even experience moderate growth. This was perhaps most clearly shown by the setting up of two camogie clubs, St Bridget's and Erin Rovers in 1975, thus ending a 16-year lapse in the playing of this sport on Chicago soil (Pridmore, 1983). The first closed-circuit telecast of an All-Ireland football final in 1974 undoubtedly contributed to this modest growth,[12] as did the hosting of the All-Star hurling and Gaelic football teams from Ireland. A visit by Cork and Dublin footballers in 1977 to play a series of exhibition games, including a high profile match under floodlights, added further lustre to the city's culture of Gaelic sports. By the end of the 1977 season there were 13 clubs competing for honours in hurling, Gaelic football and camogie (NACB, 1997).

This growth proved to be unsustainable, and by 1980 the number of Gaels in the city could fill the ranks of only eight clubs. In order to address the loss of gate revenue heralded by this decline in the number of clubs and hence, competitive matches, the Chicago central divisional board decided to increase admission prices to its regular Sunday games from $2 to $3. This ensured that the finances of the board remained relatively healthy, but the loss of another club, St Vincent's, in 1981, sounded alarm bells amongst those with responsibility for the promotion and preservation of Gaelic games. Additional energy and effort were quickly invested into the youth game and, by the following year, the Chicago minor board boasted a membership in excess of 200 children. This helped to slow the decline and the formation of two ladies' Gaelic football teams, Erin Rovers and McBrides, a year later, underscored the GAA's resilience (NACB, 1997).

The relative health of Gaelic games in Chicago during the late 1970s and early 1980s encouraged a number of members of the Association to seek out a permanent home for their sports. In the post-war era, the GAA had used a variety of leased venues for matches including Shewbridge Stadium, Rockne Stadium, Hansen Stadium, Melrose Park, as well as a range of other public parks and facilities for training. This renting of playing facilities was far from ideal, and by 1978 it was decided that an appropriate site would be sought as a solution to the perennial problem of finding a space to host Gaelic games and other Irish cultural events in the city (NACB, 1997). Four years later a 9.5-acre stretch of land was purchased in unincorporated Tinley Park in the city's South Side. Work began on the site in the autumn of 1983, overseen by a 15-strong board of directors, many of whom were GAA stalwarts. By the summer of the following year, voluntary labour, financial donations, the gifting of materials and loans of equipment from the local Irish community saw 'Chicago Gaelic Park' ready to host its first series of fixtures. The naming of the new facility clearly marked it out as a specifically Irish sporting and cultural space. This was further reinforced by the decision to record the official address with Cook County, where the park was located, as 6119 W. 147th Street. The opening four-digit number was not officially required under Cook County guidelines but, according to the NACB's official history, these digits were deliberately chosen by the Chicago central divisional board to incorporate the date of the Easter Rising (1916), hence allowing them to show their 'appreciation of (their) forebears who sacrificed themselves for Ireland' (NACB, 1997: 124). Chicago Gaelic Park was officially opened in July 1985, with a schedule of games in hurling, senior and junior Gaelic football taking place in front of an estimated crowd of 5,000 (Prescott, 1985).[13]

The remainder of the 1980s was a successful period in the history of the Association in Chicago. Continued tours by the All-Star hurlers and footballers as well as exhibition games by county teams from Cork and Kerry at Gaelic Park cemented this venue's place as the epicentre of Irish sporting activity in the city. Gaelic Park was not, however, merely the focal point of Gaelic games. The two-storey complex, built as part of the Gaelic Park project, also provided space for use by a range of Irish cultural organisations and the Irish community in Chicago more generally, allowing it to become the main hub of all Irish-related cultural activity in the city (McLaughlin, 2002). The status of the facility was officially recognised in 1991 when it was visited by Mary Robinson, then president of Ireland, during a stay in Chicago (NACB, 1997). Buoyed by this honour, the directors of Gaelic Park started work in 1992 to expand the facilities to incorporate two new stands, while the GAA's Chicago central divisional board borrowed $80,000 in 1993 to cover the costs of further development in advance of the city's hosting of the 1994 NACB play-offs (NACB, 1997).

The healthy position of the GAA in the city in this period was not only based on the construction of a permanent home for Gaelic games. While the ranks of the clubs were sustained in part by the fruits of the promotion of the games to second and third-generation Irish Americans and the involvement of a small number of players from a range of ethnic groups (Leptich, 1990; *Chicago Tribune*, 28 Aug. 1994), changes in migratory patterns between Ireland and the US and alterations in the provisions governing this process made a significant contribution in more deeply embedding the GAA in Chicago. As observed earlier in this chapter, the downturn in the Irish economy revived levels of Irish immigration – much of it illegal – into the US. As was the case in Boston, the GAA in Chicago allowed many of these migrants to negotiate the difficulties that their undocumented status created in terms of finding work. Apart from an interest in Irish sport, this was one of the draws of the GAA for illegal immigrants and ensured that the ranks of the Association were sustained by those from this sector of the émigrés.

In addition to these waves of illegal immigrants, Irish communities in the US, particularly in the cities of Chicago, Boston, New York and San Francisco (*Chicago Tribune*, 28 Aug. 1994), saw further influxes of Irish migrants as a result of two special immigration laws. The first, introduced in 1986, allocated over 16,000 of a total of 40,000 of what came to be known as 'Donnelly visas' to Ireland in the period between 1987 and 1990. [14] The Immigration Act of 1990 made provision for a further 120,000 visas, dubbed 'Morrison visas', with Ireland being given a guarantee of 16,000 per year between 1990 and 1993. It is difficult to ascertain with any certainty how many of those who acquired these visas became involved in the GAA in Chicago and elsewhere. However, the influx of legal immigrants, coupled with the continued presence of 'illegals', certainly contributed to the GAA as well as to a whole host of other Irish-ethnic institutions. The inception of two new clubs in Chicago, Padraig Pearses in football and CuChulainns in hurling in 1993 and 1994, was testament to this, as was the continued expansion of facilities at Gaelic Park.[15]

The remainder of the 1990s saw the GAA consolidate in Chicago. The strength of the 'Celtic Tiger' and a subsequent slowing in rates of emigration from Ireland precluded any substantive growth. While the century ended with a reasonable complement of four senior football teams, four in senior hurling, five at junior level in football, three ladies' football teams and one minor level team (Robinson, 2000), there were emerging concerns from within the GAA fraternity and the local Irish community about what the future might hold for their sports. The Association in Chicago had long catered for young Irish Americans eager to continue the sporting traditions of their forebears. However, in 1998, a number of volunteers took it upon themselves to expand the city's youth programme to incorporate children between the ages of five and 14. The motivation behind this development was undoubtedly about ensuring a sustainable future for Gaelic games in the city, but it was also linked to the personal desire on the part of Irish immigrants in the city to see their children grow up practising sporting activities and being immersed in a cultural space that allowed them to maintain their Irish ethnicity. As Lisa O'Flaherty, a native of County Kerry and one of the founders of this programme commented:

> The turning point came one afternoon when my son turned to me during sports practice and said 'mom, when is the time-out?'. I said to myself, that's it, I don't want him to grow up as a Yank, I want him to grow up being involved in Irish pastimes (interview, 31 July 2005).

As well as providing sustenance to the GAA, the programmes initiated by O'Flaherty and other Irish migrants in the city also afforded opportunities for second and third-generation Irish Americans to rediscover latent senses of Irishness. This applied not only to male members of the Chicago-based diaspora but also to those females who developed an interest and subsequently became involved in Gaelic games. One such individual, Lisa Kreuger, born in Central Illinois to second-generation Irish parents, began playing camogie in the late 1990s and subsequently became public relations officer and treasurer of the

Chicago central division. She recounts the importance of an awareness of her Irish family lineage and the opportunity that involvement in both Gaelic Park and the GAA provided in terms of nurturing and developing a growing awareness of her Irishness:

> I got involved because of my family. I had seen photographs but had no idea about the culture of the GAA. I got really involved in Gaelic Park and then the GAA which really helped me to reconnect with my Irish heritage. . . . It's important to me to do all I can to help promote the sport and the culture. When my great grandparents came over here, they did everything they could to blend in . . . they tried to hide their culture because they felt that they had to. They changed their name when they came over because they felt that Keane was too Irish so they changed it to Kane. Being able to reconnect with my Irishness and meeting people that you have something in common with is important to me (interview, 30 July 2005).

With this sort of commitment to promote Gaelic games amongst Irish Americans, the continued ability of clubs to pay handsomely for high profile Irish-based county stars and a ringing endorsement of Gaelic Park from Irish president, Mary McAleese, who commented during a visit in 2003 that the facility was 'one of the finest GAA centres that I have seen outside of Croke Park in Dublin' (cited in Hennessy, 2008), it appeared that the future of the GAA in twenty-first century Chicago was secure. However, a number of serious challenges had to be faced in the opening years of the new millennium, which threatened to undo all that had been achieved in the previous century. The first of these involved the terrorist attacks on 9/11 and the subsequent tightening of US border controls and thus, as a corollary, the reduction in levels of Irish immigration. The potential of these developments to undermine the GAA in Chicago and across the US was clear. What was required at this juncture was a coordinated approach between the clubs and the divisional board aimed at counteracting the likelihood of a significant reduction in recruits from Ireland. However, at the start of the millennium, Chicago's clubs were in no mood to work together or with the divisional board, and instead allowed long-standing animosities and bitter rivalries to deteriorate and fester. The rivalry between the city's two leading Gaelic football clubs, Wolfe Tones and St Brendan's, was particularly problematic, wreaking havoc with the conclusion of the 2002 championship season in Chicago and tarnishing the NACB's showpiece tournament, the All-American play-off finals.[16]

While simmering club rivalries were perceived by many within the Association as standing in the way of progress, it was an overhaul of the rules governing the import of players from Ireland and the reaction of local clubs to this that did most to damage Gaelic games in Chicago in this period. Up to this point, GAA clubs in the US could field an unlimited number of 'home-based' players; that is, those who had transferred to the club before an agreed 'cut-off' date, usually in April. Teams could also import further 'sanctioned' players from Ireland after that date but before a further deadline, typically in late July. However, only three of these players per team were allowed on the field of play at any one time. These NACB bye-laws increasingly became the cause of much consternation and dissatisfaction from clubs and county boards in Ireland, who were regularly losing their most talented players to teams in the US who were able to offer financial inducements. By the start of the new millennium, the Dublin administration began applying pressure on the NACB to reconsider its rules in order to minimise the impact of its competitions on playing resources in Ireland (interview with Joe Begley, 31 July 2005). At the NACB's convention in 2004, a meeting that many delegates failed to attend, a set of reforms were introduced for the start of the 2005 season, which abolished the rules governing 'home-based' and 'sanction' players and replaced them with provisions that permitted senior clubs to import ten players from Ireland from 1 January until 20 July with eight being permitted to sign for intermediate teams and six for junior sides (interview with Tommy Dolan, 30 July 2005).[17]

Although these new regulations were seen as a reasonable compromise in both Boston and San Francisco (interview with Dolan, 31 July 2005), they angered some of Chicago's most influential clubs and a meeting with the Chicago central division was hastily convened. During heated exchanges, some club officials suggested that the board had tamely acquiesced to the demands of Central Council in Ireland. A motion was proposed by the clubs that they should not seek affiliation with the NACB and would thus operate outside the control of the parent body in Ireland. The motion was passed with an overwhelming majority and this brought with it the very real possibility of lengthy suspensions for those players representing clubs that were not properly affiliated. Rather than face this prospect, the city's hurling and football clubs, with the exception of St Brendan's, decided that they would record their distaste for the rule changes by not entering senior teams for the 2005 season (interview with Joe Begley, 31 July 2005; interview with Eamonn Kelly, 29 July 2005). For the first time since the inception of the Chicago central division, no competitive senior level hurling or football took place in the city. These events were clearly potentially disastrous for the future of Gaelic games. However, faced with the prospect of a further year without senior-level club competition and participation in the All-American play-offs, the dissenting clubs relented and re-entered their senior teams for the 2006 season. This decision minimised any longer-term damage that might have been done and by 2008 the schedule of fixtures for the season was much healthier, involving as it did four hurling clubs, six Gaelic football teams, three ladies' football clubs, a camogie club and the Chicago youth team.

From a low ebb: San Francisco's Gaels towards the century's end

As was outlined in chapter 6, the position of the GAA in San Francisco at the end of the 1960s was decidedly precarious. The 1965 Immigration Act had wreaked havoc on the clubs and, apart from a fledgling youth programme, there was little in the way of meaningful local participation in Gaelic games. At adult level, the only games that took place in the early to mid-1970s were those organised by the United Irish societies, featuring Ireland's All-Star footballers and hurlers (interview with Mike Moriarity, 27 Aug. 2006).[18] These games did much to keep sections of the San Francisco Irish interested in Gaelic sport (O'Murchu, 1985), but the lack of immigrants and thus of new playing talent meant that a resumption of senior competition seemed a long way off. As the early 1970s progressed, however, the youth programme, led by the San Francisco GAA stalwart Danny Boyle, yielded some success and helped to maintain at least some level of local participation. The emergence of a minor Gaelic football team, Hibernians, was particularly notable. In 1973, under Danny Boyle's tutelage, the team toured Ireland, playing seven games, including two at Croke Park, and winning six. What was significant about this team, beyond its role in keeping Gaelic games alive in the city, was that all of the players were born in San Francisco and, while most had Irish parents or grandparents, some had no Irish connections at all (NACB, 1997). Recruits with names such as Salvemini and Azofeifa revealed that the youth programme in the city was predicated on inclusivity and that membership was not constrained by narrow ethnic boundaries. This was clearly a pragmatic response to a dearth of playing talent at the time, but it was also underpinned by a philosophy with roots going as far back as the early 1950s.[19]

The positive response to the fund-raising events that took place in San Francisco to facilitate the Hibernians' trip to Ireland demonstrated that there was certainly an appetite for Gaelic sport amongst the local Irish community. The continued progress being made at youth level offered some hope that the reformation of adult clubs and competition was not too far away. A further indication of the possibility of renewed GAA competition in the city came in 1974 when local Gaels were able to raise a select team to play the visiting footballers of the Irish Civil Service (NACB, 1997). Within three years of this game, competitive Gaelic football and hurling returned to the city with the inception of Shannon Rangers and San Francisco Gaels, both of which formed hurling and football teams (interview with Mike Moriarity, 27 Aug. 2006; NACB, 1997). The new senior Gaelic football championship was completed with the addition of Hibernians, who were by this stage able to offer a platform to those who had graduated from the youth programmes and who wanted to continue to play Gaelic football into adulthood. While Hibernians were unable to continue to field a senior team beyond the 1977 season, the ranks of the San Francisco GAA were added to in 1979 with the formation of the Sean McDermotts Gaelic football club (NACB, 1997).

As increasing numbers of Irish immigrants began to flow into the US following the downturn in Ireland's economic fortunes, the GAA in San Francisco was able to build on this growth. In 1982 the San Francisco Harps added to the city's roster of football clubs. The Association expanded further in the following year when Sean McDermotts added a hurling team to its activities and a group of second-generation Irishmen established the Sons of Boru Gaelic football club in 1984 thus giving San Francisco a competitive championship in both hurling and football (*The Irishman*, Apr. 1984). Such was the standard of play in evidence at the Polo Fields in the city's Golden Gate Park, then the chief venue for Gaelic games in the city, that San Francisco Gaels won the NACB hurling championship in 1985, successfully capturing the city's first national title in over 20 years (O'Reilly, 1985). Buoyed by this success, 1986 saw the formation of three more Gaelic football clubs, Young Irelands, Ulster and Clan na Gael. This not only reflected the burgeoning profile of the GAA in the city but also demonstrated the growing politicisation of Gaelic sport. The emergence of the Ulster club in particular was indicative of this trend and its militant nationalist undertones will be discussed in detail in chapter 10.

The confidence of the GAA in San Francisco at this time was so strong that they felt able to host the NACB's annual convention in 1987. By the time the city welcomed GAA delegates from all over the US, San Francisco was fielding nine Gaelic football teams and three in hurling (*The Irishman*, Mar. 1987). The 1988 season opened with an historical Gaelic football match between the visiting

All-Ireland football champions Meath and a San Francisco select and concluded with the city's first hosting of the NACB play-offs and a second North-American hurling crown for San Francisco Gaels (Burns, 1988; *The Irishman*, Mar. 1988). The contribution of this tournament to Gaelic sport in the Bay Area was inestimable, not least because GAA fans had the opportunity to witness at first hand some of Ireland's finest footballing and hurling talent, especially Jack O'Shea, the Kerry midfielder and one of the Association's greatest ever footballing talents, who lined out for Chicago Wolfe Tones (*The Irishman*, Sept./Oct. 1988). The impact of the 1988 play-offs was such that by the start of the following season two new football teams, Michael Cusacks and Naomh Padraig, had entered the fray. This saw Gaelic football reach its zenith with ten teams competing for the Western divisional crown, completing what was a decade of remarkable growth for the game in the city.

While football prospered in this period, hurling was much less popular. By the end of the 1980s there were only two hurling teams remaining in the city, San Francisco Gaels and Na Fianna. Part of the reason for this lay in the fact that hurling was a more technically demanding sport than Gaelic football and a more complex one to introduce to novices. As a consequence, the youth programmes that had been introduced to the city in the previous decade tended to concentrate on Gaelic football, a sport that possessed the basic skills that American-born children would have experienced while playing basketball, American football or soccer. This neglect of youth hurling became problematic when Irish emigration began to slow in the late 1980s and early 1990s following increases in Irish prosperity linked to the emerging Celtic Tiger. With fewer hurling-playing immigrants coming to the city and the lack of a pool of young Irish-American talent in the city, it was inevitable that the game would struggle.

In addition to the changing patterns of migration, two specific incidents in 1989 and 1990 damaged the profile of hurling in the city and almost sent the game into terminal decline. The first involved the cancellation of the annual All-Star hurling match in San Francisco in 1989, a decision that was taken, according to Danny Boyle, president of the United Irish Societies and the event's organiser, because of concerns that there was not the interest in hurling in the city to make the game financially viable (cited in Hession, 1989). While this was a blow to advocates of hurling, an incident during a game between Na Fianna and San Francisco Gaels in July 1990 at Polo Fields did the game untold damage and raised serious doubts about its future. The incident in question centred on a Na Fianna player, Bob O'Brien, who was knocked unconscious when he was struck in the head with a hurling stick by the San Francisco Gaels' player,

Andrew Jordan. When O'Brien reached hospital, it was discovered that he had suffered a fractured skull and a broken shoulder and was immediately operated on, a decision that effectively saved his life. This incident was anything but an unfortunate accident and Jordan, who had had a suspension imposed by the Western divisional board in the previous season for attacking a referee, albeit subsequently overturned by the NACB, was arrested and charged with assault. The case concluded in July 1991, when Jordan changed his plea to guilty and received a three-month jail sentence. Only a last minute plea bargain by Jordan's legal counsel saw him avoid a prison term (Matthews, 1990; 1991). This case, the first in Californian legal history that had resulted in criminal charges following a sporting injury (Hughes, 1993a: 1), although most unfortunate for O'Brien, also dealt hurling in San Francisco a dire blow. At the end of the trial, San Francisco Gaels disbanded, thus leaving the city with only one hurling club.

This, however, was the least of the Western divisional board's concerns. Shortly after the trial concluded, O'Brien initiated a $19 million dollar lawsuit against the NACB, the disbanded San Francisco Gaels and a number of individuals within the Western divisional board. The lawsuit began, and ultimately ended, with a test case against the NACB's San Francisco-based secretary, Pat Uniacke. The basis of O'Brien's case was the NACB's decision to overturn the locally imposed suspension on Jordan which he had received for his previous assault on a referee. O'Brien's legal counsel, Gerald Woods, argued that this constituted neglect on the part of the North-American GAA because they were all too aware of Jordan's 'propensity for violence' (cited in Hughes, 1993a: p. 1). Much to the relief of the NACB, the Western divisional board and those former members of San Francisco Gaels, the ruling of the presiding Superior Court Judge that Uniacke could not be held responsible for Jordan's actions effectively brought the affair to a close. Nonetheless, the circumstances surrounding the original incident and the subsequent court cases severely tarnished the reputation of hurling in the city. The affair also had the potential to make the sport a much less attractive pastime, not only for those Irish immigrants who had played the game at home and sought to continue to do so on America's west coast but also for those parents of second- or third-generation Irish-American boys, who were eager to see their children reconnect with their Irishness through involvement in Gaelic sport.

With the legal fallout of O'Brien's injuries coming to a conclusion, the GAA in San Francisco was able to concentrate once again on sporting matters. Their hosting of the 1993 NACB play-offs in San Francisco saw a return to some sense of normality in the city's GAA circles. The impetus generated by the scheduled hosting of this event also allowed the city's Gaels to redouble their efforts to revive hurling, and for the start of the 1993 season Cork and Naomh Padraig had joined Na Fianna to contest the local championship (NACB, 1997). Buoyed by these developments, the local GAA looked to the future with renewed optimism; its members actively sought ways to improve the profile of their sports and secure a prosperous future. The most significant move was undoubtedly the acquisition of a short-term lease on Kezar Stadium, the former home of the American Football franchise the San Francisco 49ers, by Cyril Hackett, a local sports promoter and playing member of the Michael Cusacks Gaelic football club. Hackett's idea to host games in the recently renovated stadium emerged from the difficulties that the local GAA were increasingly experiencing in securing permits for games at Polo Fields. With the Association actively looking for alternatives, Hackett took responsibility for renting the stadium, and in consultation with the clubs he scheduled a season of hurling, football and camogie games at the venue (Hughes, 1993b).

The hosting of Gaelic games in the modern surrounds of Kezar Stadium allowed the GAA to display their activities in a more professional manner. The Association also attempted to promote their sports beyond the city's Irish and Irish-American community by widely publicising the games through local media outlets. As Hackett commented at the time, 'We want to showpiece the uniqueness and excitement of Irish sporting games for everyone, not just Irish fans. I believe when American people see the games at first hand they will be thrilled' (cited in Hughes, 1993b: 1). When the programme of fixtures started in early June, the choice of venue and the more professional presentation of Gaelic games paid immediate dividends, with almost 400 people paying $5 per head to watch the programme of matches. This represented a significant increase in the number of spectators who would have attended an equivalent programme at Polo Fields in previous years and allowed Hackett to meet the costs of hiring the venue with ease (*Irish Herald*, July 1993). The success of the fixtures at Kezar Stadium during the 1993 season coupled with a well organised and patronised NACB play-off weekend provided a further boost to the GAA in the Bay Area. At the beginning of the following season the establishment of two women's football clubs, the Fog City Harps and Golden Gate Ladies, provided competition for the San Francisco Ladies Club which had been in existence since 1990; in doing so this added another important layer to the culture of Gaelic games in the city (*San Francisco Gael*, Mar. 1994).

Despite what was a healthy complement of clubs, the continuing drop-off in rates of Irish immigration encouraged local Gaels to continue their work to promote their games to the American-born youth market. The work of John O'Flynn, a long-standing and committed GAA member, was highly influential.[20] His ambitions for a successful youth programme came to fruition in 1994 when he, along with the help of some other local Gaels, established the Bay Area Irish Football Youth League (IFYL) (O'Regan, 1994). O'Flynn was appointed chairman of the league and, while the programme had modest beginnings, attracting around 75 children from age four and upwards in its first year, under his continued chairmanship it grew considerably (interview with John O'Flynn, 27 Aug. 2006). In a matter of just three years after its founding, the IFYL had a membership of over 500, and in 1998 an under-14 select drawn from the programme became the first team from the US to take part in the Féile Peil na nÓg, a festival held in Ireland for the best young players from home and overseas (Hughes, 1997). In recognition of their work in promoting Gaelic games to the youth of the Bay Area and, in a move which perhaps acknow-ledged that the future health of the GAA might lie in building an American-born grassroots, the clubs in the Western division donated $10,000 to this trip (*Irish Herald*, Mar. 1998). By the end of the century, the IFYL had grown further and had gained a significant foothold in some local high schools, with three teams from St Ignatius, Sacred Heart and a conglomerate select drawn from a number of other schools on the peninsula, forming and playing in regular competition (Mockler, 2000). Such was the success of this programme during the 1990s that some began to see the possibility of using it as a vehicle for promoting Gaelic games amongst children across North America. Shortly after the inception of the IFYL, O'Flynn was appointed as a liaison officer by the NACB with a view to encouraging more divisions to establish equivalent structures for under-age Gaelic games.

By the opening years of the 2000s, most major US cities had established youth leagues and O'Flynn, along with colleagues within the NACB, decided to establish a platform that would allow youth teams from across the country to play against one another. The result was the Continental Youth Championship (CYC), first held in 2004, featuring teams ranging from under-8 up to under-18 from the NACB, the New York Board and Canada (*Irish Herald*, Mar. 2004). The first edition of this tournament was held in New York and has since become an annual event, one proudly described by O'Flynn as 'the largest Gaelic sporting event held in one location in the whole world' (cited in *Irish America*, Apr.–May 2006: 66). Prior to the 2005 edition of the CYC in Foster City, California, Sean Kelly, then president of the GAA predicted with confidence that the tournament would become 'a valuable foundation stone for the future development and expansion of Gaelic games on the continent' (cited in *Irish Herald*, Aug. 2005: 3). The success of subsequent tournaments in Boston in 2006, Chicago in 2007 and Philadelphia in 2008, suggests that Kelly's confidence was not misplaced.

Conclusion

The profile of the GAA in Boston, Chicago and San Francisco from the early 1970s to the beginning of the twenty-first century was clearly dependent on fluctuations in Irish immigration to each city. The 1965 Immigration Act heralded a lull in migration during the 1970s and this brought about a sharp decline in the fortunes of many clubs, some of which were forced to fold. However, rising levels of unemployment in Ireland following an economic downturn in the late 1970s and 1980s revived the flow of Irish migrants seeking opportunities in the US, and this did much to regenerate the Association in this period. With the granting of Donnelly and Morrison visas in 1986 and 1990 respectively, and a continued rise in the numbers of undocumented Irish in the US in the early 1990s, the GAA seemed set for a period of sustained prosperity. However, with the Celtic Tiger persuading more young Irish people to remain at home as the 1990s progressed, anxieties about the preservation of Gaelic football, hurling and camogie on American soil began to resurface. The NACB's clubs were able to play down their concerns and veil the impact of slowing immigration by continuing to import high-profile players from Ireland, at least for part of the regular season. From around the mid-1990s, some began to question whether this strategy was likely to bring long-term benefits for Gaelic games in America. Following an increase in complaints from Ireland and abuses of the sanction system by clubs that were desperate to stay competitive despite the shrinking pool of Gaelic games enthusiasts resident in the US, Croke Park became involved in the debate, suspending players who had broken the rules[21] and, in 1998, tightened the regulations governing player transfers to the US.

Following the terrorist attacks on 9/11 and the closer policing of the arrangements governing immigration which resulted, many clubs continued to recruit openly and widely in Ireland and sometimes in contravention of agreed rules, much to the chagrin of county boards there, as well as the parent body. By 2002 this had created what was described by O'Riordan in the *Irish Times* as an 'exodus' of Gaelic sporting talent from Irish shores to the US (O'Riordan,

2002: 23). Complaints from clubs and county boards to Croke Park reached unprecedented levels and the GAA's Management Committee in Dublin decided to temporarily suspend all sanctions to the US. This suspension was quickly lifted, but the fact that it was imposed in the first place focused the minds of those with responsibility for the continued promotion of Gaelic games in America. Since then, some clubs have continued to call for a liberalisation of the rules governing transatlantic transfers, while others feel that the future of Gaelic games will be best sustained by nurturing an American-born grassroots. This debate, discussed in more detail in the concluding chapter, is likely to continue to feature prominently on the NACB's agenda for some time to come.

Although reduced immigration flows have clearly had a significant impact on the fortunes of Gaelic games in the US, it would be wrong to suggest that the GAA in Boston, Chicago and San Francisco sat idly by or watched passively while fluxes in migratory flows from Ireland either replenished or depleted their stocks. Those who were committed to the sustainability of the GAA in each city were proactive in their pursuit of a long-lasting and vibrant culture of Gaelic games. This was perhaps best demonstrated by the establishment of permanent home venues for the GAA in Chicago and Boston. While it was unable to acquire its own premises until late 2008,[22] the Association in San Francisco demonstrated its foresight and commitment in other ways in this period, not least through the establishment of the Bay Area IFYL in 1994, which has since developed into one of the largest and most successful GAA youth programmes in the US. Without the enthusiasm, commitment, generosity and ability of those who made these developments possible and championed the Association in other ways, it is unlikely that Gaelic games would have survived in America into the new millennium, irrespective of the numbers emigrating from Ireland.

CHAPTER NINE

Ourselves alone: the New York GAA since 1970

Introduction

By the end of the 1960s, the New York GAA was confronted with a range of mounting challenges. As revealed in chapter 6, its relationship with Central Council in Ireland had become strained and questions were being raised about the continued viability of New York's participation in National League competition. John 'Kerry' O'Donnell was becoming increasingly adversarial and public in his criticisms of the Dublin-based administration and this served only to add to the growing acrimony. The 1965 Immigration Act brought further challenges, threatening as it did the flow of new playing talent into the city's Gaelic sports ranks. Despite these obstacles, at the beginning of the 1970s the New York board was still in a healthier position than its counterparts within the NACB. However, this brought little satisfaction and there was a growing recognition that steps needed to be taken to bring about the sort of stability required to help Gaelic games continue to grow in the city's Irish communities. This chapter analyses the development of the GAA in New York from 1970 to the opening years of the new millennium. Particular attention is paid to a range of issues that came to dominate the New York board's agenda in this period. The relationship between the city's GAA and the parent body in Ireland is assessed alongside an analysis of the impact of changing levels of Irish immigration on the Association's health there. The ways in which the New York board attempted to establish a more permanent presence in the city, one that would potentially safeguard the position of Gaelic games for the remainder of the twentieth century and well into the twenty-first, are also considered here.

'A sour joke': New York–Central Council relations

A series of events in the first year of 1970 saw an already fractious relationship between New York and Central Council completely break down and left the Association in the city in a dire predicament. The year began badly when the National League's hurling decider, due to take place in May, was delayed until September following a request by the county board of Cork, New York's opponents in the final. The city's Gaels reluctantly acquiesced despite the delay causing considerable disruption to their preparations. Much worse was to follow though in the second leg of the final at Gaelic Park which concluded with a series of unseemly incidents, the most serious of which included a serious assault on the match referee, Clem Foley, who sustained a broken jaw after being punched and kicked as he left the field at the end of the game (Executive Committee GAA Minutes, 2 Oct. 1970). In the aftermath of this incident, John O'Donnell assured Central Council that New York officials would co-operate fully with any investigation. However, when the GAA Executive Committee met in Dublin in early October, this co-operation was not forthcoming. Nonetheless, following the submission of the referee's report, the two perpetrators of the attack were expelled from the Association and three officials of the New York board were severely reprimanded (Executive Committee GAA Minutes, 2 Oct. 1970).

It appeared that transatlantic GAA relations had reached their lowest ebb. Curiously though, this incident had the potential to mark a watershed in the relationship between Central Council and the Association in New York. As the Association's president at the time, Pat Fanning, suggested:

> Out of the turmoil and recriminations of recent weeks can come stability and understanding. We can devise an organisational structure that will end permanently the unseemly wrangling that has turned New York-Central Council relations into something of a sour joke over the past twenty years (Central Council GAA Minutes, 24 Oct. 1970).

Any hopes that such stability and understanding would materialise disintegrated later in the year, though, when New York's hurlers refused to fulfil a fixture against Cork in Dublin following a dispute about the date of the game. As part of their response to what they saw as a lack of consideration of their needs and aspirations, the local GAA informed Central Council that it was postponing a prearranged visit of Kerry's footballers to the city. This caused the Kerry travelling party considerable difficulties, not least because they were a day away from departing for America, creating what the GAA's president Pat Fanning described as a 'deplorable' situation. The extent of the fissures that had opened up became clear when it was suggested that the reason for the cancellation of Kerry's visit was because, 'the atmosphere and tension there were so high at present that they (NYGAA) felt they could not adequately control the situation' (*The Advocate*, 10 Oct. 1970: 13). An impasse had been reached and, worryingly, an end to the international tours appeared imminent.

That said, there were still some people in Ireland, such as Michael Duffy, the then chairman of the Monaghan county board, who lobbied for a more understanding approach towards overseas branches of the Association. In response to the stand off that developed after the cancellation of Kerry's tour, Duffy implored his Central Council delegates to remember that 'The games at Gaelic Park are the only opportunity which the Irish have of meeting once a week, and if for some reason this was to discontinue, it is our own kith and kin in the US who will suffer' (*The Advocate*, 24 Oct. 1970). Duffy's appeals ultimately fell on deaf ears as Central Council suspended all international fixtures for two years, terminated New York's participation in the National League, indefinitely, and in a move that threatened the very sustainability of Gaelic games in the city, banned players from travelling from Ireland to play for any of New York's clubs in the regular season (Central Council GAA Minutes, 24 Oct. 1970).

Beyond these punitive measures, Central Council also criticised the 'attitude and actions of the New York Board', and stressed that it was the 'absolute authority' in all affairs involving external units of the Association (*The Advocate*, 14 Nov. 1970). Comments such as these revealed that beyond the specific problems associated with the playing of international fixtures, the GAA in Ireland increasingly viewed their counterparts in New York with suspicion and distrust and regarded them as a unit that needed to be reigned in. John O'Donnell's stewardship of Gaelic games in New York contributed in no small measure to this state of affairs. As the analyses in Chapter 6 shows, he was a skilled administrator, a shrewd businessman and a forceful personality. While O'Donnell was generally a popular and much respected figure in New York GAA circles, and was central to the growth of Gaelic games in the city in the post-war era, his clear vision about how best to promote these sports coupled with his modern, business-oriented approach clearly conflicted with the more conservative, traditionalist elements of the GAA in Ireland. As King (1998: 114) has accurately observed:

During his period of dominance there were numerous rows between Croke Park and the New York Board and they tended to become personalised in the character of O'Donnell . . . the things that made him a kind of hero to New York Gaels tended to bring him into conflict with Croke Park. He wasn't willing to take dictation from headquarters but more inclined to run a semi-independent republic in New York and, as the Association was democratically run, probably reflected the feelings of the Gaels in the city.

O'Donnell's cultural affiliations were clearly to the 'old' country but his approach to the GAA in New York was steeped in progressive, modernist tendencies rooted in the 'new' world. For example, the weekly fixtures at Gaelic Park were run in a commercial fashion, much like the way they would have been run by a regular sports promoter. Alcohol was also sold at the venue and finances were secured from what would have been deemed by Central Council at that time as inappropriate sponsors.[1] O'Donnell himself recognised what lay at the heart of this often problematic relationship with what he saw as the 'old guard' at Croke Park. Indeed, in explaining his decision to turn down a nomination from Longford to stand as president of the GAA in 1970, he commented that the structure of Central Council was such that it could not be run in a 'business-like' manner and did not possess enough of the 'progressive' men required to take the Association forward (*The Advocate*, 21 Mar. 1970). It was, therefore, not surprising that relations between Central Council and a body that was heavily influenced by O'Donnell had completely broken down by the early 1970s.

Forging ahead alone

As chapters 5 and 6 have illustrated, New York's Gaels had demonstrated themselves to be resilient, persistent and self sufficient in their efforts to promote their sports in times of difficulty. If a meaningful culture of Gaelic games was to survive beyond this period then these were qualities that would have to be very much to the fore. A number of innovations that emerged early in the decade revealed that the New York board was not prepared to sit idly by and allow the suspension of international fixtures or the slowing in immigration to disrupt their activities. Renewed support was quickly proffered for a fledgling minor programme, inaugurated in 1970, aimed at restocking senior and junior football teams with American-born talent. While it is difficult to determine with any accuracy the precise numbers of American-born players that graduated into New York's senior or junior football ranks, the minor board was clearly successful in promoting the game at youth level in this period. Indeed, in 1972, the Good Shepherd minor team, based in the Manhattan Irish enclave of Inwood, became the first youth team comprised of American-born players to tour Ireland. This tour was repeated in 1975, a year that also saw the first visit to New York by a visiting Irish minor team, Coláiste Isogáin from County Cork (Byrne, 1976).

While developments at underage level did much to build a grassroots for the game, it was always going to take time for the minor programme to replenish adult stocks. Thus, the New York board was also keen to initiate measures that would have an immediate impact on the popularity of Gaelic games in the city and keep existing players interested and involved. John O'Donnell initiated a number of tours, including one to Australia and New Zealand in 1973, which did much to encourage New York's best players to continue playing football and hurling. In a move that highlighted its progressive and modernist tendencies, the New York GAA also embraced the technology available to them in the push to promote their games. Of particular note was an agreement signed in 1970 between the New York board and the cable television company, TelePrompter Cable TV, to broadcast to subscribers in upper Manhattan, weekly Monday night telecasts of football and hurling games played at Gaelic Park the previous day (*Irish Echo*, 2 May 1970). While this venture was short lived,[2] New York's Gaels did not abandon their engagement with television. In 1971 they responded positively to the efforts of Gaelic Exhibition Inc., a company owned by two Mayo-based businessmen, who offered to bring closed circuit telecasts of the All-Ireland football and hurling finals to New York for the first time, providing a further arena for Irish immigrants to watch their beloved games and socialise with one another (Byrne, 1976).[3]

Renewed links with 'home'

There were other initiatives in this period, such as the inauguration in 1972 of an annual Gaelic football championship of the Emerald Societies of various Government departments, which sought to limit the impact of the Central Council suspension (Byrne, 1976). Such ventures, whilst welcome, were clearly not as appealing to New York's Gaels as matches involving Ireland's finest county teams. Thus, with the Central Council suspension set to expire in October 1972, the city's GAA saw an opportunity to give Gaelic games a much-needed boost. The Association's hierarchy in Ireland had different ideas, however, and proposed that New York should be entered into the National League 'B' competition. In light of the circumstances that had resulted in the suspension in the first place, the New York board was not in a position to protest too forcibly and reluctantly acquiesced (Byrne, 1976).

Unconvinced about their participation in this competition and unwilling to countenance sub-standard sporting fare, the city's GAA fraternity were largely disinterested and the International Fund, set up in the aftermath of the 1947 All-Ireland Gaelic football final, was soon in deficit of around £15,000. However, the initiation of the All-Star hurling and Gaelic football series in New York in 1975 not only significantly reduced the deficit in the International Fund but also helped to maintain levels of enthusiasm for Gaelic games. The establishment of the All-Stars tour as an annual event also helped to improve relations between the New York GAA and Central Council, and an invitation to the city's burgeoning minor board to enter an under-18 team in the All-Ireland series in 1975 was further evidence of a more amicable relationship (O'Shea, 1981). With the All-Stars venture helping the New York board stay financially solvent and a flourishing minor programme in place,[4] the Association was able to cope with the worst effects of the slow down in Irish immigration and it entered the 1980s with renewed optimism.

In the opening years of the 1980s, the GAA consolidated its position. Regular championship fare continued to take place at Gaelic Park at junior and senior levels in both Gaelic football and hurling as well as youth football competitions. The 1982 season was particularly successful with the official programme of the Association's 49th annual banquet reporting that 'Attendances again increased at Gaelic Park and it would seem followers of Gaelic sports are now beginning to realise this part of our Irish heritage in New York must be supported' (New York Gaelic Athletic Association, 1982). One of the key reasons for this increased patronage was a change in the way that clubs recruited players from Ireland. Although the downturn in the Irish economy had seen an increase in the number of immigrants coming to the city, the Association was still feeling the effects of a lack of incoming Irish talent during the 1970s and in 1982 it decided to replace the three player import rule which restricted the number of overseas players who could play for a local team, with what was effectively a 'free for all' approach. This enabled those clubs with the necessary finances to fly unrestricted numbers of players from Ireland to New York for a weekend match or organise a longer stay.

The lifting of restrictions on overseas players led to a significant improvement in the quality of the spectacle on view at Gaelic Park, particularly in the latter stages of championship competition. While this was a welcome boost for the city's most solvent clubs, others were less than enamoured, fearing that their clubs would struggle to compete with those that could afford to flood their team with Irish imports. There were other reservations around the impact of this rule change on the longer term health of the GAA. Some viewed the influx of Irish players for weekend matches only for them to return to Ireland immediately after the game as a short-sighted approach to the development of Gaelic games in the city, one that would do little to encourage those resident players, often described as the 'backbone' of the GAA in New York and beyond to continue to commit to their club. As Noel O'Connell, former PRO for the New York minor board saw it:

> Bringing out the big name players from Ireland was only a short-term thrill. People weren't thinking five or 10 years down the line . . . too much resources, financially and football wise, were wasted on the weekend player. It didn't help the game here. It hurt the integrity of the game because there were players who trained all year long who, come the quarter-finals, were left on the bench and got fed up and didn't come back to their clubs (interview, 26 Aug. 2004).

Another question was how the opening up of the city's clubs in this way might impact on those who had come through what had become the largest GAA youth programme in the US.[5] While many of the city's junior football teams were sustained by American-born players during the 1970s (interview, 26 Aug. 2004),[6] by the 1980s, clubs were struggling to keep those who played at youth level involved at adult level, not least because of the myriad other sporting opportunities available to them as they progressed through the US high school and college system (interview with Liam Bermingham, 27 July 2003). This lack of progression of home-grown talent into the junior and senior ranks of the city's football and hurling clubs became a source of concern and led to a growing feeling in some quarters that more needed to be done to persuade those graduating through the youth programme to remain GAA members. The provision of realistic playing opportunities at senior level was seen as key in this aim. These arguments appeared to hold sway and at the beginning of the 1983 season, the three-player import rule was reintroduced. However, New York's leading clubs were not prepared to countenance a rule that they felt weakened them and following a 17–16 vote at a meeting of the

Association's members in 1984, unlimited player imports were reintroduced for the start of that season (Byrne, 1984).

The liberalisation of the transfer system in this way was far from welcome in Ireland, not least because it allowed New York-based teams to recruit as many players from Ireland as they desired and, in doing so, had the potential to deprive clubs there of valuable resources. The rule change also led to increased concerns in GAA and media circles in Ireland about the issue of financial incentives being paid to players who were making the trip to New York. While the city's GAA officials denied that players were paid anything other than expenses, the constant rumours coupled with complaints from individual county boards in Ireland about the loss of players for important club games, served to further sour relations between Central Council and the New York board (Byrne, 1984). It is likely that this fed into the GAA's continued reluctance to sanction New York's participation in National League competition but although this continued to rankle with the New York board, the growing strength of the games locally more than made up for this.

Although the opening up of the player import rules allowed the New York GAA to manage short-term difficulties, perhaps of greater significance for the longer term sustainability of hurling and football in the city was the rapid influx of Irish migrants between 1980 and 1990. As noted in the previous chapter, this inflow was precipitated by the continued downturn in the Irish economy, resulting in an almost four-fold increase in net Irish emigration in this period. While the issuing of Donnelly visas facilitated legal entry into the country, the numbers of official Irish immigrants were augmented by the 'tens of thousands' who arrived in the US on visitors visas and chose to stay on illegally once their documentation expired (Corcoran, 1997: 462).[7] New York's traditional Irish communities benefited greatly from these developments and as Corcoran (1997: 475) points out, it 'heralded a virtual renaissance for these neighbourhoods'. The impact of this on the Association's fortunes was well illustrated in the official programme of its 52nd annual banquet in 1985:

> The influx of many thousands of young people from Ireland in the last year has brought about a great increase in the number of players available to the clubs. With this increase in young players the ranks of the clubs have swelled and quite a few new clubs have gained admittance to the junior competitions. There were so many teams in the junior football division that there had to be games scheduled on Saturday in order to complete the competition (New York Gaelic Athletic Association, 1985).

This sort of expansion continued through the closing years of the 1980s and the GAA grew faster than at any time in the previous twenty years.[8] However, these years of growth were far from free of controversy or polemics. Continued concerns about the loss of playing talent to New York clubs and persistent rumours that these clubs were regularly contravening the Association's rules governing amateurism, prompted the GAA in Ireland to seek ways of exercising some control and influence over what had become a powerful, autonomous unit.

'Ourselves alone' or affiliation to the GAA in Ireland?

The fact that the New York board had never affiliated to the parent body in Dublin and was regarded as an 'external unit' increasingly came to be viewed within Croke Park as a problem from the mid-1980s. By 1987 Central Council began to press their counterparts across the Atlantic to affiliate with the Association in Ireland. The profile of Gaelic games in this period, coupled with fears that their interests would be compromised, not least in relation to the importing of players from Ireland, convinced the majority of New York's Gaels that they should continue to remain independent. As Monty Maloney, a former president of the New York GAA saw it:

> One of the main reasons for the reluctance was the sanction system which allowed players to come over to New York and play. The GAA at Croke Park had no control over that player. We were almost like another organisation and that was one of the reasons why we didn't want it (affiliation) because we could bring over who we wanted, how many we wanted and for as much money as we wanted (interview, 28 Aug. 2004).

It came as no surprise then that when the motion to affiliate was brought to a New York board meeting in late 1987, it was defeated overwhelmingly by 47 votes to 7 (Kilfeather, 1988). Calls from some Central Council delegates in Ireland for a complete severance of all contact with New York as a response to what was perceived to be a snub, did little to alter this view (Central Council GAA Minutes, 6 Feb. 1988), and when the city's GAA delegates met again in February of 1988, they maintained their position. In an attempt to break the impasse, GAA president at the time, Dr Mick Loftus, tried a more conciliatory approach, assuring Gaels in New York that he understood their caution as well as their fears about a potential loss of control, particularly over the issues of players imports and finance (*Irish Advocate*, 26 Mar. 1988).

Although Loftus's interjection in the debate and his more conciliatory tone helped, it was a recognition on the part of New York's Gaels of what they stood to lose should they continue to refuse to affiliate that had most bearing on their thinking. The debate over affiliation had seen a halt to the All-Stars tours to New York and Central Council made it abundantly clear that, for as long as the city chose to remain independent of the parent body, this suspension would continue, and that any requests from the city's GAA to enter National League or indeed, All-Ireland competition, would be flatly rejected. Thus, in March 1988 following a tight vote, the New York board took the historic decision to affiliate with Central Council (O'Brien, 1988). Although this effectively brought the issue of the transatlantic transfer of players under the control of Central Council, a development which saw an end to players participating in championship fixtures in Ireland and the US in the same season,[9] the New York GAA benefited considerably from this decision. The New York board now became eligible for grant aid from the parent body and attained the right to vote at Annual Congress in Ireland. In addition, the All-Stars were once again sanctioned to take in the city as part of their annual tour to the US (Central Council GAA Minutes, 4/5 Nov. 1988). Even more significant, however, was the fact that New York was once again afforded the opportunity to take part in the finals of the National League competitions in both hurling and football. Furthermore, to mark the 75th anniversary of the New York board, the 1988 football final was staged in Gaelic Park, a match broadcast live in Ireland by Radio Telefís Éireann (RTÉ). In marking the resumption of New York's involvement in this competition, John Dowling, then president of the GAA in Ireland, felt it appropriate to commend the efforts of those who had worked to preserve Gaelic games in the city and gave an indication of the position of these sports amongst those who had crossed the Atlantic:

> The establishment of the GAA over here was an important development in providing a link for our people with Ireland and in affording them an opportunity to maintain our unique traditions and culture. The Association's role has not diminished in this city over the decades. Indeed, it is now as vibrant as at any time this century.

Terry Connaughton, then president of the New York GAA, concurred with these sentiments and on the occasion of the 1988 National League football final at Gaelic Park, he stated that he was 'full of confidence that Gaelic sports will continue to be a permanent sporting exercise for the Irish in the tri-state area' (cited in New York Gaelic Athletic Association, 1988).

While some initial teething problems were associated with New York's affiliation to the GAA,[10] the early years of the next decade did little to shake this confidence. 1991 saw Connaughton establish a separate board for ladies' Gaelic football which reflected a growing interest in Gaelic games amongst the female diaspora, particularly in the Woodlawn area of the Bronx. The ladies GAA board grew rapidly from two teams in its inaugural year to eight teams just three years later, and by 1999 the New York ladies' team was competing in the final of the All-Ireland junior football championship (Fitzpatrick, 1998; *Hogan Stand*, 28 Apr. 2000).[11] If the progress that was made in the late 1980s and early 1990s was to be built upon, a period of stability was required to allow the GAA to focus on the task in hand unencumbered by major distraction. However, controversy over where Gaelic games would be played in the last decade of the century and beyond soon emerged, and served to undermine what the New York board had achieved in the previous decade.

A home for the New York GAA: Gaelic Park and the Tara Circle debacle

The status of Gaelic Park as the post-war home of Gaelic games in New York was due in large part to John O'Donnell who had secured a long-term lease on the venue in 1944. Towards the close of the 1980s, however, the relationship between O'Donnell and his family and the local GAA grew increasingly fractious. For example, a dispute between the two parties over the poor state of the facilities led to the cancellation of the replay of the 1987 football championship final (New York Gaelic Athletic Association, 1987). Thereafter, relations grew steadily worse, and by the beginning of the 1990s they had become 'tortuous' according to the *Irish Voice* (8 Oct. 1991). With the O'Donnell family reluctant to carry out any remedial work on the venue while they were in dispute with the Association, the Metropolitan Transit Authority (MTA) – which managed the site for the city – decided to seek an alternative leaseholder. By 1991 the situation had become so dire that all GAA fixtures at Gaelic Park for the entire season were cancelled. The MTA entered into negotiations with Manhattan College and the O'Donnell family in an attempt to broker a joint lease agreement which would make the college responsible for the playing field and its ancillary facilities while the O'Donnell family would retain control of the bar and restaurant facility. With these negotiations dragging on until 1992 the GAA was forced to use public parks in Woodlawn, the Bronx and Rockland, 50 miles north of Manhattan (New York Gaelic Athletic Association, 1987).

This was far from satisfactory and with the Association excluded from any discussions around the future of Gaelic Park, the New York board sought alternatives. In February 1992 they announced plans to open their own 3,000-seat venue at Ferry Point Park in the Bronx (Rohan, 1992a). This venture was quickly scrapped but Jackie Salmon, then president of the Association, motivated in part by an acrimonious relationship with John O'Donnell and a reluctance to return to Gaelic Park (Rohan, 1993a), continued to pursue other options. By July 1992, it was announced in the Irish-American press that the Association was preparing a bid, estimated at around $14 million, for the purchase of part of the estate of a community college in upstate Briarcliff Manor, which would form part of a New York Irish Centre (Rohan, 1992b). It appeared that this represented a much more viable option for the Association to acquire its first permanent home. The city's Gaels threw their full support behind a project that came to be known as Tara Circle. A committee to oversee the project, drawn from prominent members of New York's Irish community, along with members of the GAA and headed by Ed Sheeran, the Roscommon-born former vice-president of Chase Manhattan Bank, was quickly established, and it began to promote the venture in Irish circles. Negotiations continued with King's College and in August 1992, a sale price of $14 million was agreed (Rohan, 1992b).

Although the heavily indebted college was more than eager for the Tara Circle group to purchase the site (Rohan, 1992c), many of the local residents, comprised largely of well-heeled, affluent Protestants were less keen. Opposition to the venture crystallised itself in the form of a group calling themselves Residents for the Future of Briarcliff Manor Inc. which hastily organised a campaign against the construction of a GAA venue in their town (*Irish Voice*, 31 Aug. 1993). At one heated public meeting, some residents suggested that while there was no objection to the building of an Irish cultural centre, there was major opposition to the GAA's involvement and the potential traffic difficulties that would inevitably result on weekends when matches were being played (Rohan, 1993b).[12] With the resident's group successful in delaying the project, the city's GAA clubs grew increasingly impatient, not least because, in the interim, they were having to make a 100-mile round trip to Rockland State Park for matches. The GAA's attorney, Frank Hoare, was instructed to negotiate with Manhattan College about a return to Gaelic Park for the 1992 season. These discussions initially came to nothing. However, the fact the New York board were embroiled in an increasingly bitter impasse over the required planning approval for Tara Circle led to negotiations being re-opened with Gaelic Park. A deal was eventually brokered for a return to the venue which involved half of the gate proceeds going to the college and half to the Association (King, 1998; *Irish Voice*, 3 May 1994).

The return to Gaelic Park was far from an indication that the GAA was about to step away from the Tara Circle project. The Association's clubs had responded positively to requests for financial collateral and by 1994, they had gifted $100,000 to the proposed Irish Centre (Rohan, 1995a). In September 1994 revised plans, involving reduced parking spaces, spectator seating and dining capabilities and a promise that no senior hurling or football games would be played at the venue, were proposed in an attempt to break the stalemate with the residents' group. While the objectors remained immovable, this compromise proved to be much more palatable to the local Village board which granted the required approval for work to commence on the site (Rohan, 1994c). Any hopes that this would bring New York's first Irish centre and a home for the GAA closer to realisation were quickly shattered though when the residents' group began legal proceedings against the decision to grant local approval. Worse was to follow for the project when the dissenting residents secured control of the Village board at local elections in 1995. These developments appeared to strengthen the resolve of the Tara Circle committee and they responded by threatening their own lawsuit for damages from the Briarcliff Manor resident's group arguing that they were guilty of anti-Irish bigotry. Dennis Lynch, attorney of the Tara group pointed to the inflammatory comments of one prominent Briarcliff Manor resident at a public meeting in October 1994 to support this contention:

> This 'Tara hustle' is backed by the Ancient Order of Hibernians, sponsors of the outrageously discriminatory St Patrick's Day parade, which is for Irish Catholic heterosexuals . . . although closet homosexuals such as Cardinal Spellman are allowed . . . And the equally xenophobic Gaelic Athletic Association, which doesn't even allow soccer to be played in Croke Park in Dublin . . . Michael Cusack, the founder of the GAA . . . was a xenophobic, anti-semitic, anti-Protestant bully (cited in Rohan, 1995b).

The majority of the Briarcliff Manor residents distanced themselves from these comments, yet the Tara Circle group clearly hoped that by making them public in the *Irish Voice*, New York's Irish community would be galvanised and would rally behind the project. However, further requests for funding from the city's Irish associations in 1994 drew a hesitant response. Significantly, with the scaling back of the GAA's involvement in the restructured Irish centre, the Association's clubs also stalled on making any further financial contributions (*Irish Voice*, 24 Sept. 1996). Although the Tara Circle committee continued to pursue other fund-raising avenues, debts mounted and with key investors walking away from the project and opposition from local residents continuing, the venture had little chance of succeeding. It was only when the groups' president, Ed Sheeran, filed for bankruptcy in 1998, that the possibility of an Irish cultural and sporting centre in Briarcliff Manor was eventually ended (Rohan, 1998a).[13]

Import controversies

The long-drawn-out Tara Circle debacle clearly siphoned off energies and finances from the New York GAA that could have been put to much better use elsewhere. By the middle of the decade hurling was struggling with only half of the number of clubs that existed in the 1960s still competing (Belluck, 1995; Rohan, 1995c). The inability of the New York board to enthuse American-born youngsters to play the game was vital here and hampered the hurling clubs' ability to respond to slowing levels of Irish immigration. The increasing reliance on importing Irish players in both codes rather than seeking to strengthen the youth programme was also far from helpful. As noted in the previous chapter, the importing of players on a short-term basis, often for single games, gathered pace in the 1970s following the 1965 Immigration Act. The fact that those who had immigrated during the 1950s and 1960s, and swelled the GAA's ranks in that period, began to retire, only served to increase the reliance on Irish imports. As county-based and personal rivalries continued to build each year, clubs sought out quality players from Ireland rather than invest the time and resources into developing their own players from a young age. Despite or perhaps because of the tightening of the system governing transatlantic transfers, and the reintroduction of the three-player import rule following the New York board's affiliation to Central Council in 1988, abuse of this system began to increase. The suspension of the Galway hurler, Tony Keady, for the All-Ireland hurling final against Tipperary in 1989, following his illegal participation in a game for the New York Laois team in the same season generated much controversy and caused considerable embarrassment for the New York board (Rohan, 1995c). In November 1989, Terry Connaughton, then president of the GAA in the city along with Jack Salmon, a former president, were summoned to Croke Park to explain the apparent neglect of the rules governing player transfers. This meeting also provided an opportunity for the parent body to ask probing questions about continued allegations of import players receiving large sums of money for representing New York clubs. Connaughton and Salmon responded to these allegations by providing assurances that players who travelled to New York only received travelling expenses and recompense for time taken off work and promising a more rigorous approach to the implementation of the regulations on player imports (Management Committee GAA Minutes, 24/25 May 1989).

Despite these assurances, the controversy deepened. In 1991 the *Irish Voice* published an article detailing what it claimed were widespread abuses of the import system, particularly the flagrant use of illegal players, or 'ringers'.[14] It was also suggested that this practice was costing the New York GAA an estimated $150,000 per year for airfares, accommodation costs and financial incentives to players. Questions were also asked about the impact of this sort of investment on the longer term development of the GAA and it was suggested that the funds used to finance player imports, illegal or otherwise, would be better spent on youth player development (Rohan, 1991). The inability or lack of willingness to invest more finance in youth coaching vis-à-vis funding overseas transfers into the senior ranks was compounded by the fact that as well as drawing on Irish imports in their pursuit of championship honours New York's clubs regularly provided incentives to players based in some of the NACB's strongest divisions to play for them on particular weekends. While this was often a lucrative exercise for individual players and did much to sustain high levels of competition in New York, the NACB's clubs began to lose patience at what they saw as flagrant opportunism at their expense. Thus, at the NACB's convention in 1994 a ruling was passed which forbade its players from playing league or championship competition in New York. This measure had an immediate impact on hurling and one of New York's oldest clubs, Galway, which had a long history of recruiting players from Boston and Chicago, announced that it was unable to field a team for the 1995 season, the first time this had happened since the club was founded in 1914 (Rohan, 1995c).

The lack of foresight on the part of the New York board and its clubs to make provision for youth player development in hurling continued to impact on the health of this code. Although Gaelic football remained vibrant in the city, it continued to be dogged by misuse of the player import rule. By 1995, the situation reached what the *Irish Voice* (21 Nov. 1995) described as 'embarrassing proportions' as the Leitrim club was stripped of the New York championship when it was revealed that they had played three illegal players, all members of the Dublin All-Ireland winning team, in the final against Donegal.[15] While this sanction revealed that the New York board had finally decided to take a firm stand on this issue, the following season brought similar levels of abuse of the import rules. The GAA in Ireland, which had attempted to persuade their New York counterparts to bring to an end what appeared to be a tacit acceptance of flagrant rule breaking, decided to intervene in the matter, doing so in spectacular fashion. Following its own investigations into claims of rule breaking in late 1996, the GAA's games administration committee issued lengthy suspensions of between 6 and 12 months to 20 players from Ireland, many of whom were high profile inter-county stars, who had played illegally in New York during the 1996 season (*Irish Voice*, 21 Jan. 1997).[16]

The situation had clearly reached crisis point with some county secretaries in Ireland, aggrieved at the transatlantic trade in players, suggesting that the time had come to disaffiliate New York from the GAA. Armagh's Patrick Nugent suggested at the time that 'The New York board are the biggest culprits in this. Nearly two dozen players have been caught up in their incompetence. They will have to clean up their act or a parting of the ways has to come' (cited in Moran, 1997b: 15). After the difficulties and protracted negotiations involved in securing New York's affiliation in the first place, Central Council was clearly not in favour of this solution. Instead they took a more hands-on role in the management of the player import system. In 1998, a motion was passed at Congress in Dublin to tighten up the procedures surrounding both temporary or 'weekend' and long-term transfers to clubs in the US (Annual Congress GAA Minutes, 17/18 Apr. 1998). This motion coupled with the suspensions levied against players who contravened the rules on transferring to US clubs in 1996 counteracted some of the worst abuses of the player import system. The election of Monty Maloney as president of the New York board in 1998, and the tough stance that he immediately adopted towards those clubs that contravened import rules also helped in this regard (interview with Monty Maloney, 28 Aug. 2004).

The New York GAA in the new millennium

During the 1990s, the New York GAA's involvement in the Tara Circle project, the controversy surrounding abuse of the player import system and slowing levels of Irish immigration clearly hampered the development of Gaelic games in the city. Hurling had experienced a sharp downturn by the middle of the decade, and although Gaelic football was as strong in New York as it was in any of the GAA's overseas units, the number of clubs playing in this code had also begun to dwindle (interview with Terry Connaughton, 27 July 2003). Nonetheless, by the close of the century, the New York board, led by Monty Maloney, faced the new millennium bullishly. In 1999, negotiations with the Connaught provincial GAA council and approval from Croke Park saw the city's footballers compete in the All-Ireland championship series in 1999, the first time that a US team had taken part in the Association's premiere competition (*Irish Voice*, 1 June 1999; Breslin, 2000b). That the GAA in Ireland felt New York capable of producing football teams capable of playing at All-Ireland level was testament to the resilience of the city's Gaels, and their entry into this competition was a fitting way to mark the board's 85th anniversary. Further discussions between Maloney and the Ulster provincial council also led to the New York's hurlers being granted permission to enter the All-Ireland hurling series in 2000, a move which helped to reinvigorate the profile of that sport in the city.

Despite these positive developments, the opening years of the new millennium presented the Association with one of the sternest challenges that it had faced in its long history. The terrorist attacks against the US on 11 September 2001 heralded a security climate characterised in part by a much more stringent approach to the policing of America's borders. This inevitably had a detrimental effect on levels of Irish immigration and a concomitant negative impact on Gaelic games throughout the country. The effect in New York was almost immediate with the GAA there losing between 1 and 2 clubs each year because of a dearth of playing resources (interview with Terry Connaughton, 27 July 2003). This once again forced the city's clubs and GAA officials to consider how best to safeguard the longer term future of their sports. By 2003 serious consideration was being given to putting an end to the granting of weekend sanctions for Irish-based players. Indeed, at its convention in 2004, following a motion by the Monaghan club, the overwhelming majority of delegates voted to suspend the weekend sanction system. While this move was motivated in part by the costs involved in bringing players to New York for such a short period,[17] according to Seamus Dooley – a stalwart of the Monaghan club that proposed the suspension of weekend sanctions – it was designed to provide more playing opportunities to those Gaels who were resident in the city and who might have previously lost their place on the team to an expensive import. In doing so, it was hoped that a sound, locally based talent pool, sustained largely by those coming through the city's youth programmes, would emerge (interview with Seamus Dooley, 30 July 2004).

While the weekend sanction system was reinstated in the next season following a decline in playing standards and attendances at Gaelic Park, the decision to suspend sanctions in the first place revealed that there were GAA officials in the city with the fortitude and foresight to make difficult decisions to ensure the survival of Gaelic games. These qualities were evident in other aspects of the New York GAA's activities, not least in their continued partici-pation in All-Ireland competition. Buoyed by Central Council's decision to approve their involvement in hurling and football's premier competition, coupled with the prospect of hosting visiting county teams from Ireland to play championship fixtures on sub-standard facilities – including a pitch that contained a softball diamond[18] – the New York board once again focused its attentions on a permanent home. While Gaelic Park had served the GAA well over the years, it was clearly in need of a major, and probably costly, upgrade. However, some within the New York board felt that investment might be better made in the purchase of a new facility. In 2000 Monty Maloney identified a venue in Terrytown, Westchester, north of Manhattan, as a possibility. This option failed to materialise but by 2001 Maloney, along with some associates, began exploring the possibility of purchasing land on Randall's Island, located in the East river between Manhattan and Queen's. In February of that year, plans for a sports stadium were unveiled at the GAA's annual banquet and work began to convince the local Irish community, potential corporate backers and, of course, the City authorities, that the Randall's Island project would not follow the same path as the ill-fated Tara Circle Irish centre (*Irish Voice*, 26 Feb. 2002).

A management committee calling itself the Randall's Island Gaelic Stadium (RIGS) was quickly put in place, with Monty Maloney at the helm. The planning process, including the drawing up of detailed business and financing plans and early consultations with the GAA in Ireland, went smoothly, and in 2004 the City of New York bequeathed a 25-acre plot for the construction of the sports stadium free of charge. It appeared that the project was on the verge of being realised (Lewis, 2004). The city's decision to gift land on Randall's Island provided a window of opportunity and RIGS set about putting together comprehensive financing plans to generate the required funds, estimated at around $30m. At the time, Kieran O'Sullivan, a member of the Limerick hurling club who worked on the Randall's Island project was confident that this could be achieved and commented at the time that:

> The funding will come through private investment and fundraising . . . We are already in negotiations with some big corporate entities and they are all showing an interest. We have brought in some very professional people and we are confident that this funding will come through (interview, 24 July 2003).

The commitment of New York's hurling and football clubs was crucial to the business plan for the proposed stadium. However, disagreements over prospective usage rights between the New York GAA and RIGS soon arose which not only slowed fund-raising efforts but also placed the entire project in jeopardy (*Hogan Stand*, 21 Dec. 2005). The success or failure of the venture increasingly came to rest on the GAA's management committee at Croke Park which was being asked to sanction an investment of $2m. In February 2006, Central Council decided to withdraw its support on the grounds that the New York GAA would have limited control over the venue and that the capital investment and rental charges required from the Association were prohibitive (*Hogan Stand*, 21 Feb. 2006). Despite an offer by Monty Maloney to hand over control of the project to Croke Park, this proposal for a permanent home for Gaelic games in New York, like others before it, ended unsuccessfully.

Concerned about the capacity and suitability of the facilities at Gaelic Park to host senior All-Ireland competition remaining, the New York board turned its attentions to redeveloping this venue. The costs for the extensive renovation plans that were drawn up, which included floodlights and a synthetic playing surface, were estimated at $3m, a sum that exceeded what New York's Gaels could realistically raise on their own. Thus a deal was brokered with Manhattan College, in which they agreed to meet half the costs. The New York board also entered into negotiations with GAA headquarters for financial support. The Dublin administration quickly earmarked $1m for the refurbishment, and with their New York counterparts committing to raising the remaining $500,000, the finances were in place for work to commence. Gaelic Park officially reopened in December 2007 with a hurling match between the 2006 and 2007 All-Stars and in his speech to the 1,000 spectators and local dignitaries who braved freezing temperatures, Nicky Brennan, GAA president commented that the redevelopment would ensure that the venue would remain as the home for Gaelic games in New York long into the future (cited in Brady, 2007).

Conclusion

The challenges that confronted the GAA in New York in the late twentieth century were manifold and complex. In the early 1970s, the Association struggled to cope with reduced levels of immigration from Ireland as well as a suspension of participation in international fixtures. These developments had the potential to throw Gaelic games into terminal decline in New York. However, the city's Gaels rallied and responded with resilience. Renewed links with the parent body, a resumption of participation in National League competition, albeit at 'B' level, and the beginning of an annual All-Stars visit to the city, did much to reinvigorate enthusiasm for Gaelic sport. With an increase in Irish immigration replenishing the GAA's stocks in the 1980s and affiliation to the parent body in Ireland in 1988, the future seemed secure. However, the 1990s brought further difficulties, some of which were of the GAA's own making. Most notable, perhaps, were the debacle surrounding the attempt to acquire a permanent home in Briarcliff Manor and a series of much publicised contraventions of the rules surrounding the import of players from Ireland. By the start of the new millennium, the New York GAA had begun to address this latter failing and soon recovered much of its integrity in the eyes of the parent body at Croke Park, which duly rewarded their transatlantic counterparts with an invitation to play in the All-Ireland series, initially in football and subsequently in hurling. Despite a further failed attempt to secure its own premises on Randall's Island, in 2007, the facilities at Gaelic Park were finally refurbished to provide the more fitting and modern home that the century and a quarter tradition of codified Gaelic games in the city deserved.

The ability of the GAA to sustain itself and remain culturally relevant in New York and indeed, throughout the NACB's divisions since 1970, extended far beyond a simple enthusiasm for sport, an ability to cope with transient migration flows or a capacity to navigate itself through a series of internal travails. As has been the case historically, involvement with one of the city's hurling or football clubs or even the mere act of passing through the turnstiles at Gaelic Park provided Irish immigrants with entry into a cultural space that proffered much in the way of social, economic and psychological sustenance. As Kieran O'Sullivan, a member of the New York Limerick hurling club who immigrated to the city in 1986, commented:

> Gaelic games really help you settle in. You get to know a lot of people. You go up to Gaelic Park on a Sunday and you have something in common with

everyone. For a guy coming out here who doesn't know anyone here or doesn't have any connections job wise, the GAA opens up the whole American world to him. It definitely opens doors to a way of life in America. It helps you put your first foot on the rung (interview, 24 July 2003).

The socio-economic capital that could be accrued from the GAA in the city was available to the full range of Irish migrants including shorter term Irish visitors such as students hoping to make some money for a summer or adventurists seeking to spend time in a vibrant, exciting city. For those who found themselves in New York for the longer term, either as legal migrants or undocumented workers, the Association offered other benefits, not least the opportunity to maintain and nurture senses of Irishness and a connection with 'home'. This was succinctly observed by Bill Colbert, a second-generation Irish American, director of the Irish American Historical Society and a long-standing member of the Limerick hurling club, who noted; 'If nothing else, involvement in Gaelic games in New York provides you with an opportunity to ground you in your identity as being part of the Irish race' (interview, 22 July 2003). For some, the role that involvement in Gaelic games has played in the maintenance of a sense of ethnic community and cultural affiliation for Ireland is perhaps the most important facet of the GAA's role in the city. As Noel O'Connell, a long time servant of the minor programme in New York, observed:

Gaelic Park was always a hub for Irish people, not just for football but also for social gatherings . . . It's very important to keep that role, to maintain your heritage, your sense of identity, your ethnic background . . . The day the GAA loses that is the day we lose ourselves (interview, 26 Aug. 2004).

Of course, the nature of the Irishness that the GAA has allowed Irish immigrants in New York and throughout the US to maintain, preserve and articulate has been in no way monolithic or fixed. For some, the Association facilitated a connection with and expression of a benign, culturally focused sense of Irishness. At other times though and for other individuals, membership of the GAA has been a much more politically motivated act and has allowed them to give vent to belligerent, intensely ethnic expressions of Irish nationalist sentiment. While this has historically been the case for adherents of Gaelic games in the US, the onset of the Troubles in Northern Ireland in the late 1960s intensified the extent to which the GAA functioned as a conduit for the articulation of politicised, combative forms of Irishness, and it is to the role of the Association in this regard that attention now turns.

CHAPTER TEN

The GAA, Northern Ireland's 'Troubles' and Irish-American identity politics

Introduction

The vast majority of Irish Americans by the mid 1960s were largely uncon-cerned by political events in Ireland; only a few organisations in America, including the GAA, remained committed to the nationalist cause (see chapter 7). This was to change significantly with the emergence of the Northern Ireland Civil Rights Association (NICRA) in 1967 and their campaign for an end to anti-Catholic discrimination under the Unionist-dominated Stormont government. NICRA, influenced by the African-American civil rights movement (Wilson, 1995), quickly adopted a strategy involving peaceful demonstrations, street protests and marches. Some of these demonstrations were met with what were often violent counter-protests. The most notorious of these took place in January 1969 when a march organised by the People's Democracy (PD) from Belfast to Derry erupted in violence when protestors were attacked by a loyalist mob at Burntollet Bridge in County Derry. The images and accounts of this brutal attack and subsequent heavy-handed policing by the Royal Ulster Constabulary (RUC) during the considerable rioting in the nationalist Bogside district of Derry City that ensued, were picked up by the international media and reported around the world. When they reached Irish-American homes, they were greeted with anger and frustration. As a consequence, many quickly reconnected with what had been a largely dormant sense of Irishness, one that for some increasingly became characterised by an intense antipathy towards the Unionist establishment in Northern Ireland and the British presence there.

Given its long-standing association with Irish nationalism and republic-anism, it is of little surprise to note that this more politicised and militant sense of Irishness quickly found expression within units of the GAA around the US. This chapter addresses the ways in which members of the Association there expressed their Irishness in the period from the late 1960s through to the signing of the Good Friday Agreement in 1998. Particular attention is paid to examining the extent to which the GAA enabled some to espouse their politics and give vent to their identities in highly public ways. The chapter closes with an analysis of the ways in which the peace process in Northern Ireland, particularly the Provisional IRA's (PIRA) and Sinn Féin's adoption of constitutional, non-violent republicanism and the broader shifts in Irish-American identity politics that this heralded, have impacted upon the identity postures adopted by US based Gaels in recent years.

The New York GAA and the 'return' of militant nationalism in the US

The reassertion of Irish ethnic identity that emerged in America in the late 1960s and early 1970s was rooted in both empathy for the plight of the Catholic minority in Northern Ireland and growing support for the broad aims of the republican movement. While the establishment of the American Congress for Irish Freedom (ACIF) in 1967 and the National Association for Irish Justice (NAIJ) two years later helped to raise awareness of issues around civil rights and Unionist discrimination in Northern Ireland, the establishment of Noraid in 1970 and the Irish National Caucas (INC) four years later, did much to help galvanise expressions of militant nationalism that last had broad popular appeal in America in the years around the Easter Rising. This is not to say that the views of Irish Americans on the Northern Irish question were uniform or monolithic. Indeed, in much the same way that Irish nationalism in Ireland was characterised by deep ideological and political fissures, so too were Irish Americans divided over how best to express their sympathies for and commitment to Irish nationalism, with the advent of the Troubles. There were those who, encouraged by prominent political and religious figures, championed a constitutional nationalist agenda and campaigned for equality for Northern Irish Catholics. For some, largely the assimilated, well-educated, middle-class Irish Americans, once their initial anger over the civil rights issue had subsided, they retreated emotionally from what was happening in Northern Ireland (McCaffrey, 1992). However, there were others, drawn predominantly from the ranks of migrants and second-generation Irish Americans, who articulated an ethnicity that was characterised by anger at events in Northern Ireland and support for the PIRA's military campaign (Reimers, 1997). This was not necessarily a fixed position and the identities and politics expressed by those in this group were often fluid and changeable according to specific circumstances.

Even within Noraid, the organisation in America that was perhaps most closely associated with support for militant republicanism, the level of backing it received often reflected what was happening, politically and militarily, in Northern Ireland (Hanley, 2004). For example, while Noraid gained much popular support in the first two years of its existence, by the close of 1972, a year which had witnessed increasing levels of PIRA violence, public backing began to wane.

Although the GAA in America possessed moderate, constitutional nationalists in its ranks, as was the case prior to the onset of the Troubles, the Association also drew on a staunchly republican constituency in this period. These individuals saw their involvement in Gaelic games as a further affirmation of their nationalist credentials and, from the early 1970s, they were more than happy to marry their involvement in the Association with their politics. This was very much in evidence on both the Atlantic and Pacific coasts of the US. As might have been expected, New York's Gaels were very much at the vanguard of the more militant-minded view of what was happening in Northern Ireland in the late 1960s and early 1970s, and they were particularly forthcoming in their support of groups in Ireland and the US that shared their outlook. For example, in 1969 the city's GAA organised a series of fund-raising activities that were aimed, on the surface at least, at supporting NICRA (*The Advocate*, 24 May 1969; *The Advocate*, 31 May 1969; *Irish Echo*, 1 Nov. 1969). While these events generated finances for and raised the profile of the civil rights movement in Northern Ireland, the presence of Michael Flannery, one of New York's leading republican figures, on the organising committee of several of the field days suggests that at least part of the funds raised were also used to support a more militant agenda.

The New York GAA continued to support various shades of opinion across a whole spectrum of broadly nationalist organisations during the early years of the Troubles. The extent and focus of this support was largely dependent on events in Northern Ireland in this period. When Irish nationalists in the north campaigned on issues related to civil rights, New York's Gaels were eager to help in whatever way they could. Likewise, when popular support for physical force republicanism gained momentum in Northern Ireland, they also came forward with support. This was especially evident in the close association that developed between Noraid and those who organised and patronised Gaelic games in the city. That such a link developed is hardly surprising given that the men who were instrumental in setting up Noraid, Michael Flannery, Matthew Higgins, Jack McCarthy and John McGowan, were all influential figures in the

GAA (Hanley, 2004). These ties were nurtured further by others who were active in both organisations, most notably, John 'Kerry' O'Donnell. As the Troubles began to unfold in Northern Ireland, these key figures ensured that the GAA and its headquarters at Gaelic Park were at the forefront of Noraid activities. For example, a matter of months after the killing of 13 civilians by the British Army during a peaceful civil rights march in Derry,[1] the GAA began sponsoring a series of field days in support of Noraid which ran throughout the year (*The Advocate*, 6 May 1972; *The Advocate*, 24 June 1972; *The Advocate*, 1 July 1972).

In a humanitarian sense, events such as these allowed New York's Gaels to demonstrate their concerns for and solidarity with those members of the nationalist community in Northern Ireland who had experienced the loss of a loved one, either through death or imprisonment. These sentiments were very much to the fore in a tour of various US cities by county Kerry's footballers in the summer of 1972, organised, unsurprisingly by John 'Kerry' O'Donnell, to raise the finances necessary to allow groups of children from republican families in Northern Ireland to holiday in the Irish Republic (*The Advocate*, 6 May 1971). The resumption of visits by touring Irish inter-county teams to New York in late 1972 provided further fund-raising and lobbying opportunities. Indeed, at one international fixture in September at Gaelic Park, 50 per cent of the gate was earmarked for 'Relief of Distress in the North', while a number of VIP's and US politicians sympathetic to the nationalist cause in Ireland, including Ted Kennedy, were invited to attend (Executive Committee GAA Minutes, 14 July 1972).

Those in the GAA fraternity who organised and patronised these field days were concerned about the socio-economic and psychological difficulties that confronted the Catholic community in Northern Ireland during the early years of the Troubles, but they were also clearly exhibiting their support for militant nationalism. While the objectives of Noraid were ostensibly confined to providing aid for the families of PIRA prisoners in Northern Ireland, in the opening years of the Troubles, the organisation canvassed openly for funds to arm the Provisionals (Hanley, 2004). It would have been abundantly clear to those who were handing over their dollars at the entrance to Gaelic Park, and filling the collection buckets that were passed around the venue, that there was the distinct possibility that their donations were being used to buy weaponry for a paramilitary organisation. Those at the helm of Noraid's New York committee had no difficulty in outlining this possibility. For example, in one article in *The Advocate,* linked to a notice advertising a series of fund-raising games at Gaelic Park, Matthew Higgins, suggested that 'They (the republican movement in Ireland) ask for help and we send them what we can. We send it for food and clothes, and if they want they can spend it on weapons, but that is their concern' (*The Advocate*, 24 June 1972: 13).

Support for the republican movement and a desire to express senses of anti-Britishness continued to characterise GAA activity in New York for the rest of the 1970s and into the early 1980s. However, mirroring the development of Noraid, the intensity with which members of the Association expressed their republicanism fluctuated according to events in Northern Ireland. It is unclear whether the broader decline in support for Noraid after 1972 led to a dip in the militancy of New York's Gaels. What is clear though is that the hunger strikes in Northern Ireland's Maze Prison in 1981,[2] not only led to a major revival in Noraid's fortunes but also saw the GAA become very visibly involved in republican agitation, protests and fund-raising. For example, three days prior to the death of Bobby Sands, the first hunger striker to lose his life, there was a considerable, albeit unofficial, GAA presence at a protest rally outside the offices of the British Consulate in Manhattan (interview with Terry Conaughton, 27 July 2003), which involved the burning of Union Jack flags and an effigy of the then British Prime Minister, Margaret Thatcher (*New York Times*, 3 May 1981). In a further show of support for the demands of the other hunger strikers and, in a move aimed at paying its respects to the Sands family, the New York GAA cancelled all games scheduled for 10 May and handed over the gate receipts for the following week's fixtures to Noraid's Hunger Strike Defense Fund (*Irish Echo*, 16 May 1981).

As the New York GAA's relationship with Noraid waxed and waned through the rest of the 1980s and into the 1990s, the Association's members exhibited, in more subtle ways, an ethnic identity that remained firmly rooted in a hard line response to the British presence in Ireland. This was particularly manifest in relation to the New York board's attitude towards Rule 21 of the GAA's constitution, which prohibited members of the British Crown security forces and the now defunct Royal Ulster Constabulary from participating in GAA activities (Sugden and Bairner, 1993; Bairner and Darby, 1998; Cronin, 1999). New York's position on this issue became clear at the GAA's Congress in Dublin in 1998 when the former president Joe McDonagh attempted to introduce a motion to have Rule 21 removed from the Association's rule-book. McDonagh felt that he was acting in the spirit of compromise that the fledgling peace process in Northern Ireland had engendered. However, he misjudged the resolve of sections of the GAA – particularly those constituencies in the north of Ireland which had been most directly effected by the Troubles – to maintain a position that they believed was a legitimate response to what they saw as the historical suppression of Gaelic games and culture by the British state and, more specifically, as a justified protest against the continued British security force harassment of those affiliated to the Association (Bairner and Darby, 1998). Given the long-standing tradition of republicanism within New York GAA circles, it should come as no surprise that had the motion to remove Rule 21 gone to the floor of the Congress, the delegates from the New York board would have voted for the retention of the clause. When the same motion was presented to a special GAA congress in November 2001 and was eventually passed, the New York GAA maintained its stance. Liam Bermingham, a former president of the New York board, pointed to the presence in the city's GAA of a number of clubs with large parts of their membership hailing from Northern Ireland as being of particular importance:

> when the motion came to abolish Rule 21 we were under pressure from Ireland to vote for the abolition of it. But we had a meeting here and obviously we were going to be mandated by what the clubs here decided and we have Armagh, Down, Tyrone, Donegal, Monaghan, Cavan, all the Ulster clubs who asked us how we could dictate to them and they asked us that we respect their views on it and we did that and we voted to keep it (interview, 27 July 2003).

This continued support for preserving Rule 21 was perhaps the clearest example of the extent to which Gaelic games in New York, in the closing years of the twentieth century, remained linked to senses of Irishness that were intensely political, combative and republican in orientation.

The Boston GAA and Irish nationalism

Elements of the linkages between the GAA in New York and support for militant nationalism were also evident in Boston during the 1970s and 1980s. The GAA in the Boston area included members who were quite clearly republican in political orientation and were involved in organising fund-raising activities for Noraid, or were contributing from their own pockets (interview with John Hehir, 15 Aug. 2000).[3] However, in the last decade of the century there were particularities in the ways that some in Boston's GAA fraternity expressed their Irishness. As outlined in chapter 8, the 1990s were clearly significant for Gaelic games in the city in a sporting sense given the steady growth in the number of clubs and the acquisition of dedicated playing fields in the suburb of Canton. However, this decade also saw a marked increase in the extent to which Gaelic games were drawn upon specifically to mobilise an Irish nationalism that, whilst not uniformly supportive of physical force, was very much opposed to the continued presence of the British in the north of Ireland and the difficulties, perceived or otherwise, which this presented for the minority Catholic, nationalist community.

One of the earliest indications of this came in the summer of 1992 when the New England board threatened to withdraw from an Irish Cultural Centre (ICC) event, organised to raise funds for the planned construction of the Irish centre in Canton. The reason for the threat was the ICC's refusal to allow Noraid and the American Irish Political Education Committee to take part in the festival. Explaining the rationale behind this decision, Paul Gillespie, then chairman of the ICC, said that his organisation had decided 'not to get involved with political groups' (cited in Farrelly, 1992: 4). The New England board reacted furiously and its president at the time, Joe Lydon, wrote to Gillespie suggesting that this decision was 'unfair and unjust' and that 'this type of discrimination or denial process to any group' was unacceptable (cited in Farrelly, 1992: 4). Significantly, Lydon also threatened a GAA boycott and the cancellation of a series of crowd-pulling matches scheduled to take place at the festival. A meeting of Boston's GAA clubs unanimously endorsed Lydon's position and with the ICC refusing to acquiesce, the New England board rearranged the planned fixtures for its usual venue at Dilboy Field.

The New England board's stance on this issue certainly set down a marker of its politics. The following year, though, witnessed one of the clearest examples of the GAA's politicisation in this period with the formation of Aidan McAnespies Gaelic football club in Boston. This club was inaugurated in memory of Aidan McAnespie, a member of the county Tyrone GAA club Aghaloo, who was shot dead by a British soldier in February 1988 as he crossed the Irish border on his way to a Gaelic football match. McAnespie's murder was viewed by many within the Association, on both sides of the Atlantic, as a clear manifestation of what they believed to be an organised and concerted campaign of violence, intimidation and harassment, perpetrated by the British Crown forces and loyalist paramilitary groups against GAA members in the north of Ireland (Bairner and Darby, 1998). The fact that the soldier, who had fired the fatal shot, escaped trial due to 'lack of evidence' served to intensify this belief and hardened the antipathy of sections of the GAA towards the British authorities and security services (Fahy, 2001).[4]

The anger and resentment at McAnespie's murder was most keenly felt in the GAA's northern counties and served to solidify the links between the Association and the broader political agenda of northern nationalism. The waves of sorrow and revulsion at McAnespie's death were also felt across the Atlantic in Boston. Driven by a desire to express solidarity with the McAnespie family, a number of individuals involved in Gaelic games in the city decided that the formation of a new club would be a fitting and lasting tribute. Although the club was established first and foremost as a gesture of sympathy and remembrance (Fahy, 2001), membership of and support for the McAnespies also provided Irish Catholics living in the Boston area with a vehicle for expressing a more politicised Irish nationalism. This point is made explicit by John Hehir, former president of the NACB, who commented that 'the formation of the McAnespies club was about the promotion of Irish nationalism' (interview, 15 Aug. 2000). The fact that the founders also intended using the profile of the club to 'highlight political injustice in Northern Ireland' (NACB, 1998) reinforced the extent to which sections of the Boston GAA could draw on their games to demonstrate their solidarity with the aspirations of northern nationalists in Ireland.

Further attacks on GAA members in Northern Ireland in the second half of the 1990s strengthened the politicised nationalist character of Gaelic games in Boston. The murder of Fergal McCusker by the Loyalist Volunteer Force (LVF) in January 1998 was particularly significant in this regard. McCusker had played junior football for McAnespies the previous summer and intended to travel back to Boston that spring to look for work and resume his association with the club. In the aftermath of his murder, the body responsible for overseeing the development of Gaelic games in the greater Boston area took the decision to change its name from the 'New England' to the 'North Eastern' GAA board, thereby removing what was a superficial but no less symbolic connection between the Boston GAA and England. As Connie Kelly, former PRO of the North Eastern board explains, McCusker's murder was central to the name change:

> We used to be known as the New England board. Now we are the North Eastern board because a number of our players recently got killed in Northern Ireland. The board decided that we should eliminate 'England' from our name. This happened almost three years ago when Fergal McCusker was killed (interview, 30 July 2000).

The murders of Aidan McAnespie, Fergal McCusker and other prominent GAA figures in Northern Ireland such as Sean Brown, chairman of Bellaghy

Wolfe Tones GAA club and Gerry Devlin, manager of St Endas senior Gaelic football team, by loyalist paramilitaries served to further harden the political outlook and attitude of the GAA's northern counties and this continued to be reflected in Boston. This was particularly manifest in the North Eastern board's position over Rule 21. Given the responses that attacks on GAA members in Northern Ireland had elicited from the Association in Boston and the fact that the McAnespie family spoke out publicly against the motion to rescind the rule, it is hardly surprising that their views on the issue matched those of their New York counterparts (Rohan, 1998b). The difficulties which the North Eastern board had in responding more positively to the debate over Rule 21 were compounded by the fact that sections of the GAA community in Boston at the time were staunchly republican in political orientation. As one anonymous source revealed, 'there are IRA sympathisers in the GAA over here and they are going to resist removing Rule 21' (interview, 2 Aug. 2000).[5] Thus, as was the case in influential pockets of the GAA community in New York, despite the PIRA ceasefires in Northern Ireland and the decision of the republican movement to focus its energies on constitutional politics in its pursuit of a united Ireland, elements within the North Eastern board were unable to move to what might have been classified as a more progressive position on this issue.

San Francisco's Gaels and revolutionary nationalism

This sort of explicit linking of Gaelic sports clubs with an overtly political agenda was not just specific to America's north-eastern seaboard. Indeed, 3,000 miles away on the Pacific Coast a similar rationale underpinned the establishment of the Ulster Gaelic football club (GFC) in San Francisco. In many ways though, this club went further in its support of Irish nationalism than MacAnespies. The club was founded in 1986 at a time when the in-flow of new Irish immigrants to San Francisco convinced some members of the McDermotts club that there was scope to break away and establish another team. However, the rationale behind this move extended beyond sporting concerns. The majority of those behind the founding of the club hailed originally from Northern Ireland and were republican in their political outlook. The desire on the part of these earliest committee members to ensure that Ulster GFC reflected their political orientation was immediately enshrined in its constitution, article 2 of which states that:

The objectives of the club shall be to preserve and defend democratic principles enshrined in the Declaration of Independence, and the Proclamation of the Irish Republic, declared on Easter Week 1916 (Ulster GFC Constitution).

This inherently political stance was further amplified by the fact that of the five key aims of the club, four dealt specifically with its commitment to remembering, celebrating and supporting those who were involved in the movement for a united Ireland and those who had suffered hardship as part of this movement. Indeed, it was only the club's fifth aim that specifically mentioned the promotion of Gaelic games and the culture of the Irish people (Ulster GFC Constitution). The club strove to meet its objectives and satisfy its overtly political agenda in a number of ways. For example, a Political Wing Committee (PWC) was established to oversee and promote its republican underpinnings. Ulster GFC also closely aligned itself with the activities of Noraid in San Francisco and there was significant cross-membership between both organisations. This trend was not new and reflected a long-standing trend of cross membership between the GAA and San Francisco chapters of Noraid that stretched back to the early 1970s (interview with Mike Moriarity, 27 Aug. 2006; interview with Eamon Gormley, 27 Aug. 2006). As Joe Duffy, former chairman and a long-time member of the club explained, 'when I first came here, it (San Francisco GAA) was very republican minded. There was a lot of fund-raising going on. A lot of the guys who were in Irish Northern Aid, were in the Ulster club' (interview, 28 Aug. 2006).

Beyond the PWC, the club was also active in the St Patrick's Day parade in San Francisco, using it as a vehicle specifically for promoting its political position on Northern Ireland. While the San Francisco GAA took part in the parade as a way of promoting Gaelic games and Irish culture more generally, the Ulster GFC was the only club that took part in the official celebrations because it saw the parade as an ideal opportunity to publicise its political aspirations (interview, 28 Aug. 2006). In 1993, the club's contribution to the parade included a staged event involving the driving of an earthmoving vehicle through a reconstruction of a brick wall which was intended to reflect the actions of a group, popularly referred to as the 'border busters', who used earthmovers to break through barricades constructed by the British Army which closed some border roads between Northern Ireland and the Republic of Ireland (interview, 26 Aug. 2006; Black, 1997).[6] Beyond such symbolic measures, the club demonstrated its political orientation in other, more tangible ways, not least by organising remembrance masses for PIRA volunteers killed in the conflict in Northern Ireland and perhaps most notably, through its Annual Easter Brunch, organised to commemorate and celebrate those who took part in the 1916 Easter Rising. As Duffy explained, the Easter Brunch allowed the club to bring over members of Sinn Féin and the Provisionals as well as former prisoners to attend the event and express their views on matters in Northern Ireland (interview, 28 Aug. 2006). In conducting itself in this manner, the club and its members represented, perhaps, the clearest example in the late 1980s and early 1990s of GAA members not only accommodating a political component within their broader promotion of Irish cultural pastimes, but actually proactively using Gaelic games as a medium through which to promote republicanism in the US.

In many ways this hardening of attitudes amongst sections of the GAA's membership in San Francisco and on America's Atlantic coast was a reflection of what was happening more generally in Northern Ireland in the late 1980s and early 1990s. This period was a particularly bleak time in the Province, characterised by some of the worst atrocities of the Troubles and a wave of 'tit-for-tat' murders by loyalist and republican paramilitary groups. The impact of these developments on Irish-American opinion was two-fold. On the one hand, it alienated most Irish Americans who saw the PIRA's role in perpetuating the Troubles in Northern Ireland as a barrier to peace, and focused the minds of those in the US seeking to influence a constitutional solution. On the other though, it strengthened the resolve of republicans in the US to continue to support the armed struggle in whatever way they could. At this time San Francisco gained a reputation as a growing centre of Irish militancy, one aided by an influx of new Irish immigrants, many of whom were from Northern Ireland (Doyle, 1995). The fact that the GAA in San Francisco in this period was populated by these new arrivals ensured that the Association there remained sympathetic to the republican agenda. The targeting of GAA members in the north of Ireland – following a Loyalist Volunteer Force (LVF) statement declaring them 'legitimate targets' for their paramilitary activities (Bairner and Darby, 1998)[7] – also fed into this process and ensured that for much of the 1990s, the Ulster GFC was at the forefront of republican politics in San Francisco.

The GAA and Irishness in America at the century's end: identities in flux

As the 1990s progressed, political developments in Northern Ireland once again began to impact on Irish-American identity politics and, as a corollary, alter the extent and intensity of the linkages between the GAA in America and Irish republicanism. The growing move towards creating the conditions that would allow republicans to enter into a constitutional, non-violent phase of their struggle for a united Ireland was crucial in this regard. Negotiations involving the British and Irish governments and the republican leadership in Ireland brought about an IRA ceasefire in 1994. Although it was temporarily broken in 1996, the reinstatement of the ceasefire and a professed commitment on the part of the Provisionals to decommission its weapons arsenal paved the way for the Good Friday Agreement (GFA) in 1998 and the setting up of a system of devolved government in the Province. Although the power-sharing institutions associated with the GFA were beset by difficulties and suspensions, more recent phases of the peace process, particularly the Provisional IRA's statement in 2005 that their 'war was over' and the re-establishment of the power-sharing executive in 2007 have led to a growing sense that peace and democracy in Northern Ireland are permanent.[8]

This shift towards a commitment to constitutional, non-violent republicanism that occurred in Ireland was also reflected in the US, where the majority of those with republican sympathies either followed the official line of Sinn Féin and committed themselves to a peaceful, constitutional campaign for a united Ireland or simply allowed the more belligerent elements of their Irishness to slowly subside. Even Noraid re-examined its philosophy and after much discussion, it decided to reconstitute itself as an organisation that supported Sinn Féin's new position. However, as was the case in Ireland, there remained pockets of resistance to the peace process and the PIRA ceasefires. Much of this resistance found voice in the Irish Freedom Committee (IFC). The IFC was originally founded in 1961 but became increasingly moribund, following the death of Michael Flannery who had led the organisation since 1987. However, dissent in some hard line republican quarters around the terms of the Good Friday Agreement re-energised it, and in 1998 it re-emerged as a nation-wide organisation.[9] The self-professed remit of this most recent version of the IFC is similar to that of Noraid in that it raises funds for the families of republican prisoners in Ireland and Britain. The key difference from Noraid, however, is that one of the main ways that they demonstrate their support for a continuation of a military campaign against the British presence in Ireland is by concentrating their donations on the families of those jailed because of their activities with dissident republican paramilitary groups such as the Continuity IRA.

Chicago was, and continues to be, a particular focus for IFC fund-raising activity and political lobbying. This is somewhat surprising given that the city lagged behind its counterparts on the east and west coast in terms of support for Irish nationalism during the Troubles and, according to Caroll (1999), was 'at best lukewarm to appeals for help from across the ocean'. This is not to say that Chicago did not have a meaningful Irish nationalist tradition. In the 1860s, for example, money and men flowed freely to the Fenian movement in Ireland from the city. Irish Chicagoans supported the Home Rule campaigns as well as the Easter Rising, and when the Troubles broke out in Northern Ireland, sections of the city's Irish reconnected with nationalist sentiment (Funchion, 1999). Nonetheless, while a relatively small core remained in touch with and supported the nationalist movement, the passage of time, inter-marriage and assimilation meant that most Irish Chicagoans were less inclined towards politicised expressions of their Irishness, preferring instead to concentrate on the cultural aspects of their ethnicity.[10]

This trend was reflected within GAA circles in the city in recent years. While the Association contained committed republicans who periodically organised fund or awareness-raising events (interview with Tommy Dolan, 30 July 2005), in the final decade of the century there was much less of a desire to marry Gaelic sport with nationalist politics than was the case elsewhere in the country. As Harry Costelloe, a former chairman of the NACB and the Chicago central division, noted; 'The GAA in Chicago are not as political as New York or Boston. There is sympathy for Sinn Féin but they're on their own as far as fund-raising is concerned' (interview, 30 July 2005). What was perhaps a more liberal, benign strand of Irishness in the Chicago GAA was very much in evidence during the debates over Rule 21. While officials of the central division, which had responsibility for overseeing the development of Gaelic games in Chicago, toed the official NACB line in the debate on Rule 21, according to the current PRO of the NACB and Chicago resident, Eamonn Kelly, this issue barely registered in the consciousness of the city's Gaels (interview, 29 July 2005). Although Kelly was unable to offer an explanation for this, Harry Costelloe suggested that the relative lack of members from Northern Ireland within the Chicago GAA may have been a factor (interview, 30 July 2005).

The fluid nature of the identity postures constructed and articulated within Irish diasporic communities in the last decade of the twentieth century undoubtedly fed into this relative absence of an association between the GAA and overtly politicised versions of nationalism in Chicago. Oscillations in Irishness in light of events linked to the peace process in Northern Ireland also influenced the extent to which the GAA elsewhere in America remained linked to a grievance-driven Irish nationalism. There were occasional instances when the Association adopted positions that could be construed as reflective of earlier, more hard line attitudes. For example, the NACB's delegates at the 1998 Annual Congress in Dublin spoke out in support of a motion proposed by Armagh for an end to the British Army's 'occupation' of property owned by Crossmaglen Rangers (Annual Congress GAA Minutes, 17/18 Apr. 1998). However, while the McAnespies club continued to highlight perceived political injustices in Northern Ireland and the Ulster club in San Francisco persisted with their commemorations of the Easter Rising, there was no evidence of overt expressions of the philosophy that underpinned the Irish Freedom Committee at GAA venues or within clubs. If anything, the late 1990s and early 2000s saw a tangible shift in the proclivity of the GAA to openly agitate for a combative approach to the unification of Ireland or to hold a position that could be viewed as intransigent or regressive.[11] While still projecting itself as an organisation that sought to preserve senses of cultural nationalism, the Association sought to align itself to the broader philosophy that had moved the PIRA to declare its ceasefires and encouraged Sinn Féin to fully embrace constitutional politics and work in partnership with Unionist parties in a shared Stormont government.

One of the clearest manifestations of this trend could be found in the San Francisco GAA and more specifically within the fluctuating political persona of the Ulster GFC during the late 1990s and early 2000s. While acknowledging that republican sentiments remain at the core of the club's ethos, Joe Duffy, the long-standing club stalwart, acknowledges that there has been somewhat of a 'softening' in the politics of the club with most members rallying behind equality and justice issues in Northern Ireland rather than supporting physical force. His insights are particularly revealing of this process and are, therefore, worth recounting at some length:

> We always have our Easter Brunch to commemorate the Easter Rising of 1916 and we always brought out speakers from home, maybe from Sinn Féin or maybe an ex-prisoner. The club would be known for that link but not as much now because of the ceasefire. With the ceasefire, it has quietened down a lot. The young coming over now, I find, wouldn't have the same interest in these

issues compared to when I first came over here (1990). People were very Republican minded. There was a lot of fund-raising going on. As a club we wouldn't have been hiding that link. Irish Noraid would be marching in the St Patrick's Day parade and the Ulster Gaelic club would be behind them . . . part of that goes back to the days whenever we were commemorating the hunger strike or the border busters campaign that was going on in Ireland then. Now with the ceasefires you have the justice, peace and equality campaign and our club would always have been asked to help out with that and would have been glad to (interview, 28 Aug. 2006).

This slow shift to the espousal of a more liberal, less defensive brand of Irish identity within GAA circles extended beyond the confines of San Francisco and could be seen elsewhere in the Association in America. The debate around a motion, presented to the Association's Congress in Dublin in 2005, to amend Rule 42 which had hitherto banned the 'foreign' sports of rugby and association football from being played at Croke Park revealed much about the extent to which the identity positions of Irish America's Gaels were moveable and fluid. This motion emerged on the back of the planned closure of Lansdowne Road, the home of Irish rugby and soccer, for redevelopment purposes and the likelihood that games involving Irish international teams in both codes would have to be played outside Ireland because of the lack of facilities to accommodate them. The obvious solution was to play these matches at Croke Park. However, this was prohibited by Rule 42, hence the motion to amend. This was a controversial issue and caused considerable acrimony and division in GAA circles. Indeed, the debate was presented in the Irish media as a contest between the traditional and modern elements of the Association and in the build up to the Congress it was claimed that a vote in favour of the motion would be reflective of a more forward-looking and progressive Irish nationalism, while a defeat would represent a retreat into the sort of conservative and defensive nationalism that had long characterised the GAA in Ireland (Fulton and Bairner, 2007). Elements of this debate were aired within the NACB and New York board but the debate was much less polemical than it was in Ireland, perhaps reflecting the fluctuations in Irish-American identity politics discussed earlier. Indeed, while there were pockets of dissension, particularly from those divisions that possessed a high contingent of members from the six counties of Northern Ireland (interview with Eamonn Kelly, 29 July 2005), according to Michael Treacy, then NACB vice-chairman, there was resounding support amongst the NACB's clubs for the amendment to Rule 42 to allow the Irish rugby and soccer teams to play at Croke Park (www.hoganstand.com, 15 Apr. 2005). The results of an online voting poll involving over 120 clubs – which revealed that 90 per cent of those voting supported the motion to amend – said much about the extent to which the majority of GAA units in the US were unwilling to allow defensive, narrowly-defined interpretations of Irishness to stand in the way of what was perceived as a progressive move forward.

This is not to suggest that this was a view shared across the US or that the more general shift in identity politics within GAA circles was unchallenged. According to Eamonn Kelly, while the online poll revealed that most divisions were in favour of opening Croke Park up on a temporary basis to rugby and soccer, those that contained a strong migrant community from Northern Ireland were more inclined to vote against the motion. This reflected the position of most of the northern county boards in Ireland and as Kelly recounted '. . .what we noticed was that the more of an Ulster population you had in a given area you would get pretty much two to one or three to one against opening up Croke Park' (interview, 29 July 2005). The sentiments underpinning this trend were also reflected in the official NACB delegation that travelled to Dublin for the Congress. Of the seven delegates eligible to vote at the Congress, at least two cast their votes in favour of the retention of the status quo (interview, 29 July 2005). This stance was also adopted by the New York board; its delegates at the 2005 Congress elected to follow the lead of New York's northern constituents in resisting the motion to open up Croke Park (interview with Liam Bermingham, 27 July 2003).[12] What this opposition reveals is that while there has been a slow erosion of combative, militant Irishness in GAA circles in the US, some members, particularly those who hail from Northern Ireland, still struggle to move to what might be viewed as a more liberal identity position.

Events at Gaelic Park in Chicago in May 2006 may be reflective of a continued, albeit residual, desire on the part of some to draw on the GAA to ensure that their militant agenda retains some visibility in Irish America. These events centred on an invitation to the Northern Ireland international soccer team by the Chicago GAA to visit Gaelic Park during an end of season US tour. This move was significant, not least because of the sectarian abuse that had been meted out to Northern Irish Catholics, most notably Neil Lennon who retired from the national team in 2002 following death threats to him and members of his family, and because the Irish Football Association (IFA) had historically been viewed by sections of the nationalist community in the Province as sectarian (Sugden and Bairner, 1999; Hassan, 2002). In light of the relative absence of a strong republican tradition in Chicago GAA circles, it may have been easier for the Association there to extend this invitation to the Northern Ireland soccer team than might have been the case in Boston, New York or San Francisco. Nonetheless the invitation was generous, reflective of a less politicised and ethnic interpretation of Irishness and was clearly rooted in the spirit of the peace process. In his official welcome to the IFA officials and players, John Griffen, the president of Gaelic Park went out of his way to make this point explicit:

> We are non-political. Gaelic Park shares a policy statement with the Irish Football Association which we all agree on and those words are 'We condemn all things sectarian'. We know you do and we feel exactly the same. Our welcome to you here tonight is in accordance with the spirit of the Peace Process (Ferguson and Regan, 2006: 1).

Given the status of Chicago as a focal point of Irish Freedom Committee activity, it should come as no surprise that these sentiments were not shared by some in the city. Indeed, a group calling itself the Chicago Irish Committee Against Sectarianism organised a protest to coincide with the arrival of the Northern Ireland team (Ferguson and Regan, 2006). The fact that some of the protestors donned t-shirts emblazoned with the slogan 'IFA You are Not Welcome Here' while others waved black flags – a practice that originated in showing solidarity with the hunger strikers of 1981 – revealed the militant politics of this group and suggested that some, if not all, were also members of the IFC. The GAA sought to distance itself from these actions; but the fact that some of the protestors photographed were wearing Chicago GAA replica shirts revealed that at least some members of the Association there maintained political views that were characterised by a rejection of the broader philosophies that underpinned the peace process in Northern Ireland.

Despite these exceptions, the general trend in the identity politics of members of the GAA in the US since the late 1990s has been characterised by a move away from alignment with militant Irishness and towards a much more benign position. The reasons for this are manifold. Firstly, as noted earlier, it was clearly linked to the progress of the peace process in Northern Ireland and the growing sense there that eschewing the 'armalite' and embracing the 'ballot box' represented the future for the republican movement.[13] This was evident in the views of many long-standing GAA members interviewed for this study. For example, Malachy Higgins, a former chairman of the Association in San

Francisco, placed the peace process at the centre of the decline in republican activism amongst his fellow Gaelic games enthusiasts, 'It (republicanism) was very prominent when I came here first (1984) . . . but in latter years with the peace process the same support wouldn't be there . . . it's not the same now and that's just a reflection of what's going on back home' (interview, 27 Aug. 2006). This is a view shared by Terry Connaughton, a former chairman of the Association in New York, who also argued that the link between the GAA and Irish republicanism has been contingent on historically specific circumstances in Ireland:

> The link isn't as strong today . . . Today's GAA people in New York are not into that nearly as much as they were back in the day . . . I would say there is still a bit of it there but it has slowly eroded in the last 15 years. In 1981 when Bobby Sands died we had demonstrations downtown and there was a lot of GAA people at that but you wouldn't have the same response today. It's probably changing in Ireland as well. Because the Rising was so long ago the younger generations aren't that interested (interview, 27 July 2003).

In addition to the peace process in Northern Ireland and the concomitant shift in Irish-American identity politics, other factors underpinned the diminishing association between the GAA and overt expressions of support for physical force republicanism. Broader qualitative and quantitative changes in Irish immigration in America during the 1990s were especially important. The slowing in Irish emigration in light of the success of the Celtic Tiger was a key factor, as it not only put a drain on GAA units in the US in terms of playing resources but also slowed the infiltration of Gaelic sport playing immigrants who might have been politically motivated, republican, and who might have infused the Association with their political identities, as those arriving in the 1950s had. Changes in immigration patterns were equally important, most notably the fact that the majority of those immigrating to the US from Ireland from the mid-1990s differed from their predecessors. Cochrane's (2007) work has shown that recent immigrants come to the US out of choice as opposed to the sense of compulsion felt by those who emigrated in earlier decades. They are generally young, professional, economically mobile, highly skilled and confident. They are also less concerned about Northern Irish politics than those who went before them, a facet of their identity that has been accentuated with the development of the peace process in the Province. Perhaps most importantly for the discussion here, they come from what Cochrane (2007) described as a more modern, progressive and cosmopolitan Ireland. They feel less of an inclination to affiliate with the sorts of organisations that did so much to sustain their predecessors in the US or to retreat into senses of Irishness that the majority of those in the society that they were brought up in believe are redolent of the past. Thus, not only do they feel little pull towards Irish organisations in the US, such as the GAA, but they are also either liberal in their political views or are simply not interested in the politics of their homeland.

Conclusion

The relationship between the GAA in the US and Irish nationalist and republican politics has been complex, multi-faceted and fluid. At the start of the twentieth century, Gaelic games enthusiasts demonstrated a commitment both to constitutionalist and revolutionary strands of Irish nationalism (see chapter 7). Although broader support for nationalism subsided following the partition of Ireland and increasing levels of Irish assimilation into the American mainstream, the GAA helped to keep 32-county Irish nationalism alive in pockets of Irish America. With the outbreak of the Troubles in Northern Ireland in the late 1960s, Irish-American anger helped to galvanise combative, revolutionary republicanism on American shores and the GAA featured prominently as a vital conduit through which support for this strain of nationalist sentiment could be expressed. Irish-American opinion began to view the PIRA's campaign as increasingly moribund by the mid-1970s, following some of the worst atrocities of the Troubles, yet influential figures within the GAA, particularly in New York, remained firmly entrenched at the vanguard of republican politics. The hunger strikes of 1981 re-energised the commitment of Irish republicans in America to support – financially, politically and militarily – the struggle for a united Ireland, a process that was reflected in GAA circles in New York, Boston, Chicago and San Francisco and continued into the 1990s.

However, the emergence of a fledgling peace process in Northern Ireland and broader changes in the composition of Irish migrants to the US has undermined the historical link between the GAA in America and Irish republican politics. As in Northern Ireland, the peace process has had a huge impact on identity politics in Irish America. With the republican movement declaring the military phase of their struggle at an end and committing itself to constitutional politics, hard liners in the US had to reconsider their position and the ways that they expressed themselves as Irish nationalists. While there remained opposition to the new power-sharing arrangements in Northern

Ireland, most either softened their position or became increasingly circumspect about publicly expressing a form of nationalism that might be construed as narrow-minded and out of touch with majority opinion. This same process of identity contestation has been played out in GAA circles in the US and has ultimately led to a decline in the use of Gaelic games as a resource for producing and reproducing overtly politicised, militant versions of Irishness.

Conclusion

In uncovering the history of Gaelic games in Boston, New York, Chicago and San Francisco from their inception in the late nineteenth century to the beginning of the twenty-first, this study has demonstrated that the fortunes of the GAA in America have been shaped by a combination of social, political and economic forces on both sides of the Atlantic, changes in the legislative framework governing immigration into the US and the resolve and enterprise of successive generations of Gaelic games enthusiasts, officials and benefactors. The presence in America of so many Irish immigrants, the emergence of tightly-knit ethnic neighbourhoods and a desire to express senses of Irishness in foreign climes provided the foundations for the emergence and early growth of Gaelic games in the late nineteenth century. The determination, resilience and organisational capabilities of those who helped to establish the earliest GAA clubs and administrative units were also significant. The fact that involvement in Gaelic games provided opportunities for excitement, helped to alleviate pangs for home, facilitated entry into social networks that provided a job, a place to live and friendships, and ensured that those who were so inclined, could give expression to their ethnic distinctiveness and their political identities, were also fundamental in the early growth of hurling and Gaelic football.

The continuing role of the GAA in this regard has ensured that Gaelic games have retained a presence in the US since. This is not to say that the development of Gaelic games there has been characterised by linear quantitative growth. As this book has revealed, in the same way that there were periods when Gaelic games experienced rapid and substantial growth, there have been occasions when the GAA has had to face up to the very real possibility of extinction. This conclusion revisits the key challenges that the Association in the US was confronted with, and ultimately overcame, during the course of its history. In particular, it examines the impact that the heightened security climate and tighter policing of US borders following the terrorist attacks on 11

September 2001 have had on Gaelic games, and assesses the ways in which the GAA has responded to the difficulties that these circumstances have created for it. As will be revealed, one strategy has been to attempt to open the Association up beyond its traditional, Irish recruitment base. The conclusion ends by analysing what this might mean for the ability of the GAA to continue to function as one of the key markers of ethnically conceived Irishness in America.

Gaelic games in twentieth-century America

The massive waves of immigrants that poured into America from Ireland in the late nineteenth century did much to help the GAA establish itself as an important cultural, political, social and sporting resource for the Irish diaspora. The impetus that continued migratory flows provided to Gaelic games ensured that these pastimes remained healthy for the first three decades of the twentieth century, notwithstanding a brief decline during the Great War. However, during the 1930s, the Great Depression and associated declining rates of emigration from Ireland threatened to send the Association into terminal decline across the US. The numbers of adherents and clubs dropped significantly and the onset of the Second World War effectively put an end to regular competitive GAA activity in a number of cities where Gaelic games had previously thrived. As in the past though, US Gaels rallied and sought ways to breathe new life into the Association. Agitation by a number of leading New York GAA officials supported by colleagues in Ireland eventually convinced the Association's Central Council and Annual Congress delegates to sanction the playing of the 1947 All-Ireland Gaelic football final on American soil. The hosting of this match, combined with a resurgence in Irish emigration to the US in the 1950s, did much to assuage fears about the future of Gaelic games in post-war America. The inception of the North American County Board in 1959 augmented this revival and allowed the Association to enter into a 'golden era' in its development. However, the introduction of the Immigration Act in 1965 halted this growth in one fell swoop and with the Irish economy undergoing an upturn in fortunes in the 1960s and 1970s, and fewer seeking to leave Ireland, US branches of the GAA once again began to struggle.

The outbreak of the Troubles in Northern Ireland not only helped to reawaken latent senses of Irish nationalism in America but also hardened the resolve of those in the GAA with republican tendencies to redouble their efforts to promote sports forms that could function as a channel both for the expression of politicised versions of Irishness and for fund-raising to support the nationalist struggle in Ireland. This did much to ensure that despite a lack of migrants, and hence fresh playing talent, making the journey from Ireland, branches of the Association retained a presence in the sporting, cultural and political landscape of Irish America. Increasing levels of Irish emigration in the 1980s, on the back of stunted economic development in Ireland and a liberalising of the legislative framework governing Irish immigration into the US in the late 1980s and early 1990s, did much to sustain what had once again become a healthy complement of clubs. However, the emergence of the Celtic Tiger, coupled with progressive political developments in Northern Ireland convinced most Irish citizens that their futures lay in Ireland, and with levels of emigration dropping, the GAA in America was once again forced to consider strategies for survival. While some saw a need for the Association to redouble its efforts to develop an American-based grassroots for hurling, Gaelic football and camogie, others felt that this would diminish standards of play and hence the attractiveness of the games as a spectacle. Rather than invest finances and time into generating enthusiasm for Gaelic games amongst youth players, those in this latter group favoured the continued use of the sanction system and the short-term import of playing talent from Ireland and felt that this would better safeguard the health of the GAA until such a time as renewed Irish immigration replenished the ranks of the Association's clubs. This is what had happened in the past and, as far as many of those within US units of the GAA were concerned, it was only a matter of time until it would happen again.

9/11 and the challenge ahead

The events of 11 September 2001 and the stricter control of US borders that emerged in their aftermath has challenged the view that the previously cyclical nature of Irish immigration would soon restock the GAA and infuse its clubs with fresh vigour. Put simply, the post-9/11 context has made the sort of influx of Irish that nourished the Association in the late nineteenth century, during the 1950s, early 1960s and in the 1980s and early 1990s extremely unlikely in the short to medium term. Of particular significance has been the introduction of a number of measures post-9/11, that have had a negative impact on those Irish seeking to immigrate to the US. The use of more stringent procedures for entering and exiting the country, including the employment of biometric technology, has done much to discourage prospective Irish migrants from travelling to America. Fewer are tempted by the prospect of entering the country on a temporary, 90-day visa with a view to remaining there once the terms of their legal stay expire. GAA clubs in the US have suffered as a consequence as they have traditionally benefited from migrants who would often travel to play for a club during the summer championship season and, after obtaining employment and accommodation and developing an affinity for their club, would decide to extend their stay beyond their visitors' visa.[1] Prior to 9/11, migrants such as these could move relatively freely back and forth between Ireland and the US; however, the likelihood of detection as an illegal immigrant and a resultant ten-year ban from entering the US has effectively put many off taking such a risk (interview with Eamonn Kelly, 29 July 2005).

In addition to the problems associated with entering and exiting the country, the post-9/11 security climate has brought challenges for those undocumented Irish already living illegally in the US, a proportion of whom are members of the GAA. There is a growing sense within this section of Irish-American society that the stricter enforcement of the visa waiver scheme and the introduction of the Patriot Act in the aftermath of 9/11 have left them in a precarious situation, one that makes it difficult to view America as their long-term home. As Cochrane (2007: 353) observed:

> The view of many Irish people living in New York was that immigrant com-munities were being looked upon with new eyes by the US government in the aftermath of 9/11. There was a widespread belief . . . that new legislation was being enforced rigorously by post-9/11 agencies such as the Department of Homeland Security, and that existing immigration law was being applied to the letter, in an attempt to get rid of illegal immigrants and dissuade others from entering the country.

The Irish community have responded to this state of affairs in a number of ways. Some have worked intensively on behalf of organisations like the Irish Lobby for Immigration Reform (ILIR) for a reprieve for illegal Irish immigrants in the US. Others have merely continued to work without labour protection or access to state services in America's informal economy and lead what Cochrane (2007) describes as a 'shadow existence'. Many though, worried about being arrested and deported or unable to get employment or a driving license without a US social security number, have decided to leave the US and return to Ireland. While the Celtic Tiger and the peace process in the north has made this decision a lot more palatable, it has still proved to be one that has been difficult

(Brennan, 2004). Beyond the level of the individual, these circumstances have placed many Irish organisations in an invidious position, not least the GAA, who have seen their US based membership shrink as a consequence.

In this context, those within the GAA who felt that the cycle of Irish immigration to the US would eventually restock their clubs have gradually begun to realise that this scenario is unlikely. While some have responded by calling for the sort of relaxation of the sanction system that would allow clubs to recruit more players from Ireland in the short term, other influential figures within the Association are moving in an altogether different direction and are concentrating their efforts on the longer term by embarking on a renewed drive to promote Gaelic games to an American-born grassroots, and one not necessarily of Irish descent. While this trend has been evident across the US, a number of the GAA's units there have been particularly progressive in this regard. As noted in Chapter 9, the decision of the New York board to suspend weekend sanctions for the 2004 season, albeit a move that was subsequently overturned, reveals that grassroots development is high on their agenda. Since then, GAA officials and enthusiasts there, not least those involved in the New York minor board, have continued to seek out ways of building for the future. In the early 2000s assistance was sought from the GAA in Ireland to organise coach education courses for those with aspirations to promote Gaelic games amongst American-born children. Considerable efforts have also been made in attempting to introduce Gaelic football to a much broader ethnic constituency through a number of high schools in the New York metropolitan area. Noel O'Connell, president of the minor board, argues that this less ethnically limited approach to selling Gaelic games in post-9/11 America is integral to the future of Gaelic games there:

> With the problems of immigration there is going to be that gap from first generation to third and fourth generation, so we have to find a way to fill that void. Not everybody can draw on heritage so we have to try to package the sport in an attractive way. You can't promote the game on the basis of heritage if someone doesn't have Irish blood . . . I feel that we have to reach outside the Irish community to get the athletes we need (interview, 26 Aug. 2004).

In order to broaden the reach of the GAA in the way that O'Connell was advocating, in 2008 the New York board advertised for a sports development officer whose remit was partially oriented around promoting Gaelic games to children and establishing the sort of youthful grassroots that would make clubs less reliant on the import of players from Ireland in the future. This commitment to the establishment of youth infrastructures and promoting Gaelic games to Irish and non-Irish Americans has been evident elsewhere in the US, but it has been particularly marked and innovative in San Francisco.

That San Francisco has been at the forefront of this strategy is hardly surprising. As discussed in Chapter 8, the city's Gaels have long exhibited a commitment to youth development, perhaps most notably through the establishment of the Irish Youth Football League (IFYL) in 1994. The inception of the Continental Youth Championships (CYC) ten years later, on the back of the work of the San Francisco GAA stalwart, John O'Flynn, and his efforts in helping to roll out youth programmes across America was also crucial and did much to publicise Gaelic games to the broader American-born public. For O'Flynn, this approach is essential if Gaelic games are to prosper in the US: 'That is going to be our future – expanding to kids that are non-Irish. We say it is the greatest game in the world but it has been hidden. Now it is being exposed' (interview, 27 Aug. 2006). Others within the city's GAA fraternity share O'Flynn's philosophy about how best to maintain the long-standing heritage of Gaelic games, and have begun to respond to the impact of post-9/11 immigration levels in innovative ways. Eamon Gormley, former public relations officer for both the Western divisional board and the NACB, has been particularly influential in this objective. Gormley had seen his own club, San Jose St Josephs, fold early in the new millennium as a consequence of falling levels of immigration and this helped to shape his belief that the future health of the GAA is dependent on well organised youth programmes that appeal to American-born players, including both those with Irish lineage and those without. As he saw it:

> With emigration from Ireland winding down and going into reverse, American-born players must become the backbone of our clubs in the long term if the games are to survive out here. They are a huge resource that can and must be tapped (cited in *Irish Herald*, July 2005, p. 36)

Such were his convictions about how the Association should evolve in post-9/11 America that, in March 2005, Gormley organised a seminar for local GAA clubs in the Bay Area which encouraged them to market themselves more effectively as part of a strategy to 'cast the net wide to expose the masses to our unique games' (cited in Reidy, 2005: 39).[2] The presence of O'Flynn, Gormley and other like-minded Gaelic games enthusiasts, within the Western division, has allowed it to take great strides in opening up Gaelic sports to a wider constituency. For example, continued progress has been made in promoting Gaelic football in local schools[3]; American-born only teams, such as the Celts, have been established at junior level to provide a vehicle to allow young American players to progress beyond youth programmes and hurling teams have been established at Stanford University and University of California, Berkeley (Leavitt, 2009)[4]. The Western division has also drawn on information technology in an attempt to extend the reach of Gaelic games, with podcasts of matches available through itunes and translation software used to make the division's website available in Spanish, thus providing opportunities for clubs to tap into the sizeable Hispanic community in the Bay Area (interview with Eamon Gormley, 27 Aug. 2006).

In the opening years of the new millennium, the efforts of US-based Gaels to promote Gaelic games earned recognition and support from both the GAA's overseas development committee based in Croke Park and the Irish government. Beyond eulogising about the value of Gaelic games for the Irish diaspora in America, financial support was made available at various stages in this period to organise coaching courses and support the appointment of development officers. The most significant development, though, was undoubtedly the announcement, in June 2008, of a partnership agreement between the GAA and the Irish government's Department of Foreign Affairs (DFA) to promote Gaelic games abroad. As part of this partnership, the GAA invested $150,000 and the DFA $100,000 to support four posts across the US that will focus on implementing an extensive and wide-ranging youth development initiative (Irish Department of Foreign Affairs Press Release, 24 June 2008).[5]

The GAA and Irishness in post-9/11 America

This sort of support from Ireland has been well received both within the NACB and the New York board and should go some way towards guaranteeing a future for the GAA in America irrespective of levels of Irish immigration in years to come. However, the emphasis on youth development programmes, particularly the promotion of Gaelic games to non-ethnically Irish US citizens, has raised questions in the minds of some Gaels about the *raison d'être* of the Association in post-9/11 America. As has been demonstrated in this study, the GAA has historically provided a platform for the preservation and articulation of ethnic Irishness in America and it was this function that did much to sustain

Gaelic games in times of difficulty. While GAA clubs have alway
non-Irish players when circumstances dictated,⁶ the recent drive ı
Gaelic games to a range of ethnic constituencies in America has the ן
create a body that is less distinctively Irish. For some this is problε
least because it is viewed as a process that could undermine the deeply rooted,
cultural and political significance of the GAA. One long-standing San Francisco
Gael expressed these concerns in the following terms:

> One of my comments would be that people over here don't understand the history
> of the GAA or what it is about and I find that that does get lost over here more
> and more so. I find over here that the culture of being a Gael is getting lost . . .
> I was always brought up to believe that it was very Irish to play and I was very
> proud of that. I just feel that that is maybe lost a wee bit over here (interview,
> 28 Aug. 2006).

Although some feel that part of the essence of Gaelic sport might be lost in
the drive to broaden its appeal, others welcome any moves aimed at making the
GAA more inclusive and ethnically diverse. Indeed, for individuals involved in
this process, the future of Gaelic games in the US should be predicated not on
their Irishness but rather purely on their aesthetic qualities as sporting pursuits.
Speaking specifically about the spread of this philosophy in San Francisco,
Eamon Gormley commented that:

> our plan in San Francisco is about how to generate growth . . . and how to
> evangelise and say there's a new game in town, to say what are the benefits for
> them, not necessarily 'take up this game because it's Irish' . . . We need to talk
> about the inherent qualities of the games, the fact that it's faster, it's higher
> scoring, it's better to watch, there's more skill and it has the benefits of almost
> every other sport combined (interview, 27 Aug. 2007).

It is clear from these kinds of sentiments that the ways in which the GAA
has had to adapt in post-9/11 America has the potential to create fissures
between those who have a less ethnically-bound view of what the Association *is*
and who it should be *for* and traditionalists who would rather see Gaelic games
remain linked to ethnic versions of Irish identity and retain the capacity to function as vehicles for the expression of politicised nationalist discourse. Nonetheless,
despite the concerns of those who hold this latter position, the move towards
more inclusive youth programmes and recruitment strategies appears inexorable

for as long as levels of Irish immigration remain so low and the policing of US borders so stringent.

This study reveals that the GAA's response to the virtual cessation of Irish immigration following the events of 9/11 has begun to have an impact on the nature of the Irishness traditionally expressed in and through Gaelic games. It is important to recognise and account for the fact that this process has also been reflective of and influenced by broader developments in Irish America that have been occurring simultaneously. Shifts in Irish-American identity politics heralded by the peace process in Northern Ireland and Al-Qaeda's attacks on New York and Washington in 2001 and, more specifically, the security clamp-down that emerged in their aftermath, are significant here. These events have contributed to increasing levels of support for the constitutional nationalist position in the US and a concomitant decline in the propensity of Irish republicans there to publicly express a more hard line, militant view. Part of the reason for this latter development can be found in broader concerns amongst Irish republicans, particularly those who may be undocumented, about falling foul of the US Citizenship and Immigration Services (USCIS) or other arms of the Department of Homeland Security. While these concerns are by no means new,[7] they have been heightened post 9/11, not least because of a number of recent high profile cases of the detention or deportation of known Irish republicans (Cochrane, 2007). As a consequence of this clampdown and the fears within the Irish emigrant community that it has nourished, those with strongly held militant beliefs, including members of the GAA, have become much more circumspect about openly engaging in political activities that may bring them under the surveillance radar of the US authorities. In the past, influential GAA figures such as Michael Flannery or John 'Kerry' O'Donnell would have had no difficulty in ensuring that Gaelic Park in New York operated as a space that helped keep support for physical force nationalism alive; however, GAA members in post-9/11 America, particularly those who may be residing in the country illegally, are much more cautious about marrying their involvement in Gaelic games with support for Irish republicanism.

Beyond these practical concerns there are other, more ideological processes at play in the minds of GAA members with republican sympathies that have fed into their reluctance to express their politics in public ways. It is possible, if not likely, that the events of 9/11 forced America's Gaels, especially those in New York, to consider the contradictions inherent in their public condemnation of the actions of middle-eastern terrorists and expression of sympathies for those who lost their lives while at the same time remaining supportive of violent republicanism in Ireland.[8] Alongside this sort of individual or collective introspection, republicans and Irish nationalists generally have become much more conscious, than they would have been prior to 9/11, about openly venting politicised forms of Irishness because of what they perceive to be an increasingly simplistic view of Irish politics on the part of the majority of Americans. This perception has emerged largely on the back of the formation of republican splinter groups in the aftermath of the signing of the Good Friday Agreement in Northern Ireland, a development that some argue has created confusion about the aims of the increasing numbers of republican organisations that exist today.[9] This has led to concerns that public displays of politicised Irishness could be misconstrued by the American public or indeed, the US authorities, as being supportive of terrorism in its broadest sense.[10]

One of the clearest examples of this process playing itself out in a public way in Irish America can be found in the decision taken by the Irish County Associations of New York to remove a banner emblazoned with the words 'England Get Out of Ireland' from the front of the St Patrick's Day parade in 2002. This decision to break with a tradition that had been in existence since the onset of the Troubles in Northern Ireland may have been partially a response to the peace process in Northern Ireland. However, as Seamus Dooley, a former chairman of the New York GAA board and a resident of the city since 1970, observed, it was also linked to the broader post-9/11 atmosphere in the city and concerns that the banner might be misinterpreted and cause offence to the American public:

> The 'England Get Out of Ireland' banner was an issue and there were a few county associations that were concerned because of 9/11. Some people out here would have the view that if you were supporting republicanism, they might think that after 9/11 you were supporting terrorism (interview, Manhattan, 30 July 2004).[11]

Clearly then, while a small cadre remains supportive of and agitates openly for a physical-force approach to ending partition in Ireland, mainstream Irish republicans have thought carefully since September 2001 about how they espouse their political beliefs in the public sphere. This process has been reflected within US branches of the GAA and, in so doing, has helped to accelerate the broader depoliticisation of Gaelic games that began emerging in the mid-1990s (see Chapter 10). While this state of affairs has been reflective of oscillations in Irish-American identity politics, following recent events both in the US and

Ireland, it is fundamentally rooted in a growing belief that the future of the GAA will be predicated on the Association reaching out beyond its traditional constituency and appealing to young people, including those not of Irish descent, already living in America. This, it is argued, will allow Gaelic games to develop a solid, locally based grassroots that will sustain the Association well into the future. For those involved in this process, selling the ludic and aesthetic qualities of Gaelic football, hurling and camogie to a broader ethnic constituency rather than promoting them as a resource for the expression of narrowly conceived forms of Irishness will be vital to their survival and growth. Some GAA members in the US may have difficulties with seeing the Association eschew its historical association with ethnic, politicised and irredentist versions of Irish nationalism. However, should immigration levels remain where they are now, if Gaelic games are to survive and prosper in twenty-first century America it is clear that this is the path that the GAA must follow.

Notes

Introduction

1 The New York board of the Gaelic Athletic Association stands outside this governing body and is responsible for overseeing Gaelic games in the greater New York area.

2 Personal observations, Irish Cultural Centre, Canton, MA, September 2000.

3 The 1890 team was managed by Bill McGunnigle. The 1899 and 1900 teams were managed by Ned Hanlon and contained players with names such as McGann, Daly, Casey, Keeler, Kelley, Farrel, Jennings, McGuire, Dunn, Hughes, Kennedy and McGinnity.

4 The 1904 team managed by John J. McGraw included McGann, Devlin, Donlin, Shannon, Browne, Breshnahan, McCormick, Donlin and McGinnity. The 1911, 1912 and 1913 teams included Doyle, Devlin, Murray and Burns.

5 When asked to articulate the social significance of the GAA for the Irish diaspora, many of the respondents interviewed for this study noted that some Irish marriages in the US had their roots in the interactions that the Association facilitated.

Chapter One: Crossing the bowl of tears

1 James O'Toole (1999: 57) has argued, 'For the Massachusetts Puritans, the Irish were exemplars of the superstition, underdevelopment, and even barbarism which resulted from the failure to break the thrall of the Catholic religion, and their own "errand into the wilderness" was intended to provide both a refuge for the purity of religion and a model for England to emulate.'

2 The term 'Know-Nothingism' derives from the practices of the American nativist movement, particularly the Order of the Star Spangled Banner (OSSB), whose members uniformly responded to questions about their often violent activities with the standard reply of: 'I know nothing'.

3 O'Brien was succeeded by eleven Irish mayors, the most famous of which was James Michael Curley, who, during his colourful career, served as mayor on four occasions between 1914 and 1950 despite long-standing allegations of corruption.

4 Between 1871 and 1927 the mayor's office was occupied by Irish politicians for a total of only eight years. They were John Hopkins (1893–95), Edward F. Dunne (1905–7) and William E. Dever (1923–7).

Chapter Two: Sowing the seeds

1 For example, clearly demarcated boundaries were not used and the game was often interrupted by encroachments onto the 'field of play' by spectators.

2 As well as being the victims of ethnic and religious prejudice, sections of the Irish population were also the perpetrators of racial discrimination in Boston. During the second half of the nineteenth century Irish attitudes towards the African-American population were mixed. On the one hand liberal sections of the Irish-American community were staunch abolitionists. However, a sizeable proportion of that community was guilty of perpetrating the types of racism and discrimination which they themselves had experienced at the hands of the American nativist movement. For a general comment on Irish-African-American relations in this time period see Coogan (2000). For a detailed analysis of the relationship between Boston's Irish and Black communities see O'Connor (1994). It should be noted that the offending event at this picnic was included in the day's proceedings despite the presence of a number of staunch Irish abolitionists, including John Boyle O'Reilly, about whom we shall hear more of in this chapter.

3 Plans to revive the Tailteann Games were suspended until the early 1920s.

4 The book contained three detailed chapters on the ethics and evolution of boxing, training methods for athletes and ancient Irish athletic games as well as a series of short stories on the author's canoeing expeditions. O'Reilly is also described as an 'apostle of muscular Christianity' in Roche (1891: 202).

5 These included organisations such as the Irish Confederation of America (1882–9), the Federation of Irish County Societies of Brooklyn (1891–8) and the United Irish County Association (1891–7) (Ridge, 1997).

6 For example, the Kickhams were comprised almost entirely of Tipperary men and in 1904 they were renamed the Tipperary football team.

7 The Emmets, Shamrocks, Columbias and Innisfails were joined by the Grattons, O'Briens, Wolfe Tones, O'Connells, Davitts and Emeralds.

Chapter Three: Patriots and players

1 It should be noted that the practice of giving clubs in New York county names as opposed to those of nationalist heroes was not without controversy. For example, in 1916 there was a growing lobby for hurling and football teams to revive the tradition of using specifically Irish nationalist appellations. The county societies who by that stage had cemented their control of Gaelic games in the city were resolutely opposed and they insisted that all teams planning to participate in the 1917 season, of which there were 28, had to use county names. Critics of this directive argued that it was 'unpatriotic' (Hurley, 1917: 5).

2 This contention is made by drawing predominantly on newspapers, journals and magazines that were aimed specifically at Irish-American audiences. Whilst the sources used are unique for a study of this kind, there are potential problems in the 'reading' of these texts. As Jeff Hill (1996: 16) pointed out 'there are many dangers in accepting at its face value the language of the sporting press'. I recognise this fact and highlight in this chapter that the language used in these sources was intended to rouse the reader and encourage them to view Gaelic games in nationalistic terms.

Chapter Four: Preserving Ireland's sporting heritage

1   The counties represented at this initial meeting were Kilkenny, Tipperary, Cork, Sligo, Monaghan, Waterford, Galway and Roscommon.

2   Between 3,000 and 4,000 attended the games of the Kerrymen's Association at Celtic Park in late May 1904 while between 6,000 and 7,000 were present at the same venue for the games that took place as part of the Sligo Men's picnic in early June of the same year. These attendances were topped a week later during the annual games of the Kickhams athletic club at Celtic Park which featured a game between Kilkenny and Tipperary.

3   Evidence of an emerging culture of camogie can be found in the *The Irish American Advocate*, 8 June 1907, which advertised a camogie match between Birr and Nenagh. The camogie association of New York was established in 1930.

4   *The Gaelic American*, 1 Nov. 1913, reported that one outing per week took place during the 1913 season.

5   Hurley focused on one particular incident when a spectator had rushed onto the field and 'walloped' a player.

6   The *Gaelic American* carried a brief report of a Gaelic football game between Cork and Kerry in June of this year under the heading, the 'Gaelic League of New York'. *The Gaelic American*, 5 June 1915: 6.

7   Matches were played on the sports grounds of the Jesuit college, St Ignatius, in this period.

8   For the start of the 1913–14 season there were seven football teams (Celtics, Parnells, Rangers, Sarsfields, O'Growneys, McBrides and Geraldines).

9   This assertion is made on the back of comments made to this effect in a number of match reports published in *The Leader* during 1914.

Chapter Five: Fluctuating fortunes

1   The result was Tipperary 11: 4 (37) Offaly 2: 2 (8).

2   The GAA operated a 'Ban' policy at this time designed to prevent its members from playing, or using facilities associated with, 'foreign' sports.

3   Tours by Cavan, Galway and Limerick in 1934 had led to the respective county boards arguing that the US promoters had not fulfilled their financial obligations towards them and had left them with a deficit.

4   Irish immigration from Ireland to the US in the three decades prior to the 1930s stood at 390,065, 146,181 and 220,591 respectively. Between 1931 and 1940, this figure dropped to 13,167 (Fallows, 1979).

5   It should be noted that the tour of New York by Kerry and Galway in May of the following year did much to allow the GAA to recoup much of this deficit. The game at Yankee Stadium between Kerry and Galway which attracted a crowd of 20,000 was especially successful in this regard (O'Shea, 1939: 3).

6   Fund-raising games and other events were organised in this period for a number of Catholic churches in the city while a one-off GAA field day was held to raise money for Mary Scanlon, a young Irish girl who was severely injured when a fire engine accidentally crashed into her house on Christmas Day 1918. This benefit match, played on 17 July 1919 raised $328 (*The Leader*, 19 July 1919).

7   The new hurling clubs were Clare, Kerry and South of Market Boys while the football clubs were Laune Rangers, Mayo, Rovers, Celtics and Connaught. It should be noted that not all of these teams were in existence at the same time and that some lasted only a couple of years.

8   The teams involved were the Gaels, Cavan, Lees and St John's.

Chapter Six: Revival, 'Golden Age' and decline

1   Hennessey's contribution to the revival of Gaelic games in Chicago will be discussed in more detail later in the chapter.

2   The teams were St Simon Stock; Good Shepherd; St Pius; St Jerome's; St John's; Division 9 AOH; St Nick's; St Francis; Ascension; Division 4 AOH; St Luke's; Galway; Offaly; St Roses; Incarnation. This information was located in the GAA archive held at the Tamiment Library at New York University.

3   Mayor O'Dwyer's contribution was noted by Pádraig Ó Caoimh in his report to Central Council in December 1947. Ó Caoimh commented that the mayor sought frequent updates on what he referred to as 'the great project'. Mayor O'Dwyer also used his official position to secure publicity for the match in the city's principal newspapers (Pádraig Ó Caoimh report to Central Council GAA, 13 Dec. 1947). Dunne's (1997) account of the 1947 All-Ireland Gaelic football final in New York provides useful detail on some of the more general aspects of the match preparations.

4   Ó Caoimh noted in his report to Central Council (13 Dec. 1947) that the arrangements for the sale of tickets might have had a negative impact on the attendance. In their desire to prevent the tickets being bought by black-marketeers and sold on at inflated costs, the organising committee had decided not to use the services of the city's ticketing agencies and instead only sold tickets from a single location in Manhattan, controlled by the GAA.

5   By 1949 there were 65 GAA clubs in the city (special meeting of Central Council GAA Minutes, 17 Sept. 1949).

6   While New York was granted provincial status, the Association there was reclassified as an external association. The inception of the National GAA Council of the US in 1951, to be discussed later in this chapter, effectively negated the need to consider New York as anything other than an overseas branch of the Association.

7   The reason for the dispute was a misunderstanding about how the tours would proceed beyond 1951. New York felt that the GAA had agreed to two teams from the city playing the finals of the 1952 National League series in Dublin but the Dublin-based administration indicated that it would only discuss what would happen in 1952 following the conclusion of the 1951 series. This led to an exchange of terse letters between the New York GAA and Central Council. While the Dublin based administration did eventually agree to host two New York teams, O'Donnell publicly criticised Kehoe in the Irish-American press. Although he later apologised in a letter to Central Council, Kehoe refused to accept the apology and relations remained strained (special meeting of Central Council GAA, 12 May 1951; Central Council GAA Minutes, 15 Mar. 1952).

8   Tipperary won by 6-14 to 2-5 while Cork won 1-12 to 0-3.

9   The total costs incurred by the New York GAA to host five Irish county teams in 1957 was $133,000. Only a slight profit was made (*Irish Echo*, 1 Feb. 1957).

10   This move coincided with the visit to New York of All-Ireland hurling champions Kilkenny and their Gaelic football counterparts Louth (*Irish Echo*, 7 June 1958).

11   The gate receipts for the 1951 tour were £25,000. For 1954 this figure stood at £21,000 and in 1957 it had declined further to £17,000 (Annual Congress GAA Minutes, 29 Mar. 1959).

12   The last hurling final played under the auspices of the National Council of the GAA between Chicago and New York, drew a crowd of 10,000 to Chicago's Shewbridge field (*Chicago Daily Tribune*, 10 June 1956).

13   The principle players in the push for a national body included John O'Brien and Henry Cavanagh in Cleveland, Jack Courtenay and Fr Peter Quinn in Buffalo, Michael Cavanaugh of Philadelphia and Dan O'Kennedy of Detroit (*Irish Emigrant*, 22 Nov. 1999).

14   The NACB sought County Board status by encouraging affiliated delegates to put forward motions at a number of GAA Congresses in the early 1960s. This status was eventually granted by Central Council in 1993 (North American County Board, 1997).

15   The finals of the New York championship series in 1957 at Gaelic Park attracted an attendance of 3,000 (*Irish Echo*, 7 Sept. 1957). The diversity of causes that received donations from the New York GAA in this year was recorded in the body's Annual Report. The recipients included: Irish Freedom Committee; London Hostel Committee; Miscordia Hospital; Construction of Pearse Park in Galway; Construction of Casement Park in Belfast; United Irish Counties – Feis Committee; St Patrick's Missionaries; New Guinea Mission. The amount given to charitable causes in this year totalled $27,000.

16   O'Donnell's influence was formally acknowledged by the New York GAA when he was the unanimous choice as guest of honour at the Association's Golden Jubilee banquet in 1964 (*Irish Echo*, 7 Dec. 1963).

17   This is shown by record attendances and gate receipts for the various field days at Gaelic Park (*Irish Echo*, 7 Dec. 1963).

18   The match was won by Kilkenny by 4–16 to 3–13.

19   This tour was repeated by the city's hurlers in 1968 but featured a broader range of destinations including: Hawaii; Hong Kong; New Dehli; Cairo; Rome; Zurich and Paris (Byrne, 1976).

20   The 1921 Quota Act established the US's first immigration quotas. This was followed in 1924 by the Immigration Act that set an annual immigration limit of almost 155,000 per annum and allocated countries a quota based on its US population as determined by the 1920 census.

21   This was revealed to the GAA's Central Council by General Secretary Séan Ó Síocáin. One of the solutions proposed and eventually adopted, to make the tours more profitable, was to play the hurling and football matches over two legs.

22   Among O'Donnell's complaints were a change in venue for the hurling game between New York and Wexford, the failure of Cork's footballers to turn up for a game in Killarney against their New York counterparts and the failure of the GAA to provide medals for a match against Tipperary in Birr.

23   The county teams were Tyrone, Kerry, Leitrim and Kilkenny while the club teams were Kilmore (Wexford), Crossmolina (Mayo), Civil Service (Dublin), Crosserlough (Cavan) and St Eunan's (Donegal). The Connaught Railway Cup team also played at Gaelic Park, the first visit by an inter-provincial team to the US, in the Cardinal Cushing Games which had been played since the mid 1960s in order to raise funds for Catholic missions around the world.

24 In 1959 San Francisco captured the inaugural NACB hurling championship while its footballers won the Gaelic football title the following year. In 1962 Boston Galway and San Francisco shared the football title while Boston Galway secured the hurling accolade. In 1963 Boston Galway and Chicago's Shannon Rangers captured the football and hurling titles respectively. Boston Galway secured the hurling championship in 1964 while two years later Chicago's Harry Bolands won the first of its national titles. Boston Galway secured another hurling crown in 1967 and again the following year. Chicago St Patrick's achieved their first football crown in 1968 and their neighbours, Harry Bolands won their second national hurling championship in 1969.

25 The teams that affiliated to the NACB in 1959 were Galway, Kerry, Erins Hope and Cork in football and Galway, Young Irelands and Fr Tom Burkes in hurling. In 1965, the complement of affiliated clubs in Boston consisted of Kerry, Springfields, Cork, Hartford, Galway, Erins Hope, Connaught Stars, Connemara Gaels and Cavan in football and Cork Hibernians, Galway, Fr Tom Burkes and Young Irelands.

26 In hurling, the teams were St Vincent's, Limerick, Shannon Rangers and Harry Bolands while the four football clubs were John McBride's, Erins Own, Wolfe Tones and St Brendan's (North American County Board, 1997).

27 The Gaelic football clubs were Connaught, Cork, Kerry, Ulster, Leinster, Mission Gaels and Young Irelands while the hurling clubs were Cork, Sarsfields, Young Irelands and St Mary's.

28 The healthy financial position of the city's GAA was such that the Kerry club were able to embark on a six week tour to Ireland, the first by a club from the West coast (*Irish Herald*, Feb. 1965).

Chapter Seven: Lest we forget

1 The Ulster Covenant was signed by 470,000 Unionists as part of their response to the possibility of Home Rule. The establishment of the Ulster Volunteers was also a reaction to fears about Home Rule.

2 Patrick Pearse, who was executed by the British following his leading role in the failed Easter Rising in 1916, founded this school for boys in 1908. Students were instructed in Irish history and language whilst their physical education included Gaelic games. *Gaelic American*, 'Gaels preparing for St Enda's field day at Celtic Park', 11 Apr. 1914.

3 The participating clubs were Kerry, Kildare, Monaghan, Cavan, Tipperary and Kilkenny in football and Limerick, Clare, Offaly and Kerry in hurling.

4 A 'shoneen' was a slang term used to describe an individual with pro-British political and cultural leanings.

5 Beyond the Martyrs Fund, San Francisco's Gaels also organised a series of field days to raise funds for St Enda's College in Dublin (*The Leader*, 15 Feb. 1919).

6 O'Donnell's status as a republican sympathiser and supporter of the IRA was made explicit to me during a series of interviews with current and former members of the New York GAA. Interview with Terry Connaughton, 27 July 2003; Interview with Noel O'Connell, 26 Aug. 2004; interview with Monty Maloney, 28 Aug. 2004.

7 Irish Northern Aid was established ostensibly to collect money in the US to support the families of republican prisoners in Northern Ireland. However, the American, British and

Irish governments came to the conclusion that its primary function was to raise funds to arm the IRA and as such the organisation was proscribed by all three governments.

8   Flannery was also indicted in 1981 on charges of gun running for the Provisional IRA (PIRA) but was later acquitted. Until his death, he remained opposed to the peace process in Northern Ireland and was a regular contributor to republican Sinn Féin which broke off from Sinn Féin in 1986. Flannery's uncompromising stance over the Irish question brought him into conflict with moderates on both sides of the Atlantic. When he was appointed Grand Marshall of the New York St Patrick Day's parade, the Irish government refused to allow any government agency to take part. Opposition also emanated from influential Irish-American circles. For example, Governor Hugh Carey refused to take part while the Cardinal of New York, Terence Cooke also snubbed the parade, closing the gates of St Patrick's Cathedral on Manhattan's Fifth Avenue just as the Parade passed (Rohan, 1994a; Reimers, 1997).

9   O'Dwyer was part of the organising committee for the Irish Freedom Field Day held on 31 March 1957 at Gaelic Park (Meagher, 1957).

Chapter Eight: Striving to survive

1   The New England divisional GAA board changed its name to the North Eastern Divisional GAA board in 1998 (see chapter 10). The terms, New England and North Eastern are used interchangeably in this chapter.

2   Those clubs that competed in the inaugural youth league were Jamaica Plain Shamrocks, St Joseph's, Columkilles and Dedham Gaelics.

3   The camogie clubs, Eire Og, Celtics, Claddagh and St Bridget's, were formed in 1978, 1981 and 1982 respectively. The other clubs founded in this period were Shannon Blues, St Patrick's, Columbkilles, Jamaica Plain Shamrocks and Charlestown in football whilst Tipperary were added to the roster of hurling clubs.

4   For those not formally affiliated to a club, attending Gaelic football, hurling or camogie matches in Boston as a spectator has also afforded individuals with the opportunity to wear their county-based identity on their sleeves through the donning of replica county shirts. This is a common occurrence at GAA matches and events in Boston (personal observations during training sessions for the Notre Dame Gaelic football club at Soldiers Field, Brighton and during matches at Canton, MA, July–Sept. 2000).

5   A large number of Irish contractors are involved in the building trade in Boston and suburbs, many of whom are involved in the GAA as officials and/or benefactors. It is predominantly through these contacts that opportunities for work come. Clubs in Boston will also rent accommodation on short-term leases for players who fly out to the city for the summer season.

6   During the author's fieldwork in Boston between July and September 2000, it was clear that the practice of paying top-level players for their services was widespread. For example, for the 2000 season modest intermediate clubs were paying between $3,000 and $6,000 to secure the services of inter-county players. Subsequent fieldwork in Chicago, New York and San Francisco coupled with conversations with members of GAA clubs in Ireland confirmed this.

7   Notwithstanding the current payment of 'grants' to inter-county players by the Irish Sports Council from the 2008 season onwards as part of a deal brokered between the GAA, the Gaelic Players' Association (GPA) and the Irish government.

8   The term 'junior' in GAA parlance relates to the standard of play rather than the age of participants. There are three standards at adult level – junior, intermediate and senior.

9   Some of these venues included Boston Common, Victory Field, Tech Field, Hormel Stadium, Smith Field, Cleveland Circle, Foxboro Stadium, Columbia Park, Boston College and more recently Dilboy Field.

10   These clubs were Shannon Rangers, St Patrick's, Harry Bolands, St Vincent's, Wolfe Tones, John McBrides, St Brendan's and Limerick.

11   For example, the Chicago Rovers Juvenile team was formed in 1972.

12   The match was aired in the city's Ritz Theater and was attended by a crowd in excess of 1,100 (NACB, 1997).

13   Sligo New York played Castlebar from County Mayo in Gaelic football while New York Waterford played a Chicago select team in hurling. The schedule also included a Gaelic football match between Hartford and a Chicago select while Detroit faced Chicago Rovers in junior football (Prescott, 1985; NACB, 1997).

14   They were named after the Congressman who initiated the bill to have the visas introduced.

15   For example, in 1998 Gaelic Park leased a further 25 acres of land for Gaelic sporting and cultural activities, thus raising the total acreage of the facility to 50. During the 1980s and 1990s Gaelic Park became home to a rich and diverse range of Irish groups and activities including the Gaelic Players theatre group, a literary group, Irish language classes, set dancing classes, a monthly mass and breakfast, and various Irish luncheon groups. In addition, the bar shows live telecasts of Gaelic sports games from Ireland while the various banqueting facilities regularly play host to Irish-American weddings.

16   These teams met in the Chicago championship final. Wolfe Tones emerged as victors but St Brendan's immediately lodged an appeal on the grounds that their opponents had broken the NACB's rules regarding the number of 'sanction' or imported players who could be on the field at any one time. With no documentary evidence available from the referee, and with a video recording of the game allegedly being doctored by members of the Wolfe Tones club, the appeal to the Chicago central divisional board was unsuccessful. At this stage, however, the NACB stepped in and ordered that the match be replayed in order to expedite the playing of the All-American finals which was contested by the winners of the various US divisions. With both teams travelling to Boston for the finals convinced that they were the rightful Chicago champions, the replay was fixed for the morning that the tournament was due to begin. Wolfe Tones did not appear for the replay though and St Brendan's were declared victors and Chicago's representatives in the final of the NACB play-off due to be staged the following day. Just prior to this match starting though Wolfe Tones' players arrived at Canton and proceeded to warm-up on the pitch designated to host the final. Attempts at negotiation were ignored and it was not until the local police were called that the players and officials of Wolfe Tones left the pitch. Wolfe Tones were subsequently heavily fined and suspended from NACB competition for 12 months (later reduced to 6 on appeal). According to Joe Begley, former chairman of the Chicago central GAA, this affair did much to sully the reputation of Gaelic games in Chicago and added further to what had for some time been an openly hostile relationship between both clubs (interview, 31 July 2005).

17   The final clause in these new bye-laws ensured that a minimum of five 'resident' players per team were required to feature in each match.

18   These fixtures between the hurling and football All-Stars against the winners of the All-Ireland Championship in both codes began in 1971 and continued for the remainder of the 1970s.

19   In an interview in *The Irish Herald/The New Irish Gael* in August 2005, Jimmy Cotter, a member of the local GAA since 1950 recalled playing for a San Francisco Gaelic football select against their New York counterparts in a team containing a Czech-Italian, a New Zealander as well as a number of San Francisco-born players of Irish lineage (Reidy, 2005).

20   Such is his contribution to the promotion of Gaelic games at youth level in San Francisco and throughout the US that in 2006, he was selected in the top 100 Irish American's of the year by the New York based magazine, *Irish America* (Carroll, 2006).

21   For example, three inter-county Roscommon footballers received lengthy suspensions from the GAA for playing illegally for the Galway club in Boston (Moran, 1997).

22   In December 2008, the San Francisco GAA officially opened a 13-acre venue containing three playing fields on Treasure Island, a former naval base on a man-made island in San Francisco bay (halfway between Oakland and San Francisco). The Treasure Island project was facilitated by a board comprised of local GAA officials and enthusiasts, significant voluntary work by a number of Irish contractors and labourers, private donations and a grant of half a million dollars from Croke Park and the Irish government. Stage two of the $5.2 million project will involve a 25,000-square-foot community centre and clubhouse. The fields, named Páirc na nGael, were officially opened on 7 December 2008 by Nicky Brennan, outgoing president of the GAA and were visited a week later by the president of Ireland, Mary McAleese. The official opening featured a match between the 2007 Gaelic Football All-Stars and their 2008 counterparts (Ryan, 2009).

Chapter Nine: Ourselves alone

1   For example, Ballantine Brewery supported New York's 1964 'World Tour' while Schaefer Beer sponsored a range of GAA competitions in the city.

2   According to Terry Connaughton, a former president of the New York GAA board, by the time he took up this position for the first time in 1974, TelePrompter had ceased showing games from Gaelic Park (interview, 27 Aug. 2003).

3   This tradition of live coverage of Gaelic games played in Ireland continues to the current day. Advances in satellite television technologies means that all stages of the All-Ireland series are widely available, predominantly in Irish bars and cultural centres across the US.

4   By 1981, the minor board was comprised of around 2,000 American-born youth players (O'Shea, 1981).

5   The New York minor board encompassed 6 age ranges: under-10, under-12, under-14, under-16, under-18 and under-21.

6   For example, a former player of the St Raymond's club recounted to me that he won a junior championship in 1977 with a team that contained 11 American-born players (interview, 26 Aug. 2004).

7   In 1980, the number of immigrants admitted to the US legally stood at 1,006. By 1990, the figure was 4,479.

8   By 1987, the junior football competition had grown so large that it was split into two sections in order to ensure that the season's schedule of games was completed.

9   Detailed disciplinary procedures governing the movement of players to New York and North America more generally were also set out by Central Council in April 1989 (Central Council GAA minutes, 28–29 Apr. 1989).

10   For example, for the first two years that it was affiliated to the Association in Ireland, New York did not operate under the Official Guide of the parent body and instead conducted itself according to local Bye-Laws (Management Committee GAA minutes, 24/25 May 1989).

11   The swift progress that was made in ladies' Gaelic football circles in New York was achieved with limited support from the men's GAA board. For example, in 1994 the ladies' board applied to their male counterparts to use Gaelic Park for a field day to raise funds for a New York ladies select trip to Ireland. The New York board refused and instead offered a flat donation of $400 (Rohan, 1994b).

12   This prompted some Tara Circle supporters to claim that the local residents who opposed the GAA stadium did so because of anti-Irish prejudice (Rohan, 1993b).

13   Following Sheeran's bankruptcy questions were asked in the Irish-American press about where the money invested in the project, not least an estimated $150,000 from the GAA, had gone. It was later revealed that four members of the Tara Circle committee were drawing down salaries. In Sheeran's bankruptcy proceedings it was revealed that since 1993, he had been paid $1000 per month in consultancy fees from a not for profit organisation, which in all likelihood was Tara Circle (Rohan, 1998a).

14   Clubs were only allowed to import three players from Ireland for games during the regular season. In order to be eligible to represent a New York club in the play-off stage of the season, a player must have played for the club by the last game of the regular season.

15   The players were Dessie Farrell, Ciaran Walsh and Pat Gilroy. Their 'illegality' was due to the fact that they had not played for the Leitrim club prior to the final.

16   The players included Kerry's Dara O'Cinneide, Dara O'Se and Fergal O'Se, Kieran McGeeney of Armagh, Martin Flanagan of Westmeath, Vincent Mooney of Offaly, Martin McHugh, then manager of Cavan and a sizeable contingent from Donegal.

17   Many clubs in New York were becoming increasingly disgruntled by what was perceived as mercenary demands made by players in Ireland who were approached to play in the city. The logistical difficulties associated with ensuring that players could enter the US post 9/11 also raised the costs involved in flying out players. In this period a number of players flying directly to New York were refused entry by US immigration officials. To counteract this, clubs were forced to fly players from UK or European airports, thus raising the level of expenditure (interview with Kieran O'Sullivan, 24 July 2004).

18   The softball diamond was added by Manhattan College in the early 1990s when Gaelic Park was not hosting GAA matches.

Chapter Ten: The GAA, Northern Ireland's 'Troubles' and Irish-American identity politics

1   A 14th victim of the shooting later lost his life as a result of his wounds. Those involved in the march were protesting against the introduction of Internment, the policy of arresting and imprisoning people without trial on suspicion of involvement in terrorist activities. This measure was introduced in Northern Ireland on 9 August 1971.

2   Bobby Sands, a member of the PIRA, began his hunger strike on 1 March 1981. The main demand underpinning the strike was the reintroduction of special category or 'political' status for republican prisoners. When the hunger strike campaign ended on 3 October 1981, 9 other prisoners had died.

3   Hehir's observations were supported during many informal conversations with GAA members in Boston during the first phase of field work for this book in July and September 2000.

4   The 18-year-old Grenadier Guardsman charged with the unlawful killing of Aidan McAnespie claimed that he had been cleaning his weapon when his finger had slipped discharging three shots, one of which ricocheted and hit McAnespie in the back, killing him instantly. The official inquiry into the incident has proved inconclusive and the McAnespie family suspect a conspiracy and cover-up (Fahy, 2001).

5   It should be noted that Rule 21 has since been rescinded from the Association's rule book.

6   The closing of some border roads in this way was a move aimed at restricting the movement of members of the PIRA from Northern Ireland into the relative sanctuary of the Republic of Ireland.

7   This threat was repeated by another Loyalist paramilitary group, the Red Hand Commandoes (RHC), 2 years later. This was anything but an idle threat and the Association in the north of Ireland suffered damage to property and the loss of some of its members in this period (Fahy, 2001).

8   Power-sharing arrangements and government structures in Northern Ireland remain fragile. For example, for much of 2008 the Northern Ireland Executive failed to meet because of a dispute between Sinn Féin and the Democratic Unionist Party over the devolution of policing and justice powers. In addition, in the space of three days in March 2009, two British soldiers and a police officer were shot dead by members of two dissident republican groups. While it was initially felt that this would serve to destabilise the Executive, unified condemnation of the murders by the First Minister, Peter Robinson, and Deputy First Minister, Martin McGuinness, served to increase confidence in the permanence of power-sharing.

9   The IFC currently has chapters in Boston, Chicago, New York, New Jersey, Philadelphia, Indiana, New Mexico and Worcester.

10   This process was aided by the global artistic success of Michael Flatley, the Chicago-born Irish dancer, choreographer and chief force behind *Riverdance* and *Lord of the Dance*.

11   This assertion is based on my ethnographic research on Gaelic games over much of the period in question.

12   The motion to amend Rule 42 was carried allowing the Irish rugby and soccer teams to play home games at Croke Park until the completion of the redevelopment of Lansdowne Road.

13   The Armalite rifle featured prominently in the PIRA's arsenal of weaponry. The term 'the Armalite and Ballot Box' was coined in the early 1980s and described the republican movement's dual approach of paramilitary activity and democratic politics on the issue of the British presence in Northern Ireland.

Conclusion

1   This observation is made on the strength of numerous conversations with members of GAA clubs in the US during fieldwork between 2000 and 2006.

2   This seminar was repeated in Philadelphia.

3   For example, the SFGAA was able to convince Rhythm and Moves, a company which provides physical education curriculum to schools to incorporate Gaelic football into their programmes. Children from a range of ethnic backgrounds have also been exposed to Gaelic games in the city via the YMCA and Boys and Girls Clubs of America (Ryan, 2009).

4   Stanford University and University of California, Berkeley played the first ever collegiate hurling match in North America on 31 January 2009.

5   As noted in chapters 8 and 9, financial support for US branches of the GAA from Croke Park and the DFA also extended to the construction or refurbishment of playing facilities.

6   This trend has been particularly evident amongst GAA clubs set up to cater for women. Indeed, this has allowed these clubs to survive and prosper. Olivia Cahill, a founder of the Waterford Ladies' Gaelic football club in Boston, where the women's game is particularly strong, observed that while women's clubs do recruit players from Ireland many contain a significant proportion of American-born talent, including those without Irish ancestry (interview, 25 July 2000).

7   Since the early 1970s, the Federal Bureau of Investigation (FBI) was engaged in surveillance of those in the Irish community in the US who were supportive of the Provisional IRA, some of whom they believed were engaged in illegal gun-running operations (Wilson, 1995). In the early 1990s these surveillance activities intensified and according to some Irish activists, the FBI's counter-terrorism agents increasingly employed 'pressure tactics' including phone tapping and open harassment in order to dissuade expressions of support for and donations to the militant nationalist cause. Noraid came in for particular attention at this time and according to Mary McCormick, then a Noraid member and director of San Francisco's United Irish Societies, this was designed 'to scare people off' and was aimed at conveying the message that 'If you get to close to Noraid, we're going to watch you closely' (cited in Doyle, 1995: 3).

8   In the aftermath of 9/11 the New York GAA cancelled all of its scheduled games and held an open air mass that was attended by an estimated 6,000 people. According to Seamus Dooley, former president of the NYGAA board, this commemorative mass was attended by many well-known republicans (interview, 30 July 2003).

9   This view was expressed to me by numerous Irish migrants in the US during the research stages of this book.

10   Incidents such as the adding of the Continuity IRA to the US State Department's list of worldwide terrorist organisations and recent public criticism of Sinn Féin by both the Bush administration and influential sections of the Irish-American lobby, following concerns about suspected IRA criminality in 2005, has contributed to this state of affairs (Lacey, 2001; Hoge, 2005).

11 Noel O'Connell, former chairman of the New York minor GAA board, confirmed that the decision to remove the banner and the broader move to downplay Irish republican sentiments was also rooted in the fact that there were sections of American society that saw the republican movement as an element of the broader 'global' terror threat:

> The overall feeling was that those sorts of sentiments should be put on the back burner and that people should try to move on. Since 9/11 certain people who aren't familiar with Irish history have been a factor. That's another reason why people who were very pro-republican movement have decided to ease up' (interview, 26 Aug. 2004).

A similar trend has also been evident in the St Patrick's Day celebrations in San Francisco. Indeed, according to Eamon Gormley, in recent years there has been a palpable change in the tone of the Irishness expressed within the parade, one that whilst still political and concerned with highlighting perceived British injustices in Northern Ireland, is much less focused around 'a more belligerent "we're gonna kick you out of our country" nationalism' (interview, 27 Aug. 2006).

aphy

Abbott, W. C. (1929) *New York in the American Revolution, 1763–1783*. New York and London: Charles Scribner and Son.

Anderson, B. (1991) *Imagined Communities: Reflections on the Origins and Spread of Nationalism*. London: Verso.

Bairner, A. (2001) *Sport, Nationalism and Globalization: European and North American Perspectives*. Albany: State University of New York Press.

Bairner, A. (2005) 'Introduction: sport and the Irish', in A. Bairner (ed.), *Sport and the Irish: Histories, Identities, Issues*. Dublin: UCD Press, pp. 1–6.

Bairner, A. (2007) 'National Sports and national landscapes: in defence of primordialism', unpublished paper presented at Hitotsubashi University, Tokyo, Japan, Mar. 2007.

Bairner, A. (2008) 'National sports and national landscapes real and imagined', in S. Wucior and G. Maziarczyk (eds), *Literature and/in Culture*. Lublin, Towarzysto Naukowe KUL, pp. 19–32.

Bairner, A. and Darby, P. (1998) 'Divided sport in a divided society: Northern Ireland', in J. Sugden and A. Bairner (eds), *Sport in Divided Societies*. Aachen: Meyer & Meyer, pp. 51–72.

Beatty, J. (1992) *The Rascal King: The Life and Times of James Michael Curley (1874–1958)*. Reading, MA: Addison-Wesley.

Belluck, P. (1995) *New York Times*, 13 Apr. 1995, p. B1.

Bjarkman, P. C. (1992) 'Forgotten Americans and the national pastime: literature on baseball's ethnic, religious, and racial diversity', *Multi-Cultural Review*, 1 (Apr.), pp. 46–8.

Bjarkman, P. C. (1999) *The Boston Celtics Encyclopaedia*. Champaign, IL: Sagamore.

Black, M. F. (1997) 'Cultural identity: sport, gender, nationalism and the Irish diaspora', PhD dissertation, University of California, Berkeley.

Brady, F. (2007) 'Grand new era for Gaelic Park', *Irish Echo*, 5–11 Dec. 2007.

Brady, S. (2005) *Irish Sport and Culture at New York's Gaelic Park*, PhD dissertation, School of Arts and Science, New York University.

Brady, S. (2007) 'Home and away: The Gaelic games, gender and migration', *New Hibernia Review* 11 (3), pp. 28–43.

Breatnac, S. (1970) 'Should Irish eyes be smiling', *San Francisco Magazine*, Aug. 1970, pp. 16–18.

Brennan, G. (2004) 'Giving up on America', *Irish Voice*, 19 May 2004, p. 6.

Breslin, S. (2000a) 'Distant kingdom', *Hogan Stand*, 28 Apr., pp. 32–8.

Breslin, S. (2000b) 'Start spreading the news', *Hogan Stand*, 28 Apr. 2000, pp. 39–41.

Brown, T. N. (1966) *Irish-American Nationalism, 1870–1890*. Westport, Conn.

Brundage, D. (1997) 'In time of peace, prepare for war: key themes in the social thought of New York's Irish nationalists, 1890–1916', in R. H. Bayor and T. J. Meagher (eds), *The New York Irish*. Baltimore and London: Johns Hopkins University Press, pp. 321–4.

Burchell, R. A. (1979) *The San Francisco Irish: 1848–1880*. Manchester: Manchester University Press.

Burns, K. (1988) 'San Francisco all stars make game of it', *The Irishman*, June 1988, p. 16.

Byrne, J. (1969a) 'New York's hurling history', *Irish Echo*, 6 Dec. 1969, pp. 22–3.

Byrne, J. (1969b) 'New York's voice in Ireland', *Irish Echo*, 27 Dec. 1969, p. 22.

Byrne, J. (1969c) '1968 GAA review', *Irish Echo*, 1 Mar. 1969, p. 22.

Byrne, J. (1969d) 'Thoughts and reflections of 1969', *Irish Echo*, 20 Dec. 1969, p. 26.

Byrne, J. (1969e) '1968 GAA review', *Irish Echo*, 1 Mar. 1969, p. 22.

Byrne, J. (1970a) 'The Harry Bolands of Chicago', *Irish Echo*, 14 Feb. 1970, p. 22.

Byrne, J. (1970b) 'Sean Maxwell – an appreciation', *Irish Echo*, 7 Mar. 1970, p. 22.

Byrne, J. (1976) 'The New York GAA, 1914–1976', in D. Guiney (ed.), *The New York Irish*. Dublin: Gaelic Press, pp. 6–24.

Byrne, J. (1984) 'New York GAA okays unlimited player imports', *Irish Echo*, 18 Feb. 1984, p. 34.

Byrne, J. (1989) 'The Gaelic Athletic Association of greater New York: seventy five years of Gaelic sports', *The GAA Annual Banquet (75th Anniversary) Official Programme*. New York.

Carroll, L. (2006) 'John O'Flynn', *Irish America*, April–May 2006, pp. 86–8.

Carroll, J. (1999), 'Fighting Irish', http://www.newcitychicago.com/home/daily/feature/092799.html, accessed on 3 June 2008.

Celtic Monthly, 'John Boyle O'Reilly: the story of his eventful career', Aug. 1879, pp. 76–82.

Clark, D. (1986) *Hibernia America: The Irish and Regional Cultures*. Connecticut: Westport Press.

Coakley, J. and Dunning, E. (2000) 'General introduction', in J. Coakley and E. Dunning (eds), *Handbook of Sports Studies*, London, Thousand Oaks and New Dehli: Sage, pp. xxi–xxxviii.

Cochrane, F. E. (2007) 'The end of the affair: Irish migration, 9/11 and the evolution of Irish America', *Nationalism and Ethnic Politics* 13 (3), pp. 335–66.

Coogan, T. P. (1995) *The Troubles: Ireland's Ordeal 1966–95 and the Search for Peace*. London: Hutchinson.

Coogan, T. P. (2000) *Wherever Green is Worn: The Story of the Irish Diaspora*. London, Sydney and Auckland: Random House.

Corcoran, M. P. (1997) 'Emigrants, *eirepreneurs*, and opportunists, a social profile of recent irish immigration in New York city', in R. H. Bayor and T. J. Meagher (eds), *The New York Irish*. Baltimore and London: Johns Hopkins University Press, pp. 461–80.

Corry, E. (1989) *Catch and Kick*. Dublin: Poolbeg.

Cronin, M. (1998a) 'Fighting for Ireland, playing for England? The nationalist history of the Gaelic Athletic Association and the English influence on Irish sport', *International Journal of the History of Sport* xv (3), pp. 36–56.

Cronin, M. (1998b) 'Enshrined in blood: the naming of Gaelic Athletic Association grounds and clubs', *The Sports Historian*, 18 (1), pp. 90–104.

Cronin, M. (2007) 'The Gaelic Athletic Association's invasion of America, 1888: travel narratives, microhistory and the Irish American "other"', *Sport in History* 27 (2), pp. 190–216.

Cronin, M. (1999) *Sport and Nationalism in Ireland: Gaelic Games, Soccer and Irish Identity Since 1884.* Dublin: Four Courts.

Cronin, M. and Mayall, D. (1998) *Sporting Nationalisms: Identity, Ethnicity, Immigration and Assimilation.* London and Portland, OR: Frank Cass.

Cullinane, N. (1997) *Aspects of the History of Irish Dancing in North America.* Cork City: Central Remedial Clinic.

Curry, A. (1999) 'San Francisco, aspects of', in M. Glazier (ed.), *The Encyclopedia of the Irish in America.* Notre Dame, IN: University of Notre Dame Press.

Darby, P. (2001) 'The next parish over from Galway Bay: Gaelic sport, Irish nationalism and the Irish diaspora in Boston', paper presented to the Annual Conference of the North American Society for Sociology of Sport, San Antonio, Texas, Nov. 2001.

Darby, P. (2003) 'Gaelic sport and the Irish diaspora in Boston, 1879–90', *Irish Historical Studies* xxxiii (132), pp. 387–403.

Darby, P. (2005) 'Gaelic games and the Irish immigrant experience in Boston', in A. Bairner (ed.), *Sport and the Irish: Historical, Political and Sociological Perspectives.* Dublin: UCD Press, pp. 85–101.

Darby, P. (2006) 'Emigrants at play: Gaelic games and the Irish diaspora in Chicago, 1884–c.1900', *Sport in History*, 26 (1), pp. 47–63.

Darby, P. (2007) 'Gaelic games, ethnic identity and Irish nationalism in New York City c.1880–1917', *Sport in Society* 10 (1), pp. 347–67.

Darby, P. (2009a) 'Gaelic games and the Irish diaspora in the United States', in M. Cronin, W. Murphy and P. Rouse (eds), *The Gaelic Athletic Association, 1884–2009.* Dublin and Portland, OR: Irish Academic Press, pp. 203–20.

Darby, P. (2009b) '"Without the aid of a sporting safety net": the Gaelic Athletic Association and the Irish émigré in San Francisco (1888–c.1938)', *International Journal of the History of Sport* 29 (1), pp. 22–42.

Darby, P. and Hassan, D. (eds) (2008) *Emigrant Players: Sport and the Irish Diaspora.* London and New York, Routledge.

D'Arcy, F. (1999) *The Story of Irish Emigration.* Cork and Dublin: Mercier Press

Davis, T. (2006) 'Eamon de Valera's political education: the American Tour of 1919', *New Hibernia Review* 10 (1), pp. 65–78.

De Búrca, M. (1980) *The GAA: A History.* Dublin: Cumann Lúthcleas Gael.

De Búrca, M. (1989) *Michael Cusack and the GAA.* Dublin: Anvil.

De Búrca, M. (1999) *The GAA: A History.* 2nd edition, Dublin: Gill & Macmillan.

Dineen, M. (1901) 'The game of hurling', *The Gael*, Sept. 1901, p. 292.

Diner, H. S. (1997) 'The most Irish city in the union: the era of the great migration, 1844–1877', in R. H. Bayor and T. J. Meagher (eds), *The New York Irish*. Baltimore and London: Johns Hopkins University Press, pp. 87–106.

Doyle, J. (1995) 'The Irish connection', *San Francisco Examiner Chronicle*, 12 Mar. 1995, p. 3.

Dowling, P. (1998) *Irish Californians: Historic, Benevolent, Romantic*. San Francisco, CA: Scottwall Associates.

Doyle, D. N. (1989) 'The Irish in Chicago' *Irish Historical Studies*, XXVI (103), pp. 293–103.

Duffy, J. G. (1962) 'Gaelic games are vital to maintain Irish culture', *Emerald Echo*, Sept. 1962, p. 6.

Dunne, M. (1997) *The Star Spangled Banner: The Story of the All-Ireland Football Final in New York*. Dublin: Gaelic Athletic Association.

English, R. (2006) *Irish Freedom: The History of Nationalism in Ireland*. London: Pan Macmillan.

Fahy, D. (2001) *How the GAA Survived the Troubles*. Dublin: Wolfhound Press.

Fallows, M. R. (1979) *Irish American: Identity and Assimilation*. Englewood Cliffs, NJ: Prentice-Hall Inc.

Fanning, C. (1999) *The Irish Voice in America: 250 Years of Irish-American Fiction*, 2nd edn. Kentucky: University Press of Kentucky.

Fanning, C. (2000) 'Editors introduction', in C. Fanning (ed.), *New Perspectives on the Irish Diaspora*. Carbondale and Edwardsville: Southern Illinois Press, pp. 1–14.

Farrelly, P. (1992) 'Boston GAA protest Northern Aid ban', *Irish Voice*, 9 June 1992, p. 4.

Ferguson, P. and Regan, C. (2006) 'Footballers caught in "sectarian" storm', *Belfast Telegraph*, 24 May 2006, p. 1.

Fitzpatrick, P. (1998) 'Ladies GAA continues to grow and thrive', *Irish Voice*, 11 Aug. 1998, p. 42.

Fulton , G., and Bairner, A. (2007) 'Sport, space and national identity in Ireland: The GAA, Croke Park and Rule 42', *Space and Polity* 11 (1), pp. 55–74.

Funchion, M. F. (1999) 'The Irish of Chicago', http://www.lib.niu.edu/ipo/iht629912.html, accessed on 30 June 2005.

Gaelic Athletic Association (2002) *Gaelic Athletic Association Rule*. Dublin: GAA.

Gaughran, M. B. (1999) 'Football's fighting Irish', *Boston Globe*, 26 May.

Greeley, A. M. (1981) *The Irish Americans: The Rise to Money and Power*. New York and Cambridge: Harper & Row.

Hanley, B. (2004) 'The Politics of Noraid', *Irish Political Studies* 19 (1), pp. 1–17.

Hanna, F. (1999) 'The Gaelic Athletic Association', in M. Glazier (ed.), *The Encyclopedia of the Irish in America*. Notre Dame, IN: University of Notre Dame Press.

Hassan, D. (2002) 'A people apart: soccer, identity and Irish nationalists in Northern Ireland', *Soccer and Society*, 3 (3), pp. 65–83.

Hassan, D. (2003) 'Still Hibernia irrendenta? The Gaelic Athletic Association, Northern nationalism and modern Ireland', *Culture, Sport and Society* 6 (1), pp. 92–110.

Hehir, J. (2000) 'Boston and North East Gaelic Athletic Association 1884–2000', in North East Gaelic Athletic Association, *A Century of Boston GAA*. Boston: Woburn Printing Inc., pp. 2–3.

Hennessy, P. (2008) 'Chicago Gaelic Park's finest hour', www.irishamericannews.com/col_glnz.htm, accessed 30 Apr. 2008.

Hennessy, P. (2008) 'GAA promoter wanted for Chicago area', *Irish American News*, 12 May 2008.

Hession, J. (1989) 'Irish all-stars not invited to San Francisco', *The Irishman*, Mar. 1989, pp. 1–2.

Hill, J. (1996) 'British sports history: a post-modern future', *Journal of Sports History* 23 (1), pp. 1–19.

Hobsbawm, E. J. and Ranger, T. (eds) (1983) *The Invention of Tradition*. Cambridge: Cambridge University Press.

Hoge, W. (2005) 'Sinn Féin leader plays down snubs by Bush and Kennedy', *International Herald Tribune*, 16 Mar. 2005.

Holmes, M. and Storey, D. (2004) 'Who are the boys in green? Irish identity and soccer in the Republic of Ireland', in A. Smith and D. Porter (eds), *Sport and National Identity in the Post-War World*. London and New York: Routledge.

Hughes, R. (1993a) 'Multi-million dollar injury claim against GAA fails', *The San Francisco Gael*, Feb. 1993, p. 1.

Hughes, R. (1993b) 'Gaelic games for Kezar!', *The San Francisco Gael*, May 1993, p. 1.

Hughes, R. (1997) 'GAA youth team kicks off fund raising for historic trip', *The Gael*, Nov. 1997, p. 23.

Humphries, T. (1996) *Green Fields: Gaelic Sport in Ireland*. London: Weidenfeld & Nicolson.

Hurley, M. J., '"County names" a joke', *The Advocate*, 24 Feb. 1917, p. 5.

Husar, J. (1976) 'Gaelic games: rugged Irish imports', *Chicago Tribune*, 29 Sept. 1976, p. G4.

Irish Cultural Centre (1999), 'Boston and the North East Gaelic Athletic Association 1884–1999', *Commemorative Program, Irish Cultural Centre Grand Opening: Phase I*, Irish Cultural Centre, pp. 8–9.

Irish Department of Foreign Affairs (2008) Press Release, 'Minister Micheál Martin announces partnership agreement with the GAA to promote Gaelic games abroad', 24 June.

Isenberg, M. T. (1988) *John L. Sullivan and His America*. Urbana, University of Illinois Press.

Jenkins, W. (2005) 'Deconstructing diasporas: networks and identities among the Irish in Buffalo and Toronto, 1870–1910', *Immigrants and Minorities* 23 (2–3), pp. 359–98.

Keely, C. B. (1971) 'Effects of the Immigration Act of 1965 on selected population characteristics of immigrants to the United States', *Demography* 8 (2), pp. 157–69.

Kelleher, P. (2001) 'Young Irish workers: class implications of men's and women's experiences in gilded age Chicago', *Éire-Ireland* XXXVI (1 & 2), pp. 141–65.

Kelly, E. (2000) Press Release, North American County Board, 27 Sept.

Kelly, E. (2000) 'North American County Board 2000 Convention Report', accessed from www.NAGAA.org/agm2000.htm on 16 Mar. 2004.

Kilfeather, S. (1988) 'New York board gets a reprieve', *The Advocate*, 13 Feb. 1988, p. 12.

King, S. (1998) *The Clash of the Ash in Foreign Fields: Hurling Abroad*. Tipperary, Seamus J. King.

Kline, B. (2000) *Irish Dream Accomplished: Building a Cultural Center*. San Francisco: United Irish Cultural Center.

Lacey, M. (2001) 'State Department adds the Real IRA to list of terror groups', *New York Times*, 17 May 2001.

Leavitt, Z. (2009) 'Cardinal and Cal make history', *The Stanford Daily*, 22 Jan. 2009.

Lefebvre, H. (1991) *The Production of Space*. Oxford: Blackwell.

Leptich, J. (1990) 'Fans lucky as leprechauns: Gaelic football, hurling finals coming to Chicago', *Chicago Tribune*, 25 Aug. 1990, p. 8.

Lewis, S. (2004) 'GAA Manhattan transfer', *Sunday Mirror*, 4 Jan. 2004.

Lobo, A. P., and Salvo, J. J. (1998) 'Resurgent Irish immigration to the US in the 1980s and early 1990s: a socio-demographic profile', *International Migration*, 36 (2), pp. 257–80.

Mandle, W. F. (1987) *The Gaelic Athletic Association and Irish Nationalist Politics, 1884–1928*. London and Dublin: Christopher Helm/Gill and Macmillan.

Martin, D. (1994) 'Michael Flannery, an advocate of a united Ireland, dies at 92', *The New York Times*, 2 Oct. 1994, p. 64.

Matthews, P. (1990) 'Na Fianna's captain Bob O'Brien severely injured in a hurling match', *Irish American Press*, Sept. 1990, p. 22.

Matthews, P. (1991) 'GAA player gets jail term in SF case', *Irish American Press*, Aug. 1991, pp. 1–3.

McAllister, J. (1965) 'The GAA in New York: fifty years: 1914–1964', *Irish Herald*, Jan. 1965, p. 6.

McCaffrey, L. J., Skerrett, E., Funchion, M. F. and Fanning, C. (1987) *The Irish in Chicago*. Chicago: University of Illinois Press.

McCaffrey, L. J. (1992) *Textures of Irish America*. Syracuse, NY: Syracuse University Press.

McCaffrey, L. J. (1997) *The Irish Catholic Diaspora in America*. Washington, DC: Catholic University of America Press.

McCarthy, L. (2007) 'Irish Americans in sports: the twentieth century', in J. J. Lee and M. R. Casey (eds), *Making the Irish American: History and Heritage of the Irish in the United States*. New York: New York University Press, pp. 457–74.

McGinn, B. (1997) 'A century before the GAA: hurling in 18th Century New York', *Journal of the New York Irish History Roundtable* 11, pp. 12–16.

McLaughlin, J. G. (2002) *Images of America: Irish Chicago*. Chicago: Arcadia.

Meagher, W. (1957) 'Irish freedom field day this Sunday at Gaelic Park', *Irish Echo*, 30 Mar. 1957, p. 4.

Milkovits, J. (1988) 'The New York GAA: origins to Golden Jubilee', *Journal of the New York Irish History Roundtable*, 3 (1), pp. 4–7.

Miller, K. (1985) *Emigrants and Exiles: Ireland and the Irish Exodus to North America*. Oxford, New York and Toronto: Oxford University Press.

Miller, K. and Wagner, P. (1994) *Out of Ireland: The Story of Irish Emigration to America*. Washington DC: Elliot & Clarke.

Mockler, S. (2000) 'GAA thriving in the Bay area', *The Irish Herald/The New Irish Gael*, Apr., p. 32.

Moran, S. (1997) 'McHugh among 20 banned by GAC', *Irish Times*, 10 Jan. 1997, p. 15.

Mulligan, A. N. (2005) 'Absence makes the heart grow fonder: transatlantic Irish nationalism and the 1867 rising', *Social and Cultural Geography* 6 (3), pp. 339–453.

Murphy, W. (2009) 'The GAA during the Irish Revolution, 1913–23', in M. Cronin, W. Murphy and P. Rouse (eds), *The Gaelic Athletic Association, 1884–2009*. Dublin and Portland, OR: Irish Academic Press, pp. 61–76.

New York Gaelic Athletic Association (1964) 'Fifty years: 1914–1964', *New York Gaelic Athletic Association Golden Jubilee*. New York: Gaelic Athletic Association, pp. 19–43.

New York Gaelic Athletic Association (1982) '1982 GAA highlights', *Official Programme of the 49th Annual Banquet of the Gaelic Athletic Association of New York*. New York: Gaelic Athletic Association.

New York Gaelic Athletic Association (1985) '1985 GAA highlights', *Official Programme of the 52nd Annual Banquet of the Gaelic Athletic Association of New York*. New York: Gaelic Athletic Association.

New York Gaelic Athletic Association (1987) '1987 GAA highlights', *Official Programme of the 54th Annual Banquet of the Gaelic Athletic Association of New York*. New York: Gaelic Athletic Association.

New York Gaelic Athletic Association (1988) *Official Match Programme, 1988 GAA National League Gaelic Football Final*. New York: Gaelic Athletic Association.

Ní Bhroiméil, U. (2003) *Building Irish Identity in America, 1870–1915: The Gaelic Revival*. Dublin: Fours Courts.

North American County Board [NACB] (1997) *Our Story Retold: 1884–1997*. North American County Board.

North American County Board [NACB] (1998) Official Programme for the NACB Finals, Washington 1998.

North East Gaelic Athletic Association (2000), *A Century of Boston GAA*. Boston: Woburn Printing Inc.

O'Brien, P. (1988) 'New York seek place in national leagues', *The Advocate*, 27 Sept. 1988, p. 12.

O'Connor, T. H. (1994) *South Boston, My Home Town*. North Eastern University Press.

O'Connor, T. H. (1995) *The Boston Irish: A Political History*. Boston: Northeastern University Press.

O'Gorman, T. J. (2001) *A History of the Irish Fellowship Club of Chicago 1901–2001*. Chicago.

O'Keefe, T. J. (2005) 'Introduction', in D. Jordan and T. J. O'Keefe (eds), *The Irish in the San Francisco Bay Area: Essays on Good Fortune*. San Francisco, CA: Executive Council of the Irish Literary and Historical Society, pp. 1–6.

O'Murchu, S. (1985) 'All-Stars return', *The Irishman*, May 1985, p. 16.

O'Regan, T. (1994) 'Bay area Irish football Youth League kicks off', *The San Francisco Gael*, June 1994, p. 20.

O'Reilly, J. B. (1890) *Athletics and Manly Sport*. Boston, MA: Boston Publishing Company.

O'Reilly, S. (1985) 'SF hurling: Gaels win North American hurling title', *The Irishman*, Sept. 1985, p. 14.

O'Riordan, I. (2002) 'GAA moves to block players' exodus to US', *Irish Times*, 18 July 2002, p. 23.

O'Shea, L. (1913) 'Athletics and manly sport', *The Irish American Advocate*, 23 June, p. 3.

O'Shea, L. (1914a) 'Governing body formed', *The Advocate*, 12 Dec., p. 3.

O'Shea, L. (1914b) 'Gaelic Athletic Association of the USA', *The Advocate*, 26 Dec. 1914, p. 3.

O'Shea, L. (1925a) 'Governing body scouring suburbs for playing field', *The Advocate*, 14 Feb. 1925, p. 3.

O'Shea, L. (1925b) 'Everything in readiness for opening ceremonies today', *The Advocate*, 30 May 1925, p. 3.

O'Shea, L. (1939) '50,000 fans to see the Kerry–Galway clash at stadium', *The Advocate*, 13 May 1939, p. 3.

O'Shea, L. (1940a) 'Admission fee to be lowered at Innisfail Park', *The Advocate*, 6 Apr. 1940, p. 3.

O'Shea, L. (1940b) 'After Innisfail – what?, *The Advocate*, 25 May 1940, p. 3.

O'Shea, L. (1940c) 'Local Gaels looking ahead', *The Advocate*, 2 Nov. 1940, p. 3.

O'Shea, L. (1941) 'Innisfail Park lost to Gaels', *The Advocate*, 25 Jan. 1941, p. 3.

O'Shea, J. (1981) 'New York minor board GAA', *The Advocate*, 20 June 1981, p. 18.

O'Toole, J. M. (1999) 'Boston', in M. Glazier (ed.), *The Encyclopedia of the Irish in America*. Notre Dame, IN: University of Notre Dame Press.

Park, R. J. (1984) 'British sports and pastimes in San Francisco, 1848–1900', *British Journal of Sports History* 1 (3), pp. 300–17.

Peterson, R. F. (2000) '"Slide, Kelly, slide": the Irish in American baseball', in C. Fanning (ed.), *New Perspectives on the Irish Diaspora*. Cabondale and Edwardsville: Southern Illinois University Press, pp. 176–88.

Prescott, D. (1985) 'Gaelic Park opens for Irish-American games and events', *Chicago Tribune*, 19 July 1985, p. 8.

Pridmore, J. (1983) 'Hurling [Thud!] lets Irishmen [oof!] kick up a bit o' [smack!] the old sod', *Chicago Tribune*, 2 Sept. 1983, p. D3.

Puirséal, P. (1982) *The GAA in its Time*. Dublin: Purcell Family.

Reidy, L. (2005) 'GAA seminar targets marketing in America', *Irish Herald*, Apr. 2006, p. 39.

Reimers, D. M. (1997) 'An end and a beginning', in R. H. Bayor and T. J. Meagher (eds), *The New York Irish*. Baltimore and London: Johns Hopkins University Press, pp. 275–300.

Reiss, S. A. (1992) 'Sport, race and ethnicity in the American City, 1879–1950', in M. D'Innocenzo and J. P. Sirefman (eds), *Immigration and Ethnicity: American Society – 'Melting Pot' or 'Salad Bowl?* Westport, CN and London: Greenwood, pp. 191–219.

Ridge, J. T. (1997) 'Irish county societies in New York, 1880–1914', in R. H. Bayor and T. J. Meagher (eds), *The New York Irish*. Baltimore and London: Johns Hopkins University Press, pp. 275–300.

Robinson, G. (2000) 'What's new inn Chicago?', *Hogan Stand*, 28 Apr. 2000, pp. 21–3.

Roche, J. J. (1891) *The Life, Poems and Speeches of John Boyle O'Reilly*. New York: Cassell.

Rohan, B. (1991) 'The GAA and hired guns', *Irish Voice*, 5 Nov. 1991, p. 8.

Rohan, B. (1992a) 'A home – at last – for New York GAA', *Irish Voice*, 4 Feb. 1992, p. 7.

Rohan, B. (1992b) 'NYGAA to make bid on college', *Irish Voice*, 7 July 1992.

Rohan, B. (1992c) 'Tara circle: a field of dreams', *Irish Voice*, 28 July 1992.

Rohan, B. (1993a) 'Hurleystick and the ballot box', *Irish Voice*, 13 Apr. 1993, p. 18.

Rohan, B. (1993b) 'Drop the GAA, Tara Circle is told', *Irish Voice*, 31 Aug. 1993, p. 8.

Rohan, B. (1994a) 'He did not go gently: an IRA burial in Queens for Mike Flannery, 92', *Irish Voice*, 11 Oct. 1994, p. 8.

Rohan, B. (1994b) 'NYGAA snubs women's team', *Irish Voice*, 9 Aug. 1994, p. 3.

Rohan, B. (1994c) 'Tara wins local board approval: but residents group threatens lawsuit', *Irish Voice*, 15 Nov. 1994, p. 7.

Rohan, B. (1995a) 'Tara circle: keeps on tickin', *Irish Voice*, 4 Apr. 1995, p. 22.

Rohan, B. (1995b) 'No lawsuit yet', *Irish Voice*, 25 July 1995, p. 20.

Rohan, B. (1995c) 'The death of a hurling club?', *Irish Voice*, 4 Apr. 1995, p. 20.

Rohan, B. (1998a) 'Where has all the money gone?', *Irish Voice*, 14 July 1998, p. 6.

Rohan, B. (1998b) 'McDonagh's gamble fall flat', *Irish Voice*, 16 June 1998, p. 20.

Rouse, P. (1993) 'The politics of sport and culture in Ireland: a history of the GAA ban on foreign games 1884–71. Part one: 1884–1921, *International Journal of the History of Sport*, 10 (3), pp. 333–60.

Ryan, C. (2009) 'Gaelic games: a new future in the city by the bay', *Irish America*, Feb.–Mar., pp. 46–9.

Shannon, W. V. (1966) *The American Irish: A Political and Social Portrait*. New York: Macmillan.

Skerret, E. (2004) 'Irish', in J. L. Reiff, A. D. Keating, and J. R. Grossman (eds), *Encyclopedia of Chicago*. Chicago: University of Chicago Press.

Smith, A. (1986) *The Ethnic Origins of Nations*. Oxford: Blackwell.

Smith, A. (1995) *Nations and Nationalism in a Global Era*. Cambridge: Polity.

Sugden, J. and Bairner, A. (1993) ~~Sport, Sectarianism and Society in a Divided Ireland.~~ Leicester, London and New York: Leicester University Press.

Sutton, P. P. (1900) 'The ancient games of Ireland at Tailten and Carman', *The Gael*, Aug.–Sept. 1900, p. 258.

Treacy, M., cited in 'North American board say yes', www.hoganstand.com, 15 Apr. 2005, accessed online 28 May 2005.

Ulster Gaelic Football Club (1986), Constitution.

Wilcox, R. C. (1992) 'Sport and the nineteenth century immigrant experience', in M. D'Innocenzo and J. P. Sirefman (eds), *Immigration and Ethnicity: American Society – 'Melting Pot' or 'Salad Bowl'?* Westport, CN and London: Greenwood, pp. 177–89.

Wilcox, R. C. (2007) 'Irish Americans in sports: the nineteenth century', in J. J. Lee and M. R. Casey (eds), *Making the Irish American: History and Heritage of the Irish in the United States*. New York: New York University Press, pp. 443–56.

Wilcox, R. C. (1994) 'The shamrock and the eagle: Irish Americans and sport in the nineteenth century', in G. Eisen and D. K. Wiggins (eds), *Ethnicity and Sport in North American History and Culture*. Westport, CN and London: Greenwood Press, pp. 54–74.

Wilson, A. J. (1995) *Irish America and the Ulster Conflict 1968–1995*. Belfast: Blackstaff.

Other Sources

INTERVIEWS

Joe Begley, Chicago, IL, 31 July 2005.

Liam Bermingham, the Bronx, NY, 27 July 2003.

Olivia Cahill, South Boston, MA, 25 July 2000.

Bill Colbert, Manhattan, NY, 22 July 2003.

Terry Connaughton, the Bronx, NY, 27 July 2003.

Kieran Conway, South Boston, MA, 25 July 2000.

Harry Costelloe, Chicago, IL, 30 July 2005.

Louis Cotter, San Francisco, CA, 3 Sept. 2006.

Seamus Dooley, Manhattan, NY, 30 July 2004.

Joe Duffy, San Francisco, CA, 29 Aug. 2006.

Eamon Gormley, San Francisco, CA, 27 Aug. 2006.

John Hehir, Brighton, MA, 15 Aug. 2000.

Malachy Higgins, San Francisco, CA, 27 Aug. 2006.
Connie Kelly, Belmont, MA, 30 July 2000.
Eamonn Kelly, Chicago, IL, 29 July 2005.
Brendan Keneally, San Francisco, CA, 5 Sept. 2006.
Lisa Kreuger, Chicago, IL, 30 July 2005.
Monty Maloney, Manhattan, NY, 28 Aug. 2004.
Mike Moriarity, San Francisco, CA, 27 Aug. 2006.
Lisa O'Flaherty, Chicago, IL, 30 July 2005.
John O'Flynn, San Francisco, CA, 27 Aug. 2006.
Kieran O'Sullivan, Manhattan, NY, 24 July 2003.

MINUTE BOOKS
Annual Congress GAA Minutes, 1 Apr. 1934; 21 Apr. 1935; 6 Apr. 1947; 17 Apr. 1949; 9 Apr. 1950; 13 Apr. 1952; 29 Mar. 1959; 6 Apr. 1969; 17–18 Apr. 1998.

Central Council GAA Minutes, 27 July 1929; 31 Aug. 1929; 25 June 1932; 21 Aug. 1937; 23 May 1947; 13 Dec. 1947; 25 Sept. 1948; 15 Mar. 1952; 21 Nov. 1952; 24 Oct. 1970; 8 Dec. 1952; 6 Feb. 1988; 4/5 Nov. 1988; 28/29 Apr. 1989.

Executive Committee GAA Minutes, 2 Oct. 1970.

Management Committee GAA Minutes, 24/25 May 1989.

Special Meeting of Central Council GAA Minutes, 16 Oct. 1926; 17 Sept. 1949; 12 May 1951.

USA Advisory Committee GAA Minutes, 10 May 1952.

GAA CORRESPONDENCE
Delaney, Thomas. Letter to Liam Clifford, 11 Oct. 1926.
Lenihan, Paddy. Letter to GAA Central Council, 21 Aug. 1935.
Hamilton, Canon Michael. Report to Central Council GAA on US tour by Mayo, 29 May 1937.
Ó Caoimh, Pádraig. Report to Central Council GAA on 1947 All-Ireland Gaelic football final, 13 Dec. 1947.

NEWSPAPERS
The Advocate
'IAAC chief and S. J. Donleavy cheered by governing body', 20 Feb. 1915, p. 9.
'Meeting of the Gaels to be held on Jan. 9 at the Irish American AC', 1 Jan. 1916.
'Gaels are asked to contribute to fund to supply the fighting sixty-ninth with GAA material', 11 Aug. 1917, p. 5.
'The Gaelic athletes in the old sixty-ninth are calling for hurling sticks and footballs', 1 Sept. 1917, p. 5.

'Great crowd saw New York lose to Mayo', 5 June 1937, p. 3.
'GAA outposts neglected by the Central Council', 22 Jan. 1938.
'Father Hamilton sends greetings to NY Gaels', 8 Jan. 1939.
'Upkeep of clubs is expensive', 3 Feb. 1940, p. 3.
'Sports', 25 Jan. 1969, p. 6.
'Champs to visit New York', 8 Feb. 1969.
'A serious blow to NY Gaels', 24 Oct. 1970.
'New York banished', 14 Nov. 1970.
'Loftus highlights GAA problems', 26 Mar. 1988, p. 12.
25 July 1914; 3 Sept. 1914; 26 Feb. 1916; 1 Apr. 1916; 18 Feb. 1939; 31 May 1969; 24 May 1969;
    6 May 1972; 24 June 1972; 1 July 1972.

Alta California
4 May 1853.

Boston News
3 Mar. 1974.

Boston Pilot
'Field sports at the Boston Irish Athletic Club picnic', 4 Oct. 1879a.
'Irish games: the ancient sports introduced into America', 4 Oct. 1879b.
'Irish games: the coming exhibition at Oak Island June 17', 12 June 1886, p. 8.
'Shamrock Camogie interest increases', 29 July 1950.
'Camogie game Sunday', 4 Nov. 1950.

Boston Irish Reporter
'GAA cultural centre sign deal for athletic fields', Apr. 1999, p. 3.
'Irish sports youth league seeks new players', July 1999, p. 35.
'Irish Cultural Centre marks decade of progress, eye to the future', Oct. 1999, p. 20.

Chicago Daily
'Police prevent the Gaelic Athletic Association's game', 26 Sept. 1892, p. 1.
'The shamrock shines', 3 Dec. 1893, p. 4.

Chicago Daily Tribune
'Exhibition of old Irish sports', 11 May 1891, p. 6.
'Deplore the death of Parnell', 22 Oct. 1891, p. 2.
'Stopped a game of football', 19 Sept. 1892, p. 3.
'They adopt strong resolutions', 26 Sept. 1892, p. 5.
'Against the Gaelic Athletic Association', 9 Oct. 1892, p. 4.
'World's Fair notes', 30 Sept. 1983, p. 3.
'It's a beautiful scheme on paper', 7 Oct. 1893, p. 6.
'Gaels try athletic events', 27 Aug. 1894, p. 11.

'Orators who will speak at Irish picnic', 9 Aug. 1903, p. 5
'Irish field day enthuses crowd', 10 Sept. 1906, p. 5.
'Interested in approaching Chicago–St Louis hurling match', 20 Oct. 1907, p. c3.
'Donnybrook Fair was nothing like this; today's the day of the Irishmen's picnic', 15 Aug. 1909, p. 13.
'Ould sod Gaels to meet locals', 16 Dec. 1909, p. 16.
'Gaels vote $2,500 for Irish teams', 17 Dec. 1909, p. 17.
'Breach in ranks of Gaelic sport', 6 Jan. 1910, p. 10.
'Gaels may fight in court', 12 Jan. 1910, p. 12.
'Gaels to sue for money', 13 Jan. 1910, p. 10.
'Gaels have real battle', 9 May 1910, p. 13.
'Peace in ranks of Gaels', 16 May 1910, p. 13.
'Gaels announce schedule', 25 Apr. 1910, p. 10.
'Irish football team defeats Chicago, 17–3', 25 May 1931, p. 23.
'Irish football champions beat New York, 9 to 6', 18 May 1931, p. 23.
'Mayor Kelly to welcome Gaelic champions today', 8 June 1933, p. 20.
'Gaelic football team to play for title today', 4 July 1933, p. 18.
'Irish groups hold dance tonight; back Gaelic games revival', 11 Dec. 1948, p. A3.
16 Oct. 1950, p. E4.
'Decide US Irish hurling title today', 10 June 1956, p. A3.

Chicago Tribune
'Gael force Oak Forest hosts super bowl 2 of Irish sports', 28 Aug. 1994, p. 1.

Citizen
'Gaelic invasion of America accomplished', 6 Oct. 1888, p. 1.
'Letter to the editor: Gaelic athletic games', 15 Mar. 1890, p. 1.
'Letter to the editor', 29 Mar. 1890, p. 2.
'Letter to the editor: Irish athletes', 3 May 1890, p. 2.
'Letter to the editor: Gaelic Athletic Association', 24 May 1890, p. 1.
'North Side Gaelic athletes', 5 July 1890, p. 1.
'Marvellous growth and prosperity of the Gaelic Athletic Association of Chicago', 2 May 1891, p. 5.
'Gaelic sports in Chicago' 6 June 1891, p. 1.
'Letter to the editor: regarding the trouble between Mayor Washbourne and the Gaelic Athletic Association', 24 Sept. 1892, p. 1.
19 July 1884; 2 Aug. 1884; 9 Aug. 1884; 26 Sept. 1885; 3 July 1886; 6 Aug. 1887.

Daily Morning Call
'Gaelic athletes', 23 Jan. 1888, p. 2.
'Gaelic association', 30 Jan. 1888, p. 2.
'Gaelic football', 1 Aug. 1892, p. 3.
'The Gaelic football, 12 Sept. 1892, p. 2.

'Gaelic football', 1 May 1893, p. 2.
'Ireland's day', 17 Mar. 1894, p. 2.
'Parnell's beaten', 17 Dec. 1894, p. 2.
'Irish pastimes', 23 Dec. 1894, p. 4.

Donahoe's Magazine
'Irish games: the ancient sports introduced into America', Nov. 1879, pp. 460–4.
'Parliamentary fund', Apr. 1886, pp. 180.
'Irish athletes', Nov. 1888, p. 474.
'Death of John Boyle O'Reilly', Oct. 1890, pp. 359–70.

Emerald Echo
Sept. 1962.

The Gael
Vol. 1, no. 1, Jan. 1882, p. 1.
'An Irish hurling green: a ballad for the Gael', May 1887, p. 705.
'The Moondharrig hurlers: recollections of "Gaelic" days', Jan. 1900, pp. 5–6.
'The Moondharrig hurlers: on the way to the big match', May 1900, pp. 135–7.
'The ancient games of Ireland at Tailten and Carman', Aug.–Sept. 1900, pp. 255–8.
'The Moondharrig hurlers: recollections of "Gaelic" days', July 1901, pp. 218–20.
'The game of hurling', Sept. 1901, pp. 290–2.

Gaelic American
'Gaelic sports and pastimes: the GAA in America should be reorganised', 10 Oct. 1903, p. 4.
'An athletic revival', 24 Oct. 1903a, p. 3.
'Irish games at world's fair', 24 Oct. 1903b, p. 3.
'Letter to the editor', 31 Oct. 1903, p. 3.
'Gaels preparing for St Enda's field day at Celtic Park' 11 Apr. 1914.
'Ten crack teams will play in Celtic Park on Labor Day', 5 Sept. 1914.
'10,000 People attend games of national volunteer committee in Celtic Park', 12 Sept. 1914.
'Gaelic League of New York', 5 June 1915, p. 6.
'Tipp All-Ireland hurling champions defeat Offaly at polo grounds', 5 June 1926, p. 7.
'Opening of Steinway Park in Astoria for junior football', 11 Sept. 1926, p. 7.
'Speeches at GAA banquet ring out in favour of Ireland's God-given right to full freedom', 20 Sept. 1947, p. 1.
7 Nov. 1903, p. 3; 2 July 1904, p. 3; 11 Feb. 1905; 23 Mar. 1912, p. 5; 7 June 1913, p. 5; 1 Nov. 1913; 29 Aug. 1914, p. 8.

Hogan Stand
'New York ladies', 28 Apr. 2000, pp. 50–1.
'Kelly tries to smooth NY's ruffled feathers', 21 Dec. 2005.
'New York: Randall's Island is a non-runner', 21 Feb. 2006.

Irish American Advocate
'Kerrymen's day at Celtic Park', 28 May 1904, p. 4.
'To promote Gaelic football', 11 June 1904a, p. 1.
'Kickham club's big event', 11 June 1904b, p. 1.
'Irish counties athletic union', 10 Sept. 1904, p. 1.
25 May 1906; 4 June 1904, p. 1; 8 June 1907; 24 Aug. 1907, p. 5.

Irish Echo
'Ireland's games and pastimes: the National Irish Athletic Association to the fore', July 1888,
 p. 4.
'Irish athletic champions', Oct. 1888, p. 4.
'Good-will tour brings message to battle on until all Erin is free', 21 May 1938, pp. 1–4.
'By your presence in great numbers', 21 May 1938, p. 1.
'No boundary line for Irish ball-players', 4 June 1938, p. 1.
'Gaelic Athletic Association', 17 Mar. 1945.
'Undivided Ireland field day at Croke Park on July 30th', 22 July 1950, p. 5.
'UIC pres. attends GAA meeting', 19 May 1951, p. 3.
'Echoes of tour', 22 June 1957.
'Kerry and Tipperary in finals at GAA field day', 7 Sept. 1957, p. 4.
'New York annual report 1957', 1 Feb. 1957, p. 4.
'Mayo, Offaly, and Cork win at Irish freedom field day', 6 Apr. 1957.
'GAA public relations division', 31 May 1958.
'John O'Donnell is guest of honour', 7 Dec. 1963, p. 4.
'1963 GAA review', 21 Dec. 1963, p. 4.
'Let's keep international games', 8 Nov. 1969, p. 23.
'TelePrompter to present Gaelic football', 2 May 1970, p. 27.
26 May 1945, p. 5; 16 Sept. 1950; 23 Sept. 1950; 16 Feb. 1957; 27 Apr. 1957, p. 4; 7 June 1958;
 1 Nov. 1969; 16 May 1981.

Irish Emigrant
'Jimmy Maunsell', 30 Nov. 1998, pp. 64–5.
'John Hehir: a life lived in the GAA', 22 Nov. 1999, pp. 66–7.

Irish Herald
Dec. 1964, p. 6.
'Kerry club plans August tour', Feb. 1965, p. 6.
'Donegal forms football team', Apr. 1965, p. 6.
'New organizer stages Gaelic games in San Francisco in a professional venue', July 1993, p. 15.
'Irish football Youth League receives $10,000', Mar. 1998, p. 31.

Irish Independent
'Gaelic Park and Manhattan college', 2 May 2007, p. 36.

The Irishman
'Local GAA', Apr. 1984, p. 17.
'Gaelic games update', Mar. 1987, p. 12.

Irish Voice
'NY GAA makes first move for new site', 8 Oct. 1991, p. 4.
'More problems for Tara Circle', 31 Aug. 1993, p. 10.
'John Kerry: legacy of a legend', 3 May 1994, p. 10.
'Tara Circle's arrogance', 24 Sept. 1994, p. 10.
'"Illegal" Leitrim are champs no more: NY football title awarded to Donegal; protest possible',
    21 Nov. 1995, p. 18.
'GAA enforces the rule', 21 Jan. 1997, p. 16.
'Historic step for New York GAA', 1 June 1999, p. 12.
'Mike O'Connor', 5 Oct. 1999, p. 18.
'A new GAA home', 26 Feb. 2002, p. 12.

Irish World and American Industrial Liberator
'Letters to the editor', 15 Sept. 1888.
'The Irish athletes', 22 Sept. 1888.
'The Irish amateur athletes', 29 Sept. 1888.
'Irish field day', 23 Aug. 1947.
'Clan na Gael games this Sunday', 20 Sept. 1947, p. 8.
'Americans to take up hurling', 20 Sept. 1947, p. 8.

The Leader
'Gaelic games', 10 Jan. 1903, p. 8.
'Field day for Washington's birthday', 7 Feb. 1903, p. 8.
'GAA is permanently organised', 28 Feb. 1903, p. 3.
'Important meeting of the GAA', 2 May 1903, p. 8.
'Field day', 2 Oct. 1909, p. 2.
'Gaelic athletics', 20 Jan. 1912, p. 8.
'Gaelic athletic news', 19 Apr. 1913, p. 7; 26 July 1913, p. 5; 6 Sept. 1913, p. 7; 13 June 1914, p. 7.
'Hurling is the most ancient of Irish games', 29 Nov. 1913, p. 3.
'The Van Nostrand trophy', 8 Aug. 1914, p. 8.
'To aid volunteers', 5 Dec. 1914, p. 5.
'GAA news', 15 Mar. 1915, p. 3.
'Gaelic athletic tournament', 15 Mar. 1915, p. 6.
'Gaelic athletic news', 22 July 1916, p. 7.
'The Gaelic ideal', 26 Aug. 1916, p. 1.
'GAA notes', 14 Oct. 1916.
'Gaelic games', 2 June 1917, p. 2.
'Gaelic athletes out for St Enda's', 15 Feb. 1919, p. 5.
'Gaelic athletes work for Ireland', 23 Aug. 1919, p. 2.

'GAA announce series of games', 11 Oct. 1919, p. 2.
'The Young Irelands defeat Pearses', 1 Nov. 1919, p. 6.
'GAA meeting', 12 May 1923, p. 5.
'Irish Hurlers to play June 13', 20 Mar. 1926, p. 2.
'San Francisco gives Céad Mile Fáilte to Tipperary champions', 11 June 1926, p. 1.
'Clans gather to see great hurling game', 19 June 1926, p. 1.
'GAA notes', 19 Mar. 1932, p. 5; 23 Apr. 1932, p. 6; 2 July 1937, p. 6.
'B. Naughton heads GAA', 18 Feb. 1933, p. 5.
'Attendance slump', 3 Aug. 1935, p. 5.
'GAA plans sport dance', 5 June 1937, p. 5.
'NY Plans for Gaelic games', 11 Sept. 1937, p. 5.
'GAA field day for Sunday 20 March', 19 Mar. 1938, p. 5.
'Irish athletes to visit SF', 13 July 1940, p. 5.
13 June 1903; 2 Apr. 1904; 15 Sept. 1917; 17 July 1919; 23 Mar. 1935.

The Monitor
'St Patrick's Day', 21 Mar. 1903, p. 3.

New York Times
3 May 1981, p. 4.

The San Francisco Call
19 Feb. 1906, p. 3.

The San Francisco Gael
'Gaelic games return to Kezar Stadium', Mar. 1994, p. 20.

Index

Ireland
- anglicisation of, 55
- partition of, 134

Irish
- culture, 32, 52, 84: revival of, 42–3, 60
- dance, 25, 31, 103
- identity, 1, 5, 8, 10–11, 13–15, 24, 29–30, 54, 84, 213
- music, 25, 31
- nationalism, 10–12, 14, 24, 28, 40, 62, 72, 76, 79, 80, 83, 84, 95, 118, 186, 204, 207: militant, 57, 58, 65, 131, 133–40, 187–91; political, 42–3, 52, 145–6, 187
- regiments, 20
- sports, 30, 103

Irish America, 161

Irish-American
- identity, 197, 214
- involvement in Gaelic games, 103
- nationalism, 57–60, 130–41

Irish American Advocate, 40, 70
Irish American Athletic Club, *see* IAAC
Irish-American GAA club, 40
Irish Athletic Club of Boston, *see* IACB
Irish Counties Athletic Union (New York), *see* ICAU
Irish Cultural Centre, 33, 192
Irish Echo, 32–3, 34, 63, 102, 104, 105, 113–14, 116, 119, 135–6, 138, 140
Irish Emigrant, 143
Irish Freedom Committee, 139, 197–9, 202
Irish Free State, 134
Irish Herald, 126, 160, 161, 211
Irish Independent, 112
Irish Lobby for Immigration Reform, 209
Irishman, The, 157, 158
Irish National Caucus, 187
Irish National League, 64
Irish National Volunteers, 72, 76, 131, 132
Irish News, 38–9

Irish Northern Aid, *see* Noraid
Irish Parliamentary Fund, 64
Irish Parliamentary Party, 24, 59, 130
Irish Press, 112–13
'Irish question', the, 131
Irish Republican Brotherhood, 55–7
Irish Republican Brotherhood Veterans, 65
Irish Sports Youth League of New England, 148
Irish Times, 162
Irish Voice, 149, 174, 175–6, 178, 179
Irish World, 59
Irish World and American Industrial Liberator, 39, 103, 105
Isenberg, M. T., 3, 4

J1 visas, *see under* visas
Jenkins, William, 14
John Boyle O'Reilly Hurling Cup, 35
Jordan, Andrew, 159

Keady, Tony, 177
Keely, C. B., 120
Kehoe, Michael, 111–12, 116
Kelleher, P., 23
Kelly, Connie, 144, 148, 193
Kelly, E., 109
Kelly, Eamon, 1, 124, 155, 198, 200–1
Kelly, Sean, 161–2
Keneally, Brendan, 125, 126–7
Kennedy, Joseph P., 40, 52, 69
Kennedy, Ted, 189
Kilcoyne, Tom, 108
Kilfeather, S., 172
King, S., 6, 39, 40, 105, 113, 117, 166–7, 176
Kline, B., 27
Knights of the Red Branch, 63–4
Know-Nothings (Native American Party), 19, 21, 23, 24, 44, 45
Kreuger, Lisa, 153–4